A

Jew

at the

Point

PAUL JULES KANTROWICH

Cover design, text and formatting design by Stewart A. Williams | stewartwilliamsdesign.com
Photographic design and layout design by Scott Uhlfelder, Los Angeles, CA 2021 | scott@scotto.com
First edition: December 2021

The publisher is not responsible for websites that are not owned by the publisher.

ISBN: 978-0-578-33896-5 (print)
ISBN: 978-0-578-33897-2 (ebook)

The main category of the book—Personal Memoir—Other subject category 2. Personal Perspective—Other subject category 3. Young Motivational

Printed in the United States of America

DISCLAIMER

This is not an official publication of the United States Military Academy. The views expressed herein are those of the author and do not reflect the official positions of the United States Military Academy, Department of the Army or Department of Defense. This book is not endorsed, recommended or favored by the United States Military Academy or the Federal Government.

DEDICATION

For my twin sis Helen, whom I miss every day.

*To a special Band of Brothers, West Point Class of 1965,
"Sons of the Greatest Generation."
While the bumps in the road were different for all of us,
for 11 months we all traveled the same route together.*

*For all my grandchildren: Life is like a tennis match.
In tennis you can always change a losing game,
but when the match is over, there is still another match down the road.
You only have one life though, try to wake up each morning
knowing you have a chance to change your game,
compete harder and become more fulfilled, and happy.*

INTRODUCTION

A Jew at the Point covers an eighteen-month personal journey I took as a teenager while at the crossroads between adolescence and maturity. It was a very harsh period of learning.

It's about the fantasies I held growing up and the realities of life as I experienced it, first as a naïve high school senior and hotshot tennis player and later, as a terrible first-year cadet at the United States Military Academy at West Point.

All the incidents mentioned in this book took place. I did change many names of the individuals involved and some events got switched around in time.

I began writing *A Jew at the Point* more than thirty years ago, largely as a cathartic effort to put my West Point experiences into perspective. From the tennis courts of South Florida to the grassy, glistening Plain of West Point and back again, you will travel with me on a roller coaster ride of emotional torment.

At the age of seventeen, I felt alone in all aspects of my life and needed a connection to something, anything. My Jewish identity was one, or could have been, had I been an observant Jew.

Every human being has a story to tell. This is the part of my story that I felt needed to be shared.

CHAPTER 1

O n the first Tuesday of the month—July 5th, 1961—the morning sun cascaded onto the sidewalk and historical grounds of the Academy. A harsh light was bouncing and reflecting on massive cement and stone structures. A muggy, sweltering heat rose off the lush, green parade field called "the Plain" and passed in a wave over the back seat of my Aunt Miriam's old Chevy, where I sat. We drove past bronze statues and plaques, dedicated benches, dedicated trees, waving flags. A sense of history began to osmose through my body, as well as anxieties and concerns for my new life.

I wasn't acclimated to the oppressive light and heat. In Miami—my Paradise, my home—it was always comfortable, only lightly humid, with an occasional ocean breeze, or thoughts of one. As a tennis player, the outdoors was my living room; I thrived in the sensual warmth of South Florida. But this thick New York summer air weighed heavily against my body and was already forming a sheen of sweat on my arms. It pressured my chest and I felt being pushed away like I wasn't wanted. It was a new emotion for me. Deep within the recesses of my brain, a small, tinny, exasperated voice was screaming, *WALK AWAY! NO...NO...DON'T WALK. RUN!*

My mother, Aunt Miriam and I continued onto the reservation, cruising the grounds in silence. Mom and I had flown out of Miami International Airport the day before. By the end of our two-hour drive north from my aunt's home in Weehawken, New Jersey, we had run out of things to say. Now there was just a quiet acceptance of decisions made, pacts agreed to. They dropped me off in front of a sally port, where a large red sign with white letters stated "New Candidates Report Here." The arrow pointed into the sally port.

I was late. Orders stated to arrive not later than 0900 hours or 9AM regular time and it was now 9:10 AM. Only socially late, but still…this was West Point. Orders are not to be ignored.

As I got out of the car, an icy chill rippled down my back despite the heat. I didn't turn around to wave goodbye to these two women who had given me so much. *I'm alone*, I thought. I was scared, but knew I needed to pay immediate attention to the task at hand. In truth, I had done absolutely nothing to prepare for this adventure except to put my clothes on that morning. I was looking forward to my future with keen excitement but hadn't studied anything about my new home or its rules and regulations. I had made no preparations. I trusted it would all become clear over time.

On the tennis court, in a big match, I never minded being alone. I had my racquets, my serve and my trusty forehand as powerful friends that boosted me up and bolstered my confidence making me feel fearless. Alone now on the sidewalks of America's sacred military institution, I felt the reality of my youthful decision to be here mightily slamming down on me. I was scared. Once again, I heard that inner voice grumbling, gnawing within me, warning me: *RUN! LEAVE NOW!*

The sally port was a beautifully carved archway leading from the outside sidewalk into a sectioned cement quadrangle. Barracks jutted up like mighty pillars around the quad, framing the impressive cadet assembly area. At the center, presiding over all activities, was a large, white-faced, circular clock tower, supervising all that was to happen.

I traversed the darkened, cool walkway step by step, my

trepidations surfacing about the decision I'd made only months earlier. It was intensely bright at the sally port's end; condensation coat-
ed my eyeglass lenses, smearing images, distorting my vision. I heard
a crackling cacophony of sound. Celebration? I could not decipher
it. I tried to disregard the ominous heat and the persistent nagging
inner warnings of personal danger, so I kept moving, head high, chin
out, best foot forward, nervously stepping into my future.

A dazzle of harsh light clobbered my face. The sounds I was hearing weren't whoops of laughter and joy; rather, they were a loud cre-
scendo of harsh, boisterous words from angry people, lots of them.

Cadet Upperclassmen were yelling at scared-to-death "New Candidates," directing raw, vicious rants at the future leaders of our
country's defense. Young, clean-shaven, smart, athletic, patriotic,
naive boys being yelled and screamed at: why would anyone want to
treat someone like that? *WHY?!*

I had just entered an arena of warriors inadvertently dressed like
toy soldiers: crisp white pleated pants, gray felt tunics with high col-
lars, shiny black shoes, gray caps with brilliant gold shields, some with
black chevrons on the upper shoulders, some on their lower sleeves.
In a pure singularity of time, I knew I'd made a big mistake…a colossal blunder, the proverbial "Big Bang" of boners. *WHAT? WHOA!*
In 90-degree heat, I was paralyzed, numb; unable to produce sound
from my parched lips or throat. Frozen in place.

Whatever clarity I had possessed was interrupted abruptly as two
men attacked me from either side. "Drop your bag, Smackhead!"
yelled one man in my left ear. "Pick it up, Smackhead!" bellowed
another man in my right ear.

WHAT? WHOA! I quickly followed the orders as my confusion
intensified, while their furious, penetrating voices shouted as if I had
just committed an egregious offense. I didn't even have both feet into
the quadrangle yet and the men ganged up on me. "Pick it up, drop
it, pick it up, drop it, Smackhead!"

A third, taller Upperclassman joined the fray. Parked three inches from my nose he barked, "What are *you* looking at, Mister? You had better not be looking at *me*, Mister! Are you looking at *me*, Mister? Wipe that silly smirk off your stupid face, Smackhead! Pull your chin in, ram it back, further, further until it hits your spine!" He glared at me, with a venomous attitude, his mouth a jagged scar, his posture ramrod straight, dark brown eyes probing.

My competitive spirit kicked into high gear along with rising anger. I was sandwiched among these three bellicose cadres, intensely frustrated for having put myself into this position. Common sense would have said, *just walk away, Paul! You don't need this bullshit! No one does!* Instead, my competitive spirit pushed through all the noise and commotion. It rippled through my bones, telling me, *don't you dare give up.* I did nothing. I said nothing.

The Upperclassman repeated, "Pull that gourd in Mister. Now! Do it now!"

I tried awkwardly to slam back my chin, which only intensified my anger. I couldn't speak; I had nothing to say. I was simply trying to compete in this new game as my seventeen-year-old brain kept insisting this could not be for real. *Welcome New Cadet Candidate Paul Jules Kantrowich to Beast Barracks, Class of 1965 at the United States Military Academy at West Point. Welcome to a taste of the United States Army. Welcome to insanity!* As a senior in high school, I had been busily playing tennis, chasing skirts, living each day for itself, denying what was ahead. No amount of planning could have prepared me for this "Beast Barracks" scenario. Reading all the literature about West Point before coming here would have made no difference.

The intensity of my despair soon matched the volume of the Upperclassmen's voices. Fear and chaos reigned supreme. I began sweating profusely. What already seemed like a full day of torture had been less than a few minutes of real time.

"Eyes front, Mister," yelled the Upperclassman in front. "Stand at attention, pull your chin in, Smackhead. Are you looking at me again?"

"Pick up your bag, Mister!" screamed the Upperclassman to my right. "Drop your bag, Mister!" bellowed the third man. This continued until I'd picked up, dropped and picked my bag up at least ten times.

"Wipe that smirk off your puny-ass face, Mister. Where are you from?" asked the Upperclassman, whose face was practically on top of mine. Before I could answer "Florida," he said, "You are from your momma and that's why you are such a pussy-ass wimp, Mister. Remember that."

"Slap your gourd in, Mister," another of the men shouted. "Pull that chin back, back, back so it meets the back of your neck, you pussy."

"Stand up straight, put your knees closer together, look straight ahead," shouted another. "Are you looking at me again, Smackhead?"

I was five feet, eleven and one-half inches tall, with rounded shoulders and bowed legs. They were asking the impossible of me. But I kept trying to do as ordered.

Once more the Upperclassman near my nose screamed, "I asked you where you're from, Mister!" I screamed back, "My momma, Sir!"

"Are you yelling at me, Mister? Who gave you the right to yell at me, you little ass-wipe? Hit the ground and give me twenty pushups right now, Mister!" He placed his foot firmly on my back when I hit the prone position.

I was never very good at pushups. I could do pullups, situps, lift weights, run all day; but pushups were difficult for me. Adrenaline rocketed through me. When I'd completed the twenty, they made me do twenty more because I didn't count out loud enough the first time. This time I did it without his foot in place. I finally stood back up at attention, waiting for further instructions, arms starting to feel pain, body slightly weak from stress, intense anger continuing to build within me.

"Pick up your bag Mister, drop it, pick it up, drop it," the screamer on my left yelled. "What's your name, New Cadet?"

"Paul, Sir."

"What did you just say your name was, Mister?" all three yelled in unison, glaring daggers at me in disbelief. "Mister," the screamer on my right said, "You are either stupid or dumb, I can't tell which? So let me tell you what your name is and how to report."

He leaned an inch closer and yelled, "Sir, my name is New Cadet __ you fill in your last name, Sir! And that's how it's done. Got it"?

"Yes Sir!" I replied, now barking in what I hoped was a loud enough voice. Sweat now dripped down their faces, down crevices and pimples, along well-shaven, square jaws. These were the men to whom I was entrusting myself. I would be molded, guided, led and reshaped to be made into the "proverbial man" I wanted to be...by these young men who were acting like angry, spoiled children, upset that I was breathing their oxygen and standing on the hallowed grounds of their famous institution, their West Point, their world.

Who was crazy here? Them, for believing their own bullshit, or me, for thinking I could be a part of this? Not even five minutes had passed in real time, but the clock in my brain recorded it as forever. Thoughts of what my life had been like only seven months previously now flooded my consciousness.

CHAPTER 2

'm on the tennis court at the very end of the match. It is my serve and I hit a ferocious twist into my opponent's backhand and get a loopy, midcourt return. I step into the ball and pound it to his backhand again. The ball hits within an inch of the baseline, bouncing wildly towards his body above the shoulders. He can only pop it up. I move in, volley the ball away for an easy winner. Game over. Just another day at the office.

I'm seventeen, in my senior year at North Miami High, full of confidence out there on the tennis court. My other problems are gone for the time being, evaporated by a world-class forehand with an intimidating topspin that kicks deep and high. My severe western grip may look awkward, but it gives me an angle of impact to impart power and control over the ball. The amount of torque from my arm and wrist produces so many revolutions of overspin that the tennis ball looks like an egg crossing the net. My forehand is a luxury vehicle that transports me above my daytime realities…less so for my nightly conflicted dreams.

And believe me, I need transporting. During the day I bite my nails down to the quick. My dreams have me waking up in a cold sweat. I'm scrawny, just under six feet tall, a virgin exploding with love, or maybe hormones. Frankly, I'm worried and confused about that, but I can't really talk to anyone about this, not my friends and especially not my parents!

Mom and dad are hard-working people who always put the needs of our family first, but we were not exactly close. Dad is at work seven days a week at his gift shop, 'The Trade Winds', on Miami Beach. Mom's a hospital department administrator, ruling her roost there. She's never wrong and overly judgmental, not someone I'd ever want to confide in. Once, they sent me to the doctor to have "the talk." He asked me if I had any questions. I said no. That was that! End of discussion.

Sex—specifically my lack thereof—occupies a large segment of my brain. I'd be happy to learn more about it with a female, any female. Well, not Helen, my twin sister! We don't discuss anything substantial, certainly not sex! Our sister Wilma, five years and a day older than us, is out of the house, married and living in California. I think she has distanced herself on purpose to gain independence. I admire her for that.

Another thing I worry about is my lack of Jewish education. I never had a Bar Mitzvah. I'm sort of ashamed about my lack of participation in the Jewish community. I mean, I do believe in God and I'm proud to be a Jew, but between tennis and school, I don't really have any extra time. Personally, I don't think God is terribly upset with me. After all, tennis uplifts me and keeps me centered, and while I still have what they call teenage angst—horniness and heartache— my game helps me compartmentalize all that. It focuses me, keeps my mind from running in circles, gives me a path to direct all that energy. The power of my forehand lets me know I am strong and determined. I love to compete and my life, my world, is centered on being a great player. How can God fault me for that?

I'm a very good student too, by the way. My SAT scores are outstanding; I'm in mostly honors classes and I'm reasonably sure that the colleges I'm applying to will accept me just based on that. But my meal ticket—a full four-year scholarship—will be because of tennis. My free ride will allow Helen to attend college as well. Without it, my parents can't afford to send both of us at the same time.

Maybe I'll forego higher education to play professionally. Any tennis player worth his salt wants to play Wimbledon, Roland Garros, Melbourne, Forest Hills: the big four slams. I believe I have the tools and skills to go wherever I want. I just need to decide what I want to do, what will be the greatest help to my family and what will be the most satisfying for me as well. Either way, I plan to work hard for my future.

Meanwhile, I live and breathe tennis. I string my own racquets; I sleep with them at night. They're connected to me, extensions of my arm, mind and soul. As I fall asleep, it's as if they're telling me that I can always raise my game, feel the ball better, be freer on the court. That sense of freedom stays with me when I wake up and lets me know I can beat anyone. My singles ranking has shot up every year. My doubles play has been amazing as well. So, maybe what I feel those racquets are communicating to me is the truth.

My twin is my opposite. I'm skinny, she's stocky. She has a lot of friends; I'm more of a loner. I'm serious and she's jocular. She's the family communicator—when she's not in lockdown in her room— and I'm the student. But while I'm the family peacemaker, she often initiates small guerilla wars at home.

I've got ocean blue eyes, a deep tan, an easy smile and cheeks that my Aunt Gertie loves to pinch. Helen is not—how shall I put it— much in demand by the boys; she's never actually dated. I feel bad that she doesn't have a boyfriend. I can see how upset and hurt she gets. As her twin, I feel what she feels; I can see the pain under her anger, especially when she deals with Mom. I love Helen, but on a day-to-day basis, we only occasionally like each other, tending to bicker instead of talking…and once again, my focus returns to tennis, to my future success.

Helen is my biggest fan and I'm grateful for that. I can look back during tough matches, and there she is, giving me the message, proud to be my sister. She's an excellent tennis player herself, with crushing groundstrokes and a powerful serve. She owns a high state ranking in the Juniors, like I do. But, on the court, she blasts every shot as if she wants to blast her way through life. She won't hear any suggestions of guile, finesse, change of pace, any refinements. I practice longer, harder, more intensely than she does. I think out there. I notice, I learn. Helen mostly wants to bash the ball, so she loses matches that she shouldn't. But her losses don't bother her as much as mine bother me.

I've reached one decision about my future: I do *not* want to be a teaching tennis pro. I have no patience for others. I don't want to be out on the court tossing balls and telling people all day long, "Get your racquet back and watch the ball!" I was a ball boy for Jack Kramer's tour when they played the Miami Beach Auditorium. I've seen the world's best players perform with their power, control and ease. Their racquets are like magic wands, creating mind-boggling shots that I go over and over in my mind. That's who I want to be.

I think I can wait until the end of the spring tournaments in June, right around graduation, when I will decide whether I should go to college. I have six months to give it careful thought and determine if I have what it takes to play professional tennis. As a measure of good sense, though, I've sent out a brief resume to a lot of colleges to see if I'm wanted or needed in their athletic programs. I'm worried, because I'm pretty sure I have only one shot at making the best decision possible. What if I make the wrong choice?

CHAPTER 3

've played a lot of tennis matches where near the end, I was flat-out exhausted and drained from several hours of acrobatic turns and jumps, hugging the fence for the three inches of shade there, licking the inside of the tennis can filled with water for the last two drops, squeezing as much perspiration as possible from my white tee shirt to reduce the weight I carried. Often my tennis racquet turned leaden, my legs felt rubbery, and my feet were weighted with clay-encrusted socks and sneakers.

It was now only my first five minutes of Beast Barracks although it seemed like an eternity. But that was just the beginning! It made those exhausting tennis times now seem like a picnic. I sweated through my short-sleeved shirt and down into the seat of my trousers, building up a body odor I couldn't avoid smelling. I was quickly back to the reality of my "new candidacy" and the terrors at hand, surrounded and confused by the noise and venom of angry men here in Beast Barracks.

"Chin in, eyes front!" the men screamed. "Shoulders back, legs together, no grinning, no smirking, no talking, Asshole!"

Peripherally, I saw I wasn't the only "New Candidate" being abused. There were hundreds more young men bracing against the words barked at them, perspiring down the front of their clean-shaven faces, all beginning to learn how to be West Pointers. I didn't feel alone any longer, but I still felt brutalized and angry.

Unfortunately, anger was the least appropriate emotion I could afford to feel. It had always been my weakness, usually directed at myself for losing focus or blundering. My anger was generating an explosion of tremendous self-doubt within me. *Better calm down, Paul, keep the ball going, one more stroke, don't get sucked into their game plan.*

The leader of my little group decided he'd had enough of me and sent me on my way forward. I had taken only a few steps before two more Upperclassmen stopped me.

"Why are you walking, Boy? You are supposed to 'double-time run' wherever you go. So, start double-timing in place so we know that you know how to do this!" Both these two new fellows, one with a southern accent, were shorter than me, but they glared even more intently than the others, yelling louder, twisting their faces into grimaces, talking at me closer to my chin.

"Did you know, Boy, you are lower in the scheme of life than dog shit?" The first Upperclassman, laughing and taking great delight in making sure I was thoroughly educated to this fact. I said to myself *…Okay…since I now know I'm dog shit and you know I'm dog shit, why keep pissing on me?* I was moldable material and would have responded to constructive criticism. There was nothing constructive about this.

"Pull your gourd in, Mister, eyes front!" yelled the first Upperclassman. "Keep double-timing until I say stop."

"Chin in, Mister!" the southerner shouted. "We call that bracing and you are to always have your chin in unless you are in your room with no Upperclassmen around, or you are ordered to 'fall out.' Go over to that group of worthless little girls and stand in line with them!"

I stopped thinking and double-timed over to the "little girls" lined up in a row at attention. Obedience and immediate reaction seemed far better than thinking: *do what you're told, follow the rules, get with the program, suffer through the next five minutes.*

Another Upperclassman was cruising the "little girls'" line with a clipboard. "Name?" he asked, sternly.

"New Cadet Kantrowich, Sir!" I answered, chin pulled in, shoulders pulled back, arms flush against my sides, my little travel bag in my left hand. My face was a sweaty swamp. As he moved past me, I turned my head to follow him. He had a face you wouldn't remember, some type of gold decoration on the upper sleeves of his gray tunic, with an air of administrative competence as he referred to the clipboard in his left hand.

An officer in a green uniform walked by and the Upperclassman saluted him with his right hand: rigid, angled, fingers together, quick and precise. The officer returned the salute smartly and walked away. As the Upperclassman turned around and saw me watching the receding officer, his face reddened, his mouth formed a scar of irritation, eyes flicking angry waves of daggers at me. He reversed his route and came back towards me.

"Kantrowich," he yelled, "What are you looking at? Eyes front always! Give me twenty pushups, hit it."

I laid my wet palms on the hot pavement and began, struggling by number twelve, faltering at fifteen, dying at twenty, pain radiating through my biceps and triceps, saved again by my pal adrenaline. I got back up to attention, glasses awry, chin trying to hit the back of my neck, mind cloudy from exertion. "Kantrowich," he barked, "Report to the Man in the Red Sash near the Clock Tower."

It was now about ten minutes into Beast Barracks, the longest ten minutes of my life. I turned toward the Man in the Red Sash, about fifty feet away, standing adjacent to the Clock Tower, and began double-timing toward him.

Within a couple of steps, I could see what a majestic figure he was, a proud warrior. His posture was ramrod straight, his chest proudly pushing his gray tunic outward while his black beaked cap rested firmly and squarely on his head, the gold USMA shield centered above the beak and shining like a star. Knife creases fronted his immaculate white trousers; startling bolts of light reflected off his black shoes. His wide shoulders tapered to a narrow, athletic waist. Trimmed in black, his tunic seemed painted on his upper torso. A white belt with a golden plate in its center angled from his right shoulder across his body to the left side of his waist where it interrupted a wider, red sateen sash circumscribing his waist. A shapely, large, red tassel dropped down along his left leg. He carried a silver sword hitched down through a special holder, in a silver, gold-tipped scabbard. Resplendent, graceful, commanding, he exuded confidence, standing there holding a battered clipboard thick with sheets of printed paper. For the first time since this nightmare started, I felt hope.

Ten feet into my quest, I was stopped by another Upperclassman. "Where are YOU going, Mister? Slap that gourd in, wipe that smirk off your ugly face, why is your shirt coming out of your trousers? "IRP!"

I assumed the word "IRP" meant "speak." "Going over there, Sir," I said, pointing towards the Clock Tower and the majestic man.

"Mister, you should be at attention when you talk to me. Slap your chin in, eyes front. No pointing! Now tuck that shirt into your trousers before the Officer of the Day sees you looking so slovenly." I didn't think, I just reacted, tucking as ordered.

"Move out quickly now, get away from me. I detest slobs!" I moved out, double-timing towards the Clock Tower, where I could clearly see the time: 0917. Only seven minutes had transpired since I was dropped onto the sidewalk, entered the sally port, screwed up my courage and stepped into this quagmire called the United States Military Academy at West Point.

After only less than ten minutes into this new life, my thoughts swiftly drifted back to seven months previous, and home.

CHAPTER 4

I t's still hot at twilight as I finish practice. I towel off and drink two tennis cans of fuzzy water to rehydrate; refreshing, but it's an acquired taste. Reviewing my practice sessions in my head, I realize that my backhand needs a lot of work. Slicing is no problem; I can slice a thousand backhands and rarely miss, but it's still a defensive shot. It keeps me in the point but it sure isn't going to win me any matches against better players. I also need to work on my low forehand volleys. But it's my flat and topspin backhands that I should concentrate on.

Mike Belkin from Florida and Bill Lenoir out in Arizona are the only players around with two-handed backhands. I've tried it, but for me, the two-handed swing is awkward. I must continue to perfect my one-hander. I need to address the ball more aggressively by positioning my racquet head lower and not overstepping my right foot laterally. Hitting a million proper backhands would also help!

Abe Revman, my cigar-chomping tennis pro, agrees. "Firmer wrist...don't whip it too much, Paul," he says as we leave the court. "Good practice today, good job," he adds, patting me on the back and sending me home.

Abe took over from my first pro, Nick Bollettieri. Abe's my kind of guy, always smiling, encouraging, kindly but honest. He's short, stocky and tan, in his fifties. Nick was slightly taller, late twenties, the tannest white man I've ever met and a bundle of energy who decided, at some point, that he belonged in greener pastures. With Abe, it's all about you as a player and as a young person maturing. With Nick, it was always about Nick. While Nick was instrumental in helping Helen and me in the beginning, it's Abe who has helped us develop into excellent players and, hopefully, more well-rounded individuals.

As I walk the more-than-two-miles home, my confusion about college returns. I've received the first response to my mass-marketing yesterday from Colgate University, offering me a grant-in-aid. Since it's not a full four-year scholarship, I sent the coach a nice "thanks, but no thanks" note. Something tells me I'm going to meet him eventually down the road of collegiate tennis if I do decide to go to college at all.

Helen wants to attend the University of Florida in Gainesville and be a Gator! But since there are no tennis scholarships for women and because of her iffy grades, I honestly doubt she'll be admitted. Every day that passes without her hearing from "Gatorville" is another day of gloom and doom in the house. Her anxiety over this issue, plus the ongoing war between her and mom, makes her no fun; not that I'm around her much. She gets home, sees there's no letter, loudly slams her bedroom door and I don't see her until the next morning at 6:30 AM while we're rushing to school.

The time is rapidly approaching for both of us to participate in the annual Orange Bowl Junior Tennis Championships at Flamingo Park, down in Miami Beach. The tournament usually takes place during the Christmas holidays; it's considered the world junior tennis championship. Juniors come from all over the United States, Europe, South America and Australia to participate, although the largest contingent comes from Florida. Arthur Ashe from Richmond, Virginia, Charlie Pasarell from Santurce, Puerto Rico…there are no slackers in this group. Helen and I are both getting excited about it and upping our preparations. I can't wait to smack some tennis balls around with all these terrific players and prove something to myself.

Helen has something to prove to herself as well; she has her heart set on playing a girl named Judy Alvarez. All the Florida players are laying-in-wait to pounce on anyone from outside our domain. Flamingo Park will be humming and vibrating with an energy rarely witnessed by the "snowbirds"—older folks who come to Florida in the winter to escape the cold and relax.

Abe is working with both of us on strategy for the tourney. We've discussed the slicing and pushing by the South Americans, the aggressive serve/volley by the Australians and a host of other tactics. He keeps his eyes on Helen, saying "But most of all, we have to be consistent...reduce unforced errors and keep the damn ball in the court!" We all laugh at that remark; Helen knows she'll keep on blasting the ball. I know it too, and she knows that I know. (As twins, we can sometimes read each other's minds.) But God bless our coach Abe. He's ever the optimist and honestly believes he can make Helen listen to him.

I always listen to Abe; Helen rarely does. I listen because Abe isn't judgmental, just factual. I don't usually take even constructive criticism well; I'm always on the defensive and I know it's a weakness of mine. But Abe's kindness and thoughtful comments have helped me learn and listen better. I want to be a great tennis player and I know his coaching can help me get there. With this big tourney a little over two weeks away, I'm determined to concentrate on my game, in fact, harder than ever before.

But Helen, she's different. Part of her is a closed book. Having a boyfriend is her deepest desire and that's just not happening. She doesn't talk about it, and she doesn't want anyone else discussing it either.

CHAPTER 5

Seven months previous, Helen's success and happiness was on my mind. At this moment, however, I should be only thinking about my new mission, to report to the "Man with the Red Sash," now only thirty feet away. I started towards him again, double-timing with my chin in, twenty feet, fifteen feet....

"Where are YOU going, Mister?" yelled an annoyed voice from behind. I stopped without turning, stood at attention, at a loss. Another Upperclassman, in a highly agitated state, confronted me three inches from my face.

"IRP! I asked you a question, Smackhead. Where are you going?"

I panicked, unable to speak, clutching my small bag in my left hand, tensing that hand into a fist, feeling my face flush, grinding my teeth. The words finally burst out, and I screamed, "Sir, I am to report to the Man in the Red Sash, Sir!"

"Are you angry at me, Mister, yelling at *me*? You'd better have a damn good reason for being angry at me, Mister! IRP!"

"No Sir" I said, trying to convey a less hostile tone.

"You had better not be angry at me, Mister," he said. "Stand up straight, shoulders back, chin in more, listen up. When you pass an officer or a cadet Upperclassman, you are to stop, assume the position of attention and smartly salute that person until they pass by. That's the courtesy we extend to our superiors. It's recognition for who they are, get it? It upset me when I saw you totally ignore that officer."

"Yes Sir!" I replied quickly.

"You got THAT Mister?" he said as he moved to my right. "Yes Sir!" He was now behind me. "Move out," he snapped, "Now!"

I raced the last fifteen feet toward the majestic figure who would hopefully put these crazy past ten minutes into perspective. Facing him directly, I stood at attention. Shoulders back, knees closer together, feet aligned, I smartly saluted. "Sir", I announced, "New Cadet Kantrowich reporting to the Man with the Red Sash as ordered, Sir!"

The Man with the Red Sash seemed the epitome of a West Point cadet, a vision of what people might imagine he should be. Posture straight, elegant uniform and a serious but relaxed expression on his face. He said nothing at first. He looked directly into my eyes. Finally, quietly he asked, "First name, please?"

"Paul, Sir," I replied, a light tremble in my voice. The Man with the Red Sash scanned me up and down, then referred to his clipboard for what seemed forever. "Last name please" he continued. Eventually he said, in a voice raised only slightly, "Welcome to West Point, New Cadet Paul Kantrowich. There are over nine hundred and fifty of your new classmates here today. Some will be gone before 1700 hours, some gone tomorrow, some gone every day for quite a while. Good luck, Kantrowich, you are going to need it! Make your family and your country proud of you."

I considered his words. They sounded very sincere. I needed a little sincerity today.

"Report to Fourth Squad, First Platoon, 'A' Company, First Battalion," he continued. "They are over there." He pointed to a corner of the yard. "Now move out!"

"Yes, Sir!" I replied, and double-timed off in the direction he indicated, moved by his kindness after all the screams and insults previously by the maniacs I had met. *This is the way it should be here,* I thought. I now had an image in my mind that could boost me up when my spirit sagged, a hero I could admire and emulate, a calm and generous leader to look up to. As I looked back, just a quick glance, to keep his image firmly in my mind, The Man in the Red Sash seemed to glow with a bright aura about him.

"WHOA, where are you going, Sonny Boy?" yelled an Upperclassman. I halted, stood at attention, bracing, chagrined. "My Squad, Sir!"

"Well, who gave you the right to look around and check things out like you were just a tourist looking at the sights? Are you a tourist, Boy? Are you here on vacation, Boy?"

"No, Sir," I carefully replied.

"You were looking around like you are a tourist. Are you lying to me, Boy?" His expression could have scared a rabid dog.

"No, Sir," I replied again.

"Give me fifteen pushups right now. Hit it!" he barked. My arms collapsed after twelve.

"Looks like Sonny-Boy is really a little girl after all," he chuckled. "Start over again and give me fifteen more, or you'll just stay with me and keep starting over. What's it going to be, little girl?"

Adrenaline saved me again. I ground out the fifteen pushups with him standing over me. Finished, I stood back up at attention as he edged closer to me, perspiration dripping off both our faces, anger on his face, fear on mine.

"Listen, New Cadet and listen good…your eyes are fixed straight ahead at all times, no one gives you the authority to look anywhere else, ever. You got that, little girl?"

"Yes, Sir!" I stated.

"And another thing. You keep that chin in, Smackhead, always. No one gives you the authority to let it out. You got that too?" He didn't wait for an answer. "Now get out of my sight. Move it!"

I grabbed my bag, saluted, and started running double-time, realizing I'd lost my bearings; I didn't know which direction was which. There were so many New Cadets running helter-skelter, so much yelling and black rage. I stopped to salute an Officer, started up again. I stopped to salute one Upperclassman, then another. When I stopped to salute two Upperclassmen conversing with each other, they didn't move, so I didn't move after saluting them. Not knowing what to do, I stood erect, fixed in place. As they approached me, their cheerfulness and laughter dissipated, their demeanor now provocative.

"What do you want, Smackhead? Where are you going? What are you doing? Do you know what you are doing?" "Why were you looking at us?" raged the redheaded cadet with two chevrons on his tunic's lower sleeves.

"Slap your silly gourd in further, Mister!" added his apparent buddy, who had four chevrons on his upper sleeves. I had no answer. "Where are you going?" they asked again.

"Sir, Fourth Squad, First Platoon, 'A' Company, First Battalion, Sir!" I finally answered. Both men laughed loudly, their mood lightened.

"You are in luck, Smackhead, that's where we're going...follow us!" I had just run into my Squad Leader and my Company Commander, although I had no clue who they were and where they were taking me. They walked, I double-timed. No more talking, no more thinking; I just followed my leaders.

Traversing the quadrangle, we entered the North Area, adjacent to the Cadet Mess. We stopped at the stoops of the first set of barracks on the west side, now cast in brilliant sunlight. Barracks rose on three sides of the quad, while the fourth opened to a walkway out to the Plain and the Mess Hall. Men were starting to assemble in groups. Their cacophony punctuated the oppressive atmosphere in this smaller and more confined area.

If I did an about-face right this minute I could walk out of my present situation to freedom, to a saner environment, to safety. Part of my brain was screaming, *Get the hell out of here, Paul!* while another section was bitching, *don't give up, go one more minute, go one more hour, go one more day!* But my resolve to survive was eroding away.

Feeling dehydrated, abused and confused, I wondered why such degradation was necessary from an institution where I had been invited to attend. Not a moment had passed that my mind didn't question the validity of this experience so far. I hadn't expected champagne and caviar, but I hadn't expected torment either. I didn't realize I had signed onto something that would strip me of my individuality, punish my creativity and replace it with obedience. I had to believe that the inner messages I was receiving about bolting were valid.

Competitive tennis, however, was greatly instrumental in strengthening my resolve in tough situations. Within me was a stubborn resolution to overcome adversity; to persevere when others might quit. It was as if I were in the last set of a grueling tennis match, down match point, trying desperately to win: *One more point Paul...just one more point.* I had arrived at my new home for the next eight weeks, Beast Barracks, with its long-standing traditions, good or bad...and I would try hard to play through to the last point. I dreaded it but loathed the idea of quitting even more.

As I followed my Squad Leader, my mind drifted again, swirled off on tangents. Disconcertingly, one specific thought right then was about a guy named Herb who, recently, played a big role in my life. Herb!

CHAPTER 6

Helen came home from school today and slammed her room door shut with the loud bang we'd all gotten used to. I hadn't seen her all day. We never had the same classes together at school. On my way out to the tennis courts, I check to see if she's coming with me to practice; we share a beat-up, dented, dark puke-green 1950 Buick my dad bought for us for fifty dollars. It uses more oil than gas, but it's all ours; well, we alternate "ownership" of the car. Sometimes we fight over whose turn it is to drive and whose turn to fill the tank, but mostly we luxuriate in the fact that we have our own car.

Today is Helen's day to own the car. I cross the three feet past the bathroom we share and knock on her door. "Go away," she says.

"It's me," I say.

"GO AWAY!" she shouts.

When Helen makes up her mind about something, you don't mess with her. With the big Orange Bowl tournament coming up in less than two weeks, I would have thought she'd be practicing every chance she gets. She remains locked up in her room instead.

Since it's not my day to drive, I begin walking to the tennis courts. I checked the mail when I got home from school; Helen still hasn't heard from the University of Florida. That's probably what's eating her, since some of her friends have already gotten early acceptance letters. I feel badly for her, but it's out of my control. She's probably also upset that the offers have been rolling in for me: free rides from The University of Wisconsin, Duke, Florida State and Notre Dame, so far.

Walking along 163rd Street, the main drag in North Miami Beach, I start to obsess about my backhand. Today's practice will be all about that stroke. To do well in the tournament, I must work on firming up my wrist before the racquet head contacts the ball. I know what to do...I just must focus and do it!

As I walk, I keep shifting into a backhand preparatory stance and concentrating on a firm wrist prior to the start of my swing. If I can swing my racquet every twenty feet on my way to the courts, it will take me twenty minutes longer to get there, but I will have swung my backhand with a proper, firmed up wrist six hundred and sixty times. I can sense improvement already. I can't wait to hit tennis balls to prove it.

At the courts, Abe comes over to me, shifts his fat Macanudo cigar from mouth to hand, and asks me to do him a favor. "Paul...I would appreciate it if you could hit with someone for a little while. I think you'd enjoy it and I know he would."

Oh, sure. All I want to do is hit backhands. Oh well. If someone can provide pace on the balls, it doesn't matter to me whether my opponent is a ten-year-old kid or a seventy-year-old lady.

"Okay, Abe," I say. He points across the grass towards court number four: it's a short, stubby, forty-something-year-old man. We make our way over to him and I'm thinking, *all righty then.*

"Herb," Abe says, "I would like you to meet Paul. Paul is a high school senior and a highly ranked junior in the state, so please try to take it easy on him!"

I look over at Abe and turn so only he can hear me. "Abe, I think you have it backwards; I promise I'll take it easy on him!" My self-confidence was kicking in and I needed to show Abe I had belief in myself…something he continually preached to all his players.

I turn and approach the middle-aged guy and say, "Hi Herb, nice to meet you. Let's go out there and bang a few balls around."

Herb bends over to pick up his two racquets. "Pleasure to meet you, Paul. Thanks for playing with me."

"Sure," I say.

We shuffle over to court number four. Herb has a certain aura about him, a quiet air of confidence as he glides onto the court. All his movements are precise and rhythmic. I have a sneaking suspicion I may have badly misjudged my new opponent.

The moment Herb takes a few practice swings, I know I've been an idiot. His strokes flow like chocolate syrup poured over cold, vanilla ice cream; his footwork barely imprints the court's surface. His approach and addressing the ball are pure silk, smooth! Always smiling at me, he seems so relaxed. Herb epitomizes the essence and form I've always looked to achieve as a player but still obsess about.

After a few minutes of warming up I ask Herb to play rather than just hit. Hitting stroke after stroke bores me; I always prefer a match. "Sure," says Herb, "Let's play!"

After I barely win a very close first set, I ask Herb to play another, and then another…and another. Watching him play—seeing the depth of his shots with the control that he has and the variety of spins and power he demonstrates—I'm in awe. That doesn't mean I'm going to let him beat me! But I must use every trick in my repertoire to eke out a victory. Balls are flying over the net as if they were shot out of a cannon. Two hours go by; Herb looks as fresh and relaxed as when he started playing. He keeps smiling the whole time while I grimace, fight and struggle. He's not taken aback by my talking to myself at times; he just keeps grinning at me. This short, stubby guy is a fantastic player, a true gentleman with a lot of class.

As Herb and I part ways he asks, "Why did you run around your forehand so much and hit so many backhands during our game? You had such a powerful topspin forehand that gave me fits. Why didn't you capitalize more on that?"

Sheepishly, I tell him my backhand needs more work and I'm determined to concentrate on it. He laughs and says, "You kept a nice firm wrist when your racquet head was low, but it got a little floppy when I saw your concentration level shift. Best of luck and I hope we have an opportunity to meet again. I have a feeling that might happen sooner than later. Take care, Paul," he adds as he glides away.

Afterwards, Abe tells me that Herb Lewis had been a great player in the "good ole days" and is now actively involved with the tennis umpires around the state and the country. Now he tells me!

It turns out that Herb was indirectly interviewing me for a possible invitation to attend West Point. Abe never said a word about it because he felt that just being myself would be good enough. That's how much faith and confidence he had in me.

I walk home, tired. My mind drifts away from tennis practice and towards a host of different topics: women I like; what I'd like to be doing with the women I like; possible colleges; my future.... Then I start to obsess again about my failure to become a Bar Mitzvah. I've had very good reasons for this, but I think that ship has sailed. Helen and I were "confirmed" at age fifteen in temple studies, but neither of us can speak or read Hebrew at all. The best I can do is recite some memorized prayers at the friday night services we occasionally attend with our parents. We've both picked up a little Yiddish from relatives conversing at holiday get-togethers, but that's it. Maybe I should start being a more conscientious Jew....

Sleep does not come easily, even though I'm beat. My mind keeps drifting to love and sex and the confusion I feel between the two. *Focus, Paul!* Right now, my backhand deserves all my attention, but damn…it's hard not to think about girls, especially Jill.

CHAPTER 7

A t my twentieth minute here at West Point, I stood bracing hard in a line with eight other sweaty and sun-baked New Cadets, standing parallel to the worn, wooden stoops of our gray, stone barracks in the North Area. My chin was pulled in as far as humanly possible. We had formed the nine-man Fourth Squad of First Platoon, "A" Company, First Battalion. Rather than bearing the present burden of Beast Barracks as individuals, we were now in a collective state of despair. A solitary figure, our Squad Leader, observed our motley crew. I closed my eyes awaiting the next command, the next insult, the next physical abuse. Scattered, colored dots sped steadily across the darkness beneath my eyelids and inside my brain as I desperately tried to relax.

My thoughts traveled south to my home, to my twin sister Helen. Did she sense my confusion, my discomfort and physical ache? Was she still in bed, having gone out to the movies the night before, or over to Miami Beach and Jahn's Ice Cream Parlour? What happy, fun, exciting things did she have planned? Was she practicing at the tennis center, now that I was no longer around to cajole her into improving her game? There was always another tournament to prepare for at that time of year in Florida; was she working on her consistency? Was our tank of a car still working? Did she get the oil changed? Had she met any guys she was interested in or were interested in her?

Oh Helen, I never thought I would miss you after only forty-eight hours! I'm jealous of the freedom you have…the vast, open opportunities to explore new worlds, while I'm trapped in line here with my Squad…sweating, aching, following strict, meaningless and denigrating commands. Do all these small tortures lead to manliness? I wish you well, Helen, please… think of me occasionally before they kill me.

I thought about the University of Florida, which Helen would joyfully attend, and where, just three weeks prior, I was playing Junior Davis Cup Tennis with Letzring, Johnson, Belkin, Shuert, Turville, Harris and Kenny Marcus. Fresh from winning the Florida State Junior Boys Doubles with Kenny, I had beaten three top ten junior singles players enroute to the semi-finals of the singles. I smiled, remembering the best ten days of my life. A sense of peace arose in me as I recalled how wonderfully alive I felt during the short breaks after splitting sets in a tough match; changing my drenched tee shirt, maybe switching to a tighter racquet, while drawing up a new strategy to win….

I opened my eyes to a red-haired, freckled-faced, wide-grinning Squad Leader parked just a few inches north of my nose. "Are we having fun today, Kantrowich?" he asked calmly. "Are you thinking about how much fun I have planned for you and your friends today, Kantrowich? I tell you what, Kantrowich, I'm going to ask the entire Squad except you to hit the ground and knock off fifteen pushups… and then, when they finish, maybe fifteen more. You can just watch and observe their troubles, caused by you. Do you think any of them will be happy about this, or about you afterwards?"

My Squad labored through the punishment as our Squad Leader explained, "When one New Cadet screws up, the whole Squad will pay the price. That's my first rule. Know it well!"

The last Squad member grunted, completing his pushups as the

Squad Leader continued, "So fellas, you know who to thank for this little lesson? Kantrowich!" I had no doubt they were all going to kick the shit out of me once we were alone. At seventeen, which is worse: mortification, or the fear of physical harm and pain?

The Squad Leader continued. "Gentlemen, now that you've heard my first rule, let us move on to my second rule. You will do everything, all day, all night, as if you are nine segments of one unit. You will eat together, sleep together, shower together, train and learn together...everything you are and will ever be for the next eight weeks, you will do together. And remember, everything you are and will ever hope to be is because I allow it, and you will owe all your future success to me.

"Furthermore, there will be absolutely no failure here. No failure allowed. For the next eight weeks, I will be your mother, your father, your teacher, your spiritual guru, your harshest critic, your judge and your jury and your best friend. You will blindly follow every order I give, every suggestion I make, absorb every precious word out of my military mouth. You will soak up every fact and statistic my brilliant, military mind will project to you."

He paused for us to absorb his wisdom. *Jeez*, I thought, *he sounds as if he really believes this bullshit!* "My name is Cadet Corporal Danford (Danny) Brite, your Squad Leader, your benefactor and the finest human being you will ever set your eyes upon! Today we are going to do the following: first you are going to learn how to march. Then you'll get all your uniforms and learn how to wear them, get all your military gear and learn how to store it, get your rifles and bayonets, get your haircuts, learn to set up your footlockers and your rooms, learn how and when to report, learn how to eat, march and salute. And we are going to do all that and be ready for your swearing-in ceremony at 1730 hours at Trophy Point! That is, of course, if any of you are still here by then." He paused for effect. None of us dared interrupt to ask questions.

"Your parents or the guardians who brought you here today will be in attendance at that ceremony," continued Cadet Corporal Brite, "So you must look sharp, engaged and prepared! Be informed and advised: any one of you can leave these grounds anytime you choose. Simply walk through that sally port and home to your momma. Make sure you wipe away your tears before you go because you wouldn't want your momma to think, instead of her bright-eyed shining man of the family, you are actually a whining, wimpy little girl."

He continued to announce our new orders, demonstrating the drill: "Here is how you stand at 'parade rest,' how you stand at 'attention,' how you 'right face,' 'left face,' 'about face.' You always start marching with your left foot forward first. You halt by bringing both feet together sharply. Now follow my commands. Group AT-TEN-HUT! Forward march!"

I knew all this stuff from years of experience in marching bands, from third grade through high school; here was something I could do without screwing up. It's when the fellow in front of you screws up—even if you are marching properly—that makes you and everyone else look stupid and out of synch.

Alas, the Squad mate in front of me had two left feet, no sense of rhythm and poor marching skills. Our Squad Leader yelled "Halt!" and our clumsy Squad mate ran into the fellow in front of him who had halted while he hadn't. We proceeded to do twenty pushups because of his *faux pas*.

Several more mishaps occurred and so did more series of pushups as our reward. Finally, our Squad's effort seemed to smooth out and we became a reasonable marching unit.

Next, we marched as four Squads in Platoon formation. Not particularly challenging but, with poor control throughout other Squads, the Platoon Leader was yelling his head off: "Stay in line, left foot first, shoulders back, head straight, column left, column right, HALT!"

The Platoon Leader singled out our awkward Squad mate. "What are you, a moron? Don't you know left from right? Are your ears clogged up? What year of school did you finally finish, eighth grade?"

Perhaps the Platoon Leader thought that, if he humiliated this New Cadet enough, it would motivate him to produce better results; a strange way of exemplifying leadership, from where I stood. Or perhaps this West Point Upperclassmen simply strived to take humiliation of New Cadets to its highest possible art form.

My own attitude started slipping from anxious to ho-hum. Just twenty-five minutes into being a New Cadet and the old impatience I felt during long rallies on the tennis court had returned. This attitudinal shift was neither smart nor profitable.

As the Platoon Leader screamed at my Squad mate, my brain began nagging, *GO HOME, not worth it!* I began thinking about home again, Jill and my very best friend and doubles partner Don. Instead of all my concentration totally absorbed with the present situation, I found myself drifting, drifting back to the previous Jewish holidays in December 1960.

CHAPTER 8

'm trying to deal with end-of-semester exams...decide about college...figure out how to buy four or five Hanukkah gifts on a weekly allowance of five bucks...and keep enough money in reserve to take Jill David out on a date Saturday night. I should only be thinking about studying and tennis, with the Orange Bowl looming large, but...my attention span—what little I have—is probably the equivalent of a gnats, because I'm madly in love with Jill! She's a five-foot tall, dark haired, bronzed Jewish princess with the most beautiful smile I have ever seen. I bring Cheez Whiz sandwiches to school every day in order to save money to take her out. Since an average date consists of a movie, gas or oil for the car, and burgers, fries and cokes at McDonalds, I need a buck-fifty left over to swing it. I don't have an after-school job—tennis is my job that will earn money for me later—so I'm not exactly rolling in dough. I'm sick of the taste of Cheez Whiz, but its creamy texture does remind me of Jill's lips, so...it's a reasonable trade-off.

I'm lucky to be on the Spalding Free List, which provides all my tennis racquets and shoes. Otherwise, with my lack of finances, I'd never be able to get through the week; I wear out about twelve racquets a year between hitting the ball, restringing and picking up loose balls around on the court. I mean, I'm a big fan of the blue-throat-ed Kro-Bat models but in my position, I'm grateful for the white, extended-throat Pancho Gonzales racquets they give me. Both racquets have extreme flexibility in the upper shaft and a nice whip effect from the head. Also, I saw Pancho play this year and honestly, I'm thrilled to use the same racquets as he does.

Okay...since I'm also on the Victor String Free List (lucky again, because I string my own racquets), I think I'll give a set of Imperial gut to Helen and string one of her racquets as her Hanukkah gift. I'll give dad a set of nylon strings and restring his racquet as well. Mom and Jill will each get a solitary red rose. Friends and other family members will have to be content with my good wishes for a happy holiday. I'm not cheap, just poor! Gift issues solved, check.

My future in tennis is still undecided, but my focus is on the forth-coming Orange Bowl Junior Tennis Chcompioships. I'm also going to put off choosing a college for as long as possible, because more offers are coming in: University of Miami, Rice and Georgia Tech, to name a few.

I usually allot two hours each evening to study for final exams, but only after I restring my three racquets for the next day's practice. Hitting with topspin is murder on natural gut strings, even worse on nylon fiber. I use the old "pick and dowel" technique for stringing a racquet and I've gotten to be an expert at it. It works very nicely, especially when you have no money and a shitty allowance. I'm going to patch rather than completely restring the racquets tonight, saving both time and string. I'm going to need as much string as I can get for my racquets during the tournament.

I usually restring my racquets in my room while listening to the radio...Miami's WQAM. It's a rock 'n' roll station; that's how I learn all the latest and greatest songs. I dig rock 'n' roll vibrating down to my very bones! As a drummer in both the high school marching band and the orchestra, I often think about becoming a professional percussionist. I even tried to get a couple of guys together to form a band once, but that didn't work out. Our best set included "Miami Beach Rhumba," passé at best. We stunk! I met Buddy Rich's niece at a school hop not long ago and since then, I've been practicing more than ever, dreaming of being like Buddy, one of the world's greatest drummers. If I practice even harder, maybe someday…who knows?

Everything about music cheers me up; it makes me get off my butt and I dance. Helen and her friends taught me all the latest moves like the Watusi, the Stroll, the Locomotive, the Mashed Potato, the Twist and the Frug. I feel like a star at friday night dances, doing the Lindy, the Jitterbug and the Dirty Boogie. Music and dancing relax my mind and ease the pressures of my life. I love Chuck Berry, the Big Bopper, Buddy Holly, Cozy Cole, Chubby Checker and Fabian, among others. "Turn Me Loose" by Fabian is one of my favorite songs. That's what I want, to be turned loose: unencumbered by my parents, released from all the everyday rules and regulations…free to travel and experience the world; that's a goal I have in my lifetime.

Stringing racquets keeps me focussed on tennis, but music and dancing ease my whole body and soul. Unfortunately, they don't relieve my horniness! Slow dancing is quite awkward with a constant woody. On the court, tennis helps alleviate the problem temporarily and for a short while afterwards. But, um…pop-ups can still ocurr; always at inappropriate times.

Jill does *not* relax me. I remain a virgin. If I could just get to "second base," that would be a championship moment! But I'm too much of a gentleman. To be honest, I don't especially know what I'm doing or when to do it. I haven't learned the difference between passion and love, liking someone or being in love with them. I am so crazy about Jill, it must be love? Why does love sometimes hurt so much? It seems all very confusing to me.

★ ★ ★

Finally, it's Friday afternoon. The school doors have slammed shut for the holidays. All the students pile out, looking forward to ten days off; no homework, no more tests, and the freedom to romp and play. Nothing beats the holidays in South Florida; the sun's out and it's not too hot in the tropical breeze, but things are heating up in other ways. We boys eagerly anticipate meeting debutantes from up North, visiting here with their pale, exhausted parents. The girls are looking forward to changing their hair styles, perfecting their tans and flirting with cute northern boys looking to meet a southern belle!

Jill went up north yesterday to visit relatives, affording me less distraction during the Orange Bowl competition. The last time she came to a tournament, I had a one set lead, up a service break in the second set against Eddie Turville. He was seeded number one in the tournament; ranked higher than me in the state. I was just about to upset him in this semi-finals match.

During the first half of play I used my head, my big brain; in fact, I was beating him by focusing on that firmer wrist for my backhand, a calmer, more relaxed approach towards the ball, more aggressive picking up of short balls and by attacking the net. But as soon as I thought about Jill, my little brain took over and dominated my wavelengths during the second half of the match. When I remembered her being only one hundred feet away from the court and watching me...*BAM!* Concentration gone and before you could open a new can of tennis balls....pssssst....match lost. I must give Turville credit for upping his game by sensing my lack of focus and capitalizing on it. But, ugh!

That was then. Today is the day to set the tone for the tourney. I picture myself stepping onto the tennis court with the best players of the junior world and beating them. I am willing my self-confidence to be strong. Tennis is a much more involved sport than just the physicality of it; I've got to project strength, consistency and power out into the airwaves to set my path for the next ten days.

Helen has come out of her funk, and we work out together for a while. She practices her volleys and I blast backhands at her. We talk about her not trying to knock the cover off the ball and keeping more groundstrokes inside the baseline. Abe and I thought we'd convinced her that this was a winning tactic, particularly against players like Carol Ann Prosen, Stephanie deFina and especially Betty Harris, her hated rival. She dislikes Betty because Betty is everything Helen wants to be, taller, gorgeous, long flowing blond hair and a figure that would stop a large, moving truck. Helen keeps shaking her head and saying, "Okay, okay, I got it!"

After my workout, I take a bucket of balls over to a back, unused court and start working on my serve. It's powerful, reliable and consistently good. I rarely double-fault and it usually pulls me out of a jam in a match. Most of the time, I hit an "american twist," but I can flatten it out or slice and slide it. A little more depth is what I need, so I work on my toss, trying to throw it consistently a little farther in front of me, particularly if I'm going to follow it into the net.

I start hitting my serve as hard as I can, making adjustments as I add more depth and action to make it more formidable. After serving a half dozen bushels of balls, I walk off the court, satisfied and eager for the tournament to start.

When you're physically fit, grooved into the methodology of approaching and striking the ball—when your footwork is smooth, your mind clear of chatter about little bullshit things—the ball looks bigger; you can sense the spin and depth of the ball more sharply; you glide easily to wherever you want to be on the court; you can even sense your opponent's thoughts. You can beat anybody. That's how I feel today. My head is in the game. My focus is sharp. *Bring it on Baby, BRING IT ON!*

This will be my last Orange Bowl. Next year, I'll be out of the junior boys division and into the big show, men's tennis. I have my sights aimed straight ahead for winning. As I sit down on a bench to cool off, I know everything's going to be just fine. Tennis is played using one's head the most and my head is in the right place now...at the right time.

I'm also intent on doing well in the doubles competition with my partner and best friend, Don Losman. We've won a lot of tournaments together. We mesh extremely well and complement each other's game. Donnie is about my height, handsome, a religious Jew whose dedication I—as a lazy Jew—admire. Helen has a crush on him that she won't admit, while Donnie's oblivious. Coming from a divorced home, he scrambles his way in the world. We've played each other only once in a singles tournament and I beat him in three hard-fought sets; we became great friends after that first meeting.

Some doubles tournments we've played together flowed smoothly; some were like a war, digging deep within ourselves to pull the match out. We can sense each other's mood and physical limitations to shape our strategy. While we have different temperaments, different styles of play and different strengths, we blend to form a brotherhood. My forehand blasts from the deuce court allow Don to roam freely and volley with impunity. His steady backhand returns give me the freedom to move around and create havoc at the net. More importantly, we have a true, honest friendship we both can draw upon when needed.

Last year, Don and I beat the Abrew/Rochte combo at Fort Lauderdale in the semifinals. It was an interesting match, to say the least. During the second set, Don jumped the net, swinging his racquet at Rochte's head! I jumped over to stop Don, grabbed him, swung him around and said, "What the hell is going on, Donnie?!" He blurted, spittle oozing from his mouth, "That prick called us a couple of kikes!"

Immediately I joined him in going after Rochte, racquets flailing, our wood racquet frames smacking his. There was no body contact, no fists flying, but lots of yelling. We were defending ourselves against more than just an ignorant remark.

Anyway, the tournament director Jimmy Evert broke us up and threatened to default both teams if we didn't calm down, apologize and play tennis like good sportsmen. I took Don aside and reasoned with him that beating those assholes would be the equivalent of defeating the nazis. Hey, whatever works, right? We blew them away in the third set and went on to win the tournament, never to see them as a duo again.

This was only the second time in my life I'd ever been around such an ignorant, biased and ugly individual. The first time anyone called me a kike was several years ago; I didn't even know the meaning of the word. The third and last time I met an anti-Semite, I almost busted a knuckle driving my right fist into the left side of his jaw. I couldn't hold my racquet for almost a week afterwards! That taught me never to use my right hand in a fight unless it was absolutely necessary.

CHAPTER 9

The atmosphere at Flamingo Park, site of the Orange Bowl International Junior tennis champioships, is electric. If you listen carefully, you might discern ten different languages spoken. You can also see at least 100 gorgeous girls in the 18 and under division, strutting around in pretty, short white tennis outfits. Mary Habicht stands out: a lovely American/Brazilian mix with long, tan legs; a radiant smile; and dark, short, coiffed hair: athleticism and beauty wrapped up in one amazing package. *Concentrate on tennis, Paul....*

The Junior Orange Bowl players never see the draw sheet until the first day of the tournament. When you get to the courts, you find out who your first-round opponent is, what section of the draw you're in and who the seeded players are. I plan on winning the tourney, so I'll have to beat a few seeded players along the way; it doesn't matter what order they're in.

I glance up at the large white draw sheet and see that my first opponent is from Israel with a 10 AM starting time. I'm ready. We're introduced at the scorer's table and walk out onto the court to warm up. Forty-five minutes later, we shake hands and return the three balls we've been using to the scorer's table. I've ripped through this guy very quickly: 6-2, 6-1. The hard work on my backhand has proved worthwhile. *Welcome to South Florida, buddy...sorry to ruin your day!*

I'm joyful, confident and on a roll. It's now 11 AM with a clear blue sky overhead, virtually no breeze through the tennis complex. Since my next match won't start until roughly 3 PM, I scout the match where I'll have to play the winner. As I watch from the grandstand, I note both player's shortcomings. Now I'm off to watch Helen's first round match.

I find her on an end court annihilating her attractive but smaller opponent. The midwest cutie is having trouble adjusting to Helen's powerful strokes as well as the Miami heat; she's wilting. Helen's power can almost match many of the top male juniors, and although often her winners barely outnumber her unforced errors, today she can't miss. She's using our new strategy of not going for outright winners on every stroke and it's paying off.

Helen comes off the court sweating heavily but happy. It warms my heart to see her special grin after all those joyless days waiting to hear from Gatorville.

I tell her how well she'd played and try to make the point that the new strategy is working for her. She smiles and says, "Wow, Abe sure knew what he was talking about for my game!" As we walk back to check the main draw sheet, I quietly remind her that I helped with that strategy as well.

"Oh yeah, of course, you too!" she replies. Looking up to see who her next opponent will be. "Did you win?" Helen asks. I answer "Yes" but her smile diminishes immediately, her whole demeanor changes. Her eyes cloud over, and a dogged determination sets onto her face. Judy Alvarez is one of the top seeds in the Junior Girls division, expected to have a great chance to win the tournament...and that's who Helen is scheduled to play next. Helen has wanted to play Judy, but she hoped to get a few more rounds in beforehand.

Judy personifies the tactics of attack tennis. She rushes the net quite often, following her serve in to hit a first volley even on the slower clay surface of the Flamingo Park courts. She brims with self-confidence. Helen dislikes anyone who brims with self-confidence, since she and I usually have so little of that.

"I have to beat her" she mumbles back to me. "I know I can beat her!" I can feel the anxiety and desperation pouring out of her skin. I must help start building her belief in herself again. It's not going to be easy.

"Helen," I tell her, "I have a great game plan and strategy that is going to help you upset her and win the match, but you have to listen to me!" She gives me a look and then leaves, wandering off into the lady's locker room to hide. I guess I'll see her later. For now, off to the coca cola machine to grab some sustenance. I'd better rebuild my positive energy, since Helen just sucked it all out of me.

While sipping on a coke, I hear faint music and drumming wafting by. Regardless of all the great matches going on and all the fantastic junior girls bopping around, this melodious drift pulls me in its direction. I have time until my next match, so I follow the music.

The sound grows in intensity as I amble across the park grounds. I begin to hear horns blending in; then rhythmic percussion sounds which remind me of street beats from a marching band. I can see banners and flags and colorful uniforms moving back and forth. Lo and behold, I've stumbled onto the U.S. National Drum and Bugle Corps Competition! It's an individual, group and band competition with people from all over the country coming together to compete for special honors.

I've been in marching bands since third grade. I know and love percussion and parade drums. As I've said, I have often thought that professional drumming could be a fantastic second career for me. Intrigued, I hurry over to observe the spectacle.

The first division to compete consists of individual drummers on single parade drums. The first contestant I see is a nine-year-old boy playing paradiddles, double paradiddles, triple paradiddles, flam paradiddles—all drum rudiments—so fast and with so little effort that I'm flabbergasted! Never in my wildest dreams could I have imagined this speed and fluidity with such little effort from such a little kid. He's light years ahead of me: *sensational, wow!*

I watch and listen a little longer until I can't stand it and rush away. The realization smacks me in the face that, after more than ten years of practice, I'm not nearly as good as that nine-year-old...and there's a whole park filled with others just like him! That settles it: obviously I'll never be good enough to be a professional drummer. Tennis is where I need to focus. Drumming can be a hobby. For me, this is an emotional setback.

I run back to the courts to calm down, readjust my emotions and rededicate myself to winning this tournament. I observe, from the grandstand, players I think might be a future opponent but I can't get rid of the image of that kid's drumsticks moving like a blur, smoothly hammering out the beats. Clearly, I needed that reality check. Now I can eliminate that pipe dream as a professional musician from my future and concentrate on what's important...tennis! Slowly I try to rebuild my confidence. And there isn't a nine-year-old in the entire world that can ever beat me in tennis anyway.

It's time to get ready. I walk over to the draw sheets posted on large cork boards near the pro shop. They've just posted the doubles seedings and pairings.

Yikes! Crap! The second reality check of the day has just hit me squarely in the face. They posted the junior boys doubles draw and it looks like Donnie and I are in a really difficult position.

CHAPTER 10

had to pull my wandering thoughts back off December's previous Orange Bowl to work through Platoon marching. This lackadasical mind-travel back and forth from the chaos here of Beast Barracks to the comfort of thoughts of home was getting problematic. I had better become more aware of the present and quickly reset as "A" Company was called to order by our Company Commander.

Four chevrons on his upper tunic sleeves, stern facial grimace, ram-rod straight posture, hands along his outer trouser seams, he yelled the order: "Alpha Company, Atten-Hut!" His command was clear and concise; in control of everyone present. Time for me to start focusing on the here and now.

Cadets were supposed to be vibrant and vital, generation after generation, war after war. My Squad mates, with the other three Squads forming our Platoon, now learned to march in Company formation *en masse*. Some Upperclassmen simply observed us, grading and critiquing from the sidelines. A lot of chevrons and designs adorned their gray uniformed shoulders. These men of the cadre were responsible for supervising operations for all New Cadet activities. They also liaisoned with the Officer Corps, the faculty, the

43

Commandant and the Superintendent, helping smooth the flow of the Corps of Cadets throughout the year. These Upperclassmen had just become Firsties (Seniors) and had to prove their own personal mettle to the selection board of officers so that, when the academic year started, they would be awarded the highly ranked jobs for running the Corps of Cadets during the academic year.

It was exhilarating to be marching along with a hundred other men, in proper step, turning when ordered, stopping when ordered, saluting when the Commander bellowed, "Present Arms!" Now that we were back into Company formation, the orders of the day were announced, saluted and immediately put into effect.

Feeling part of a small unit but, even more so, part of a bigger whole, gave me quick but conflicted satisfaction. It was agreeable to my personal sense of orderliness, symmetry and unity, and I had strong, proud confidence in my marching skills. For the first time during this initial hour of Beast Barracks, I chanced the thought, *Things will get better. Maybe I am overreacting to the negative incidents and disregarding the positive?*

Our Company Commander released the Platoons, the Platoons released the Squads, and our Squad Leaders marched us into the barracks, up three and four flights of stairs. We were assigned rooms: three bunkmates to a three hundred square-foot area, sink in the room, but toilets and showers in the basement, four or five flights down. Following that we formed up again to go shopping for everything a New Cadet was supposed have on his person, leave in a footlocker, store in his closet or gun rack or place in his desk. No need for academic books yet.

Since crossing through the sally port sixty minutes prior, we'd either been bracing, double-timing, forming up, doing pushups or being yelled at. As we double-timed over to the Cadet Supply Center, the weather was still pasty, hot and humid, no breeze. None of us had any water since we arrived; none was offered.

Bracing burned up tremendous energy and was the rule of the

day. A New Cadet had to stand at attention with his back straighter than a wooden yardstick; shoulders back as if you had a knife embedded between your shoulder blades; chin slapped in trying to reach the spinal cord; knees and feet together with downward, extended, pointing fingers gripping the sides of your legs like you were trying to avoid urinating. The second part of bracing consisted of having one or several Upperclassmen simultaneously screaming near your nostrils or eardrums, or both.

Our Squad Leader was a world-class "bracer" but not a screamer. Apparently, he believed in the power of words, quietly and eloquently spoken, as opposed to an upsurge of frenetic volume. He would reason with my Squad mates, quietly explaining why our backs should be straight; why our chins smacked in; and why our place in the hierarchy of the military establishment was lower than dog shit.

Once we'd assembled for our shopping formation, the Squad Leader singled me out for being the last to arrive and for failing to stand at attention properly. He braced me hard and said, without raising his voice, "I have my eyes on you, Kantrowich. Better shape up, get with the program! Pull those shoulders back, smack that weak-assed chin in, head up, eyes front! Right at this moment you are on my personal shit list!" My inefficiency and tardiness earned the Squad fifteen more pushups.

We double-timed as a Platoon across the Area, towards the Cadet Supply Center, passing barracks after barracks. A simple railing traveled around the skirt of the stoops of each barracks, with a single door entryway for each stone section, glass windows facing outward from each orderly room overlooking the stoops. The barracks towering over us made me feel I was in a canyon.

The center of all New Cadet activities, the Area, was a giant, miasmic life-force sucking out our energy. It had four sally ports, like the major directions on a compass: North, South, East and West, typifying unity, symmetry and uniformity. It seemed to possess a rhythm all its own, vibrating from hundreds of shoes pounding atop it, screeching from leather soles scraped across its rough textured surface. It reverberated with the many colorful profanities spewed into the air and directed at us from the Upperclassmen's vulgar mouths, punctuated by that most common of yelled phrases: "Slap your stupid chin in, Smackhead!" The echoing shouts of the Upperclassmen blended with the hollow sounds from the statues of heroes long deceased on the West Point campus: Thayer, Sheridan, Lee, Grant and Patton among them.

Surrounded by history, we advanced to the Cadet Supply Center where our Squad Leader ordered "Halt!" I tried to remember the last time I had gone shopping; it seemed so long ago. Every August, prior to the start of each new school year, my mother would take Helen and me to buy new school clothes. I was always allowed to pick out four shirts and three pairs of pants, plus socks and underwear, if mom agreed with my choices. What started out as an exciting adventure would soon turn sour when I realized I wasn't going to be allowed to get what I really wanted. Perhaps shopping at the Cadet Supply Center would prove to be more fun. I really did need a little fun just then.

CHAPTER 11

The junior boys doubles draw sheet seems to melt in front of me. Not only are Donnie and I not even seeded in the draw, but the tournament officials only seeded four teams instead of the normal eight. We must play the seeded team of Arthur Ashe and Cliff Buchholz in a first round matchup.

With my next singles match coming up, I need to snap out of a downward emotional spiral that began with Helen's anxiety over her next match and increased with my losing any chance of a second career in music! I need to talk to my coach Abe or my buddy Don to work through my feelings. Talking about my problems is always therapeutic and helpful.

But...Abe's not around; he's out helping the 13-and-under kids navigate their first big tournament. Don has his own problems out on court number twelve with a tough-looking Floridian named Howard Letzring. He's not going to be a barrel of laughs if he loses that match.

It could be worse, I guess. If Ashe were playing with Cliff's older brother, Butch, it would be an even tougher match. Butch is a better player than Cliff but out of the juniors now. Lucky for the both of us. Still, Cliff is damn good on his own too.

But I digress; I have other things to worry about. The strings in all three of my racquets are starting to fray and I still have my singles match to play. I go looking for Helen and find her on the other side of the grandstand, chatting up her best tennis buddy, Lenore. All my little annoyances have been building up and wreaking havoc with my confidence. Maybe the girls will draw me out of this funk.

Trying to talk to them is like interrupting a couple of magpies chowing down on roadkill. They speak in rapid-fire, hushed tones while the matches proceed below us. Eventually they notice me; I tell them everything. Lenore says, wisely, "You don't have to play doubles until the day after tomorrow, so concentrate on your singles match today!" She's right, of course.

"You are going to beat them anyway," Helen chimes in, always my cheerleader. "So why are you so worried?" Yeah, this was a good idea, talking to my sister and Lenore. I shouldn't get so down on myself; it's nuts.

After a moment, Helen asks, "What's the great strategy you claim to have for my match against Judy? I really need to beat her in the worst way!"

Feeling chuffed, I switch from insecure and needy to big-shot brother-mentor mode. "Okay, listen closely. Number one: when she comes to the net behind her serve, just lob over her head high enough so she can't hit an overhead. When she runs back to the baseline to recover, drop shot her immediately. You won't win every point," I warn her, "but she'll get tired in this heat. Number two: soft ball her when you can; she thrives on power so let her create her own. Number three: hit a lot of slices, keep the ball low and deep in the court. If you make her bend lower for the ball, she won't be able to drive forward to the net as often. Number four: you can expect her to attack the net a lot, so only blast the ball when you have an open lane to fire at. Lastly: clear your mind of who she is and concentrate on what you need to do on the court. You CAN beat her Helen! It won't look pretty out there, but my tactics will work!"

I leave the two of them looking at each other and go off to start my own pre-match preparation. First, I eat a baloney sandwich from home, drink another coke from the machine and finally, take a long pee in the men's locker room. You never want to interrupt a match you are winning to take a bathroom break.

In the junior boy's 18 and under division, you don't sit down for a two-minute break when you switch sides, you don't take a fifteen-minute break if you have split sets and there are no injury timeouts. Play is continuous. If you call for an umpire because your opponent is an asshole and cheating calling the lines on his side of the court, you wait for the ump to show up; that's the only brief respite you ever get!

At the appointed time, I'm ready to play a short, speedy Chilean—Eduardo Guell—who slices the crap out of the ball. He makes me dig down low to get under his shots, both forehand and backhand. Since he has a lousy serve, I'm able to figure out his game quickly. I become aggressive, hammering both my serve and forehand confidently. In about an hour, I waltz off the court, no worse for wear. Another win, another step in the right direction.

My thoughts turn to Helen, so I rush over to watch her compete against Judy. The old saying goes, "From your lips to God's ears!" Well, apparently God never listened to the tactics I taught Helen, and neither does Helen. Judy is crushing my sister in straight sets. Helen is caught up in the idea of playing on a featured court; I figure she's embarrassed to soft ball and lob. She keeps blasting away, hit or miss, all through the match…more misses than winners.

After losing the match, Helen storms off the court and I don't see her for the rest of the afternoon. Her doubles partner Lenore appears to be in hiding, avoiding her. I can't say I blame her. The car ride home is a nightmare with me not knowing what to say. Helen is just ignoring my presence anyway.

Back at home, Helen slams her bedroom door shut and that's the end of that. I feel her loss, deeply. But since tomorrow is going to be such a big day for me, I've got to shake it off and plot my moves for the next day's matches. I have two singles and a doubles match; my third-round singles opponent is Edud Dagen, another Israeli. I know nothing about him.

After showering and restringing my racquets, I assemble more stringing gear to take with me in the morning, while thinking and dreaming about my plan to win both the singles and doubles matches. First, I play the matches in my head; then I develop a strategy from my thoughts. At last, I feel ready to win this thing. I know I may not be the best tennis player in the tournament, but I have the greatest motivation and drive of anyone here and I am ready to boogie.

CHAPTER 12

Thinking about ready to boogie, I have been at West Point now for only an hour and five minutes. It seems like a lifetime; I think I might be ready to boogie the hell out of here! I have tried hard to keep my thoughts from flying back and forth between the harsh reality of Beast Barracks and tennis. I know it's time to stop this spotty lack of concentration and fully participate in the activities of this insane environment. I am just not feeling right though; like someone stole my wallet and I am missing my driver's license, my personal identity, who I really am.

As we New Cadets entered the Cadet Supply Area, we were allowed to "fall out"—to let our chins out from the back of our necks. Relief! Immediately, we were each given two large, brown, strong duffel bags, both capable of holding at least sixty to seventy pounds of new gear.

We were also permitted to interact with the civilian staff who measured us, clothed us and filled our bags with the proper gear and apparel. They had all the sizes in all the clothing needed for more than 950 New Cadets, right there at hand. It was truly amazing! Their smiles and chatter were infectious. This was the first time since entering Beast Barracks that I associated with friendly, sincere and helpful people, none of whom were interested in breaking me down or breaking my balls.

We all were issued a dress uniform; an army field outfit (fatigues); a parade uniform; an athletic uniform; a bathroom uniform; a khaki cadet uniform; a classroom uniform; two overcoats (one long, one short); a raincoat; a gray jacket; a black hooded parka; a heavy plasticized poncho; five hats (one gray hat with a black beak, one soft gray triangular hat, one "tar bucket" parade hat, one brown baseball-type cap for the field outfit and one metal, brown, pitted helmet with a liner); two pairs of black shoes; one pair of hightop black boots; one pair of Keds basketball sneakers; multiple pairs of black dress socks and white athletic socks; white tee shirts and white boxers; two black belts; two brass belt buckles, unattached; and two larger brass buckles—one for the waist, one for the chest.

As we moved through the various outfitting stations, our Squad Leader said, "You are all going to have to learn to wear all these different uniforms so, as a special reward, we will have clothing formations to practice doing that." *Oh, joy!*

Each of us also received a shoeshine kit; a brass cleaning kit; a letter-writing kit; a bathroom kit (toothbrush, toothpaste, razor, shaving cream, deodorant, nail file); a gun-cleaning kit; a blanket; two sets of flat white sheets; two pillowcases; one pillow; a large, "brown boy" comforter; two large towels; two smaller towels; two hand towels; a bar of soap; and a plastic soap dish. Next, we were each issued an M-1 rifle with attached leather shoulder strap; an elongated silver bayonet; an accessory belt; a water canteen; an ammo pouch; and a field bayonet and holder. A backpack, entrenching tool, mess kit and compass rounded out the equipment. My two duffel bags bulged from all the weight. I weighed one hundred thirty-five pounds, all muscle, but still it was quite a load to carry back to my room.

All of us were also given a small book of wisdom and knowledge called *Bugle Notes*—the cadet bible. Being well-versed in *Bugle Notes* allowed New Cadets to (possibly) eat while seated in the Mess Hall; go to the bathroom when in the barracks; take a shower during the shower formations; and, basically, satisfy the sadistic need of Upperclassmen to hear from us every song, story, fact and statistic from the book, repeatedly, *ad nauseum*. *Bugle Notes* is part of the history of the "Long Gray Line;" every USMA West Point Cadet since 1802 has had to memorize the "poop" contained in that little volume.

As I quickly flipped through my copy, I realized I knew absolutely nothing about anything in it: not one fact or song, not one scintilla of information. A foreboding spirit seemed to emanate from its purportedly inspirational pages full of legends, traditions, creeds, chants, regulations and "cadetiquette."

We, sons of to-day, we salute you
You, sons of an earlier day.
We follow, close order, behind you,
Where you have pointed the way.
The long gray line of us stretches
Thro' the years of a century told,
And the last man feels to his marrow
The grip of your far-off hold…

My thoughts were interrupted by our Squad Leader, forming us up to double-time (yes, double-time) back to our barracks while *schlepping* our overflowing, weighty duffels. Our chins remained slammed back in as we made the awkward trip back to our assigned rooms to dump our gear. We then rushed back to formation for the next activity: haircuts at the Cadet Barbershop, located in a subterranean dwelling under the Cadet Headquarters Building. All New Cadets had to get a haircut before the 1730 hours swearing-in ceremony. We double-timed over there, proceeded down a short stairwell and stood in line to get clipped. With about forty-five to fifty New Cadets in line and four barbers working, the wait was about eleven minutes long.

Awaiting my turn I thought about Gino, my Italian friend and barber for the last five years in North Miami Beach. All the pictures on the walls of his shop were of the great Italian cities—Rome, Venice, Florence—and Gino sang Italian opera while he worked. It was like taking a trip to Italy every time I got a haircut.

Gino had a typical red, white and blue swirling barber pole in front of the shop. Inside were chairs with small tables between them, cluttered with old magazines, the same ones for as long as I could remember. *Life*, *The Saturday Evening Post* and several girlie magazines filled with gorgeous, half-naked women. I would always glance over at them but was too embarrassed to pick them up.

We'd visit for a bit before my trim. As Gino relaxed into his favorite oversized Belmont chair, he would always ask me, "So did you get laid this week?"

"I wish!" I'd answer. I may not have been getting any action but I felt a lot of joy inside at Gino's shop.

Here at the West Point Cadet Barbershop...no joy. No joy at all! The haircuts were supervised by an Upperclassman who made sure we didn't converse and that each haircut was within the regulations. He took his job seriously, chastising several New Cadets who simply acknowledged their barbers with "Hi!" or "Hello." As they worked, the barbers never spoke to us because they knew we weren't supposed to talk to them. We heard only the incessant buzz of electric clippers, like a swarm of insects attacking a carcass. No banter, no jokes, no laughter, no moaning about the recent losses of our favorite sports teams and certainly no interest in my sex life!

A barber would mow our entire head in one minute. The clipped hair piled up so high around each barber chair, it looked as if the clients were seated atop giant fur balls. In a chair next to me, one New Cadet with longish blond hair had tears in his eyes as his curls were shorn. I thought I heard him groan slightly as the barber took just four or five swipes across the kid's scalp, the fur ball around his chair increasing significantly. The poor guy left his Belmont chair dazed.

Looking in the large mirror in front of my chair gave me a panoramic view of the Barbershop and its four Belmonts. The mounds of hair piling around each chair—straight and smooth, curly and kinky—reflected colors of black, brown, red and blond from the sunlight filtering through the shop's small windows. The harsh lighting above shone jagged and bright on the hair piles, making them appear as small bonfires.

The New Cadets had blank expressions on their face, very little hair on the top of their heads and white sidewalls above their ears. Piles of hair, shaved heads, ears sticking out...I couldn't help but think of those grainy, speeded-up newsreels that show the concentration camps in Europe...emaciated men with the same hairstyle we now sported.

Ugh, no! Cancel, cancel, Paul. You're not an inmate here. Just power through.

By the end of the afternoon, that supervising Upperclassman had overseen more than nine hundred haircuts. I barely recognized my reflection, my head like a furry peach, my face sunken with sadness. Not one of those buzz cuts, including mine, was remotely as good as what my buddy Gino might have given me.

My thoughts continued to channel back to home and tennis again. With this constant surge of reminiscing, I was making myself crazy and placing myself in jeopardy here.

CHAPTER 13

Wouldn't you know it: it was supposed to be my big day at the Orange Bowl yesterday, but rain postponed all the matches. By the time the sun finally peeked out, it was too late to start; damn it. I could feel my energy and momentum sliding away as my disappointment built up. If I'm going to have any success in this tournament, I've got to be ready to play on a moment's notice, and not get rattled by delays.

Last night I had a nightmare about breaking the strings on all three of my racquets and not being allowed to patch them up during the match. That's the equivalent of hitting tennis balls that have no air in them. I woke up this morning with a clammy sense that my Orange Bowl was losing air and I couldn't locate the leak.

So now, after a ragged night's sleep, I have my singles round of sixteen with a possible berth for the quarterfinals. Doubles also, since they got postponed too; great.

It's not just another day at the office. It's a huge day with two big matches for me and Helen is still in the doubles draw with Lenore, struggling to stay in the tourney. At eight AM, dad's already at his Trade Winds shop. In 1959, after the big economic recession that caused havoc around here with many hotels closing, he managed and then bought the gift shop, where he works his butt off seven days a week to keep us fed. He surely knew what the day had in store for Helen and me like who we'll be playing against, where we are in the draw.

Next, mom rushes off to her administrative job at the Osteopathic Hospital. She's all business and has shown no interest in the tournament. Few words are even spoken in this house in the morning anyway and today is no exception; not so much as a "good luck." On her mind is probably the three loads of laundry from the day before, waiting for her when she returns from her workday.

After a breakfast of juice and cereal, my gear all ready, I collect my sister to leave the house. We make the 40-minute drive south to the courts without much discussion or debate. My first singles match is at ten AM, against the Israeli kid. It goes quite well; I beat him 6-2, 8-6 although I struggled in the second set losing my focus. I started looking ahead instead of concentrating on the task presently at hand.

But now, after several hours, I step onto the court to meet my next opponent with the winner going into the quarterfinals. My feet seem cast in cement buckets, my racquet heavy and unwieldy. The balls don't seem to bounce normally. Over my years of tournament play, I've only felt this way once before. Trouble was headed my way then. Will this be a repeat performance of that horror show? I can't shake the feeling. Maybe my brain will clear if I can just play more efficiently, run faster, power the ball harder. Or maybe I should pretend to be someone else....

My opponent is a sleek, stylish Spaniard, Juan Gisbert, a year older than me, seeded seventh. He has an all-around game, good serve, groundstrokes that seem to flow easily. He walks with confidence, his eyes bright and sparkly. He's ready to play. I need to bring my best game to this match. This match will direct my future path in life.

But my sense of foreboding doesn't vanish. *Come on man, let's go ...COME ON!* I try whistling a Gary U.S. Bonds song: "Don't you know that I danced, I danced till a quarter to three"—*my tennis racquets, my tennis racquets and me.* But every attempt to rid myself of this raw, disconcerting feeling is failing.

I step onto the feature court, warm up, try to find rhythm, timing, relaxed swings. My body feeling awkward; all elbows, stiff knees, flat feet.

Juan serves and wins the first game easily. He has a slippery slice serve and a wicked reverse spin on his twist serves. He's able to hack the ball low on both groundstrokes, making me dig down for my topspin forehand and causing me to flatten it out a little more than I want to.

We trade serves again and again and then, at 2 all, his serve, he catches a net cord off a lucky backhand reach and steals the point. *Shit.* He follows with two great serves and a backhand passing shot down the alley. I had powered my trusty forehand deep to his backhand corner only to see his return flash by me like a bullet, out of my reach, within the baseline. *Ouch.* We switch sides of the court. He's leading 3 games to 2.

My serve now. I've got the "yips" and double fault the first point. *Fuck!* On the second point, he moves in and hits a backhand winner off a reasonably decent serve. But I'm regaining my momentum. *Yes!* From love-30, I reel off four points in a row to win the game using serve and volleys, however, I'm not playing freely. Every shot I hit seems forced and rushed. Even so, the score is 3 all.

Juan's elegant strokes are disrupting my concentration and I wind up losing the first set, 6-3. I'm not playing controlled and relaxed. My ego takes over. I can feel myself grandstanding, disconnected from myself, playing to the crowd. I try to hit artistic drop shots, amazing first service aces, topspin lobs. I know I should play safe shots when I need to. I *know* I should allow myself to get back into points by good defensive measures, by hitting harder. What the hell is wrong with me? My shots miss long by an inch, wide by an inch, with no margin of safety. The second set is rapidly decomposing for me.

No excuses: Juan's playing a smarter, more disciplined match, winning all the important points—and I'm just a fool, playing like a Joker. He breaks me in the seventh game on a beautiful forehand drop volley at ad out and he doesn't look back. When he hits that shot, all I can do is clap my racquet, indicating "great get." He holds serve and breaks me again.

Juan doesn't beat me; I beat myself. End of second set 6-3, end of match, *finito*. A good, competitive match, hard fought, if that is any consolation…but I'm not looking for consolation. My serve, my reliable weapon, has let me down. I've let myself down. I've let all Floridians down. My game has imploded along with my world. I'm a loser….

I realize that the greatest shortcoming is not my backhand, not my service toss, but my impatience. It shows up in a variety of ways: hitting low percentage shots, failing to get enough depth on approach shots, not putting first volleys deep enough into the court, not adjusting my game to compensate for aggression, watching the crowd reactions to my good shots while not concentrating on the next point.

Well, I must shake this off very quickly, accept my shortcomings and learn from my mistakes; the outcome of my upcoming doubles match with Donnie depends on it. The Ashe/Buchholz encounter promises to be a difficult match, even with the excellent strategy we've mapped out. I'd better get my head back into the game right away.

Arthur Ashe plays the forehand court in doubles, usually returning a flat ball. On our serve, we plan to poach the heck out of him at net. Buchholz usually chips his backhand serve return, so we'll attack him with serves as wide as possible, forcing him to hit over a higher portion of the net. Our basic strategy: when the ball is in play, avoid Ashe like the plague and hit everything to his partner!

It works beautifully! We split the first two sets, break them in the third and I serve 5-4, 40-love, triple match point to Buchholz. With the sun to my back and only the slightest cross breeze gently caressing the American flag four courts and a grandstand away, we are one point from victory…just one good Kantrowich serve is all we need…one point!

Arthur, lounging at the service line, shakes his head, looking like he's just lost his best friend. But then… "Hey Cliff", he says, turning to his partner smiling. Ashe has a fantastic smile that can light up a room.

"I think NOW it's time to turn up the heat a little!" he says light-heartedly. Arthur's always a gentleman on the tennis court, a real sportsman. He's not trying to psyche us out; he's just frustrated because he knows they're going to lose in this dire situation. It's gallows humor. Besides, who ever wins a tennis match being down triple match point with the opponent serving? Not impossible…but crazy.

Buchholz laughs, Donnie laughs, I chortle. And I'm going to power my serve, win the point and take this match and this victory quickly to the bank right now!

So, at 40-love, triple match point, I hit a wide twisting serve to the ad court. Don takes a step to the left to poach Buchholz and is trapped when the ball comes screaming back at his body. He can't get out of the way and dumps his backhand volley into the net, 40-15, double match point. Now I am serving to Ashe.

Previously I'd been hitting hard, flat serves down the middle of the court to Ashe's backhand and Don usually has been able to pounce on the returns and flick them away for winners. This time, I serve a slice wide to Ashe's forehand after which, ninety-nine times out of one hundred, he'd go cross court. This time, he goes down the line into the alley for a sharp winner.

Don howls, "Good shot" as I go over to calm him down. 40-30 single match point; I'm serving again to Buchholz. Don and I meet at the service line to talk strategy for the final point of this match. I plan to hit a slice into Cliff's body cutting down his ability to direct his backhand return while Don's on the lookout to cut off the return, volley it away for a winner, match over, goodbye!

I serve a wicked, hooking slice that hits the back service line tape to the left side of Buchholz's body. He makes a late hit on the ball. Don sees Buchholz's return angled down the backhand alley, but he's already committed to one step crosscourt, where he thinks the ball will go. When the ball comes off Cliff's racquet, it's a mishit with the ball fluttering to Don's right as he moves left. His reaching backhand volley is dumped into the net. Now it's deuce and we're losing our edge.

Ashe and Buchholz are pulling off the truly crazy impossible! Don and I lose two more points in a row to lose my serve. In the next game, Ashe serving, I try a ridiculous passing shot that would have drawn applause, had it gone in. We both tank on Arthur's service game and, with Don serving, we both keep making one error or another on volleys and groundstrokes to lose the final game and the match. We blow the final set, 7-5.

Drained of energy, we all approach the net. Don and I are fresh out of spirit, dejected; it's as if someone has stolen our skin. Ashe shakes my hand and says, "I really thought you had us, Paul! We were lucky to win and sometimes you need a little luck. We had it today! Great match!" In my haste to run and hide, I reply, "Yeah!" *D'oh.*

I feel like shit. While it's a privilege to play Arthur Ashe, it is not a privilege to lose to him. This match will probably haunt me for the rest of my life.

It's a long, arduous drive home. Helen and Lenore also lost their doubles, so we're twin tennis losers. Swell! I leave Flamingo Park with a bruised ego but hopefully a lot smarter. I want to continue doing well in the remainder of the Florida tournaments until the end of my stay in the Juniors. I need my singles ranking to climb higher, if only to prove to myself I have it in me. With this turn of events, however, I'm pessimistic about having a professional tennis career. I've placed so much effort into the Orange Bowl, without much reward: no title, no nothing.

So perhaps at this point, I should be more optimistic about going to college. Over four years, I might mature as an individual as well as a player. Maturity should certainly help my level of concentration. Maybe there's still hope for me to go pro. Maybe I just need some time to get my confidence back.

★ ★ ★

Near the end of February 1961 more offers arrive from other schools: Amherst, Penn State, Georgia. Doors are opening. Luckily, Helen finally got her acceptance letter from the University of Florida—her heart's desire—so she's much more amiable and in tune with the world now.

Herb Lewis---the guy I thought I was just practicing with to humor Abe--- called Abe who, in turn, called my father to ask if I would be available to work out with the West Point tennis team down in Coral Gables. They're in Florida for winter break to play the U of M Hurricanes in a practice match and they need some good Juniors to help them. If they're perchance recruiting players for the next attending class, Abe doesn't mention it, but dad's all excited. To me, it's just practice.

I don't know much about the Military Academy, other than they march a lot, wear uniforms with bright buttons and go into the Army upon graduation. I watched part of "The West Point Story" on TV once. It was so boring, I turned it off to watch "Gunsmoke," my favorite program, instead. But one of dad's good friends, John Campbell, is a retired Air Force Colonel. When he found out I might practice with the West Point team, he went nuts and badgered my father to make sure I don't back out!

Since I really like Herb, and to get dad off my back, I said I'd go, but I really have no interest other than practicing in a nice environment. I mean, me in the U.S. Army? I can't even stand up straight and I abhor rules and regulations. In my mind, rules are made to be broken. It's not a great attitude, I know, and probably not a good fit. But, when the time rolls around, I drive the old Buick down to the U of M Campus to meet the Army coach Leif Nordlie, his assistant

MSGT Bill Milliken and the Officer-in-Charge Lieutenant Colonel Harry Buckley. While walking into the tennis complex, I pass by the U of Miami tennis coach Dale Lewis and chat with him for a couple of minutes, then locate the Army team.

I go up to meet the West Point Tennis Coach Nordlie who then introduces me to his staff and several of their players and we all go onto the court to play a few sets. Now, I'm just here to play tennis. I don't mention that I've already secured a four-year scholarship to the U of M, to compete on these very courts on which we are now playing if I want it. Better left unsaid, I figure; I'm not here to prove anything to anyone.

So, I don't do anything special with the Army players. Except mow them all down.

MSGT Milliken comes over and asks if he can play a set with me as well. He goes down 6-0, 6-0 and he's exhausted, but he won't quit, urging me to play another set with him. Even LTC Buckley tells him to take a break

After practice, Coach Nordlie asks me to call my parents; he wants to invite them out to a lovely restaurant for dinner tonight. While we're there, he makes a strong pitch to convince my folks I should go to West Point, Class of 1965, starting July 1961. They'll arrange everything as they have an open appointment from a Congressman from the State of Ohio. I must pass a medical physical exam and a battery of psychological tests; a mere formality, it seems. Nordlie is quiet but adamant about having me on his team. After all, I fill many different categories of students that West Point needs: an excellent athlete, with a great academic record, and Jewish too!

Coach Nordlie must know I have many college offers. He seems like a peach of a guy and it's nice to feel so wanted and needed. It's a real boost to my self-confidence. One of the salient features of the evening's discussion is just how prestigious an institution the Academy is and that there is always employment after graduation. The word "deployment" is never, ever mentioned, of course.

I'm guessing the free meal at a decent restaurant is what seals the deal for my folks, but they are also deeply impressed. Me, not so much. Regimentation is low on my list for a lifestyle, and I still have a potential tennis career to consider. Going to West Point would just about kill any hopes of tennis stardom for me. It's something I really need to ponder seriously.

I thought I had most everything figured out before. Now I'm in a state of total confusion about the future...again.

CHAPTER 14

Once the entire New Cadet Squad was coiffed, we again assembled in front of the Cadet Barbershop with our scalped tops and white sidewalls, our civilian hair on the floor greeting more New Cadets entering the shop. Our new hairstyles (or lack thereof) went well with our dehydrated, bedraggled, exhausted appearances.

"Squad form up," our Squad Leader announced. "Atten-hut, forward march, now double-time," he ordered as we headed back to the barracks. "Kantrowich...slap that neck in now!" he yelled at me, so I made like Mussolini while I double-timed.

"When you get back to your rooms, you will set up all your gear in your closet, footlocker, desk, make your beds and meet your bunkmates," he barked as we ran through the Area. "You will perform all those tasks within forty-five minutes, then re-form as a Squad in front of the barracks! Uniforms will be fatigues. Group halt!" he barked when we arrived at our barracks.

"Kantrowich, stay in place! The rest of you, fall out!" Everyone moved away, leaving me as the solitary figure in line, chin in, dripping sweat, anxious.

"Kantrowich..." the Squad Leader asked quietly, "What am I going to do with you? You have the attention span of a moth, your posture is atrocious, your face always looks like it's smirking, and your eyes wander here and there, instead of straight ahead at all times. What do you have to say for yourself?"

I said nothing.

"IRP!" he said. I stood silent, wondering how I could ever satisfy this man. He was about three years older than me, yet he seemed much more mature and worldly. My entire situation here relied on him having more confidence in me.

Just like in a tennis match, if you are losing, you must find a way to change your game in order to win. *Try to listen harder, Paul.*

"Kantrowich," he said more quietly, "The correct response would be, 'No excuse, Sir!'"

"No excuse, Sir!" I repeated loudly.

"Kantrowich...stand up straighter, eyes to the front, lips relaxed, concentrate on a target straight ahead of you and pretend you want to burn a hole through it. That's better. Remember what you are doing right now and keep doing this when you are at attention...got it? You are making me look bad, Kantrowich, and this isn't good for either of us. I've got to answer to the Platoon Leader, and he's got to answer to the Company Commander about your abilities; and it also reflects on my abilities, so shape up or I'm going to ship you out!"

This remark gave me pause. We both wanted me to do better. "Yes, Sir!" I quickly replied.

"Now get out of my sight and get your bunk squared away. GO!"

I bounded up the stoops, through the solitary door and started up the stairwell, reflecting on what the Squad Leader had just said. I needed to get to the fourth floor, where my new room and my roommates would be. It was imperative I find sanctuary to quietly reflect on the day thus far. I also felt that conversing with my new roommates would help unclog my mind of all the bullshit that had transpired; amongst us, perhaps we could put things into proper perspective. The fourth floor would be my oasis.

At the first stairwell landing, I was passing an Upperclassman from another Squad when he shouted, "Stop! Where are you going? Hit that wall, Mister! Who are YOU?"

I stopped dead in my tracks, not knowing what "hit that wall" meant. "New Cadet Kantrowich, Fourth Squad, Sir!" I reported.

With open hostility, he yelled, "Hit the wall, Mister!"

"I don't understand Sir!" Bad error: New Cadets were instructed that there were only three proper responses to questions asked by Upperclassmen. "Yes, Sir! No, Sir! No excuse, Sir!" I had violated a sacrosanct protocol.

The Upperclassman positioned me with my back firmly against the wall, at attention, chin in, head up, back of my heels and my neck pressing against the wall. "That's the way this is done, New Cadet whatever-your-name-is! Now, take one step forward...now hit the wall!" He physically slammed me back into the position he had just taught me.

"One step forward...now hit the wall!" This time I slammed myself back into the wall. "Again...one step forward...now hit it!" He had me practice that several more times.

"Every time you see an Upperclassman on the floor of the barracks, before you pass him, you stop, hit the wall and then ask that Upperclassman if you may pass."

"Yes, Sir!" I correctly replied.

"Now, get going," he said as I bounded towards my destination, which took about ten minutes, since I was stopped many times, on every floor, to "hit the wall" for each of the assorted Upperclassmen I passed enroute...all of them with a keen interest in yelling at me and bracing me.

When I finally arrived at my room, my bunkmates were way ahead of me in performing all the required tasks our Squad Leader had ordered us to do. Since I was last to arrive, I got a top bunk instead of a preferred bottom. Top bunks were more difficult to make up daily.

I introduced myself around only to find my bunkmates hostile towards me for causing them all the extra pushups earlier. Their chilliness continued throughout the remaining time we had before re-forming up. I took note of what they had all done to lay out their gear and which uniform they put on for the first formation. Perhaps they would all warm-up to me later when they saw what a wonderful human being I really was.

Because of my delay in getting to the room, I was last to arrive at the formation, in the required uniform but not appropriately dressed. My shirt wasn't bloused properly, I hadn't correctly pleated my trousers into my combat boots, and I wasn't wearing a hat. My Squad Leader quietly told me to go back to my room at least get my hat as he loudly announced to the rest of the squad, "Okay guys, let's knock out fifteen pushups while your buddy Kantrowich goes up to get his hat!"

The way back to the room was a carbon copy of my prior trip. I had to honor all the Upperclassmen wandering each floor by hitting the wall. My displeased Squad mates had to do three series of fifteen push ups each by the time I arrived back with my hat.

Since we were forming up as a Company by Platoon, I wasn't the only New Cadet to foul up as other Squads and other Platoons were experiencing the same punishments, perhaps for other reasons. The annoyance and hostility in the air was palpable.

Before the Platoons and Company came to attention, our Squad Leader explained we were going to the Mess Hall to eat lunch. We lined up in formation and proceeded to march, then double-time to the Cadet Mess Hall. It was twelve o'clock, and with all the activity we had done, I was ravenous and looking forward to sitting, having a cool drink, chowing down and relaxing awhile; maybe getting to chat with my new roommates for a few minutes and bond with them over a quick repast.

I started to remember listing all the pros and cons of wanting to come to West Point just five months ago. It seems like so many of my con remarks were coming true.

CHAPTER 15

D o I want to go to West Point? Mom and dad certainly want me to go. Dad's friend John has been relentlessly bombarding and regaling him with stories about all the glory and heroics he witnessed throughout his career as a World War II and Korean War Veteran. Since dad had helped build radar for the U.S. government and was in a deferred military status of some sort during those conflicts, he was fortunate not to have seen the horrors of war himself. But John's war tales seem to have left my dad with an impression about what "real" men do. The thought of his own son being invited to become a West Pointer is probably the major reason he wants me to go. Dad's fascination with this idea borders on temporary insanity.

Both my parents are also convinced that my attending West Point will solve their college financial woes. I'm sure they're still struggling to pay bills from the 1959 recession that hit the country very hard, especially the Miami Beach area. Either they forgot that I have a multitude of terrific scholarship offers, or they're brainwashed by the prestige of West Point and simply choose not to acknowledge the other schools any longer. With her bookkeeping and accounting background, mom controls the money in our family. She manages her and dad's weekly income with such dexterity, we're able to make ends meet every month, but money is always an issue at our house. I'll be helping relieve some of the financial stress.

Mom and dad also seem to forget that West Point has strict rules, long-standing conventions, uniformity and no room for "free spirits." Either they're not thinking straight, or they ignore the reality that their only son Paul marches to the tune of a different drummer. Marching in a parade is one thing, possibly marching off to war is a far larger responsibility.

Helen has voiced no opinion to me about what school I should attend. I overheard her tell some friends she was "afraid for me," but she didn't elaborate. She also told her friends that she can't wait to leave home for the University of Florida and how lucky I am to be able to leave in early July instead of late August.

The question remains: do I want to attend West Point? As a future engineering major, I'm sharp in math and the sciences and feel I can handle the academics. I sit down at the small wooden desk in my room and decide to list all the pros and cons of this decision; a decision which will help me either to agree or disagree with my parents. I reach over to adjust the goose-neck lamp on my desk, the one I made in junior high school shop class, and realize it is time to focus on reality.

I begin writing: SHOULD I GO TO WEST POINT??

GOOD REASONS:
1. Make a "man" out of me.
2. Get me to stand up straight like mom always bitches to me about.
3. Steady job for four years upon graduation. I can then slowly make up my mind about a future career (except, perhaps, professional tennis player!)
4. Great engineering degree.

5. Helen gets to attend the college of her choice.

6. I get away from home.

7. Learn to play squash.

8. Coach told me I could play the European clay court circuit after graduation, on the Army team. An opportunity to showcase my tennis outside of the college arena.

9. No expenses for my parents, ever.

BAD REASONS:

1. School eleven months of the year (nine academic, two training).

2. Classes six days a week (Over twenty-four semester hours every semester).

3. Go into the Army upon graduation, four-year commitment.

4. Conventional rules and strict discipline is always required.

5. No women.

6. Only approximately twenty-four hundred students.

7. Cold weather!

8. Must wear uniforms, even uniform underwear!

9. Must wear hats most of the time. I hate hats!

10. No indoor tennis facilities, play tennis only four or five months a year.

11. Starts July 5th, no summer tennis circuit this year. Summer training called Beast Barracks instead, whatever that is!

12. No Christmas or Spring Breaks the first year.

13. No academic electives.

14. 3.0 grading system, not 4.0 (with minimum of 2.0 to pass).

15. Confined to reservation all week and need a pass for weekends.

16. No drinking.

17. No public display of affection. (And no women.)

18. No more summer tennis tournaments around the country, ever.

19. No car until last semester of senior year.
20. No offcampus living.
21. Cannot marry until after graduation.
22. Early rising, 5:50 AM every day.
23. No choice of food in the Mess Hall.
24. Must have short hair.
25. Demerits, confinement and "punishment tours."
26. Room inspections daily and/or weekly.
27. Plebe year starts after Beast Barracks, a full year of insanity.
28. Must attend religious services every Sunday.
29. Cannot flunk even one course or you are expelled from Academy.
30. Other reasons not even contemplated!
31. Did I mention no women?

So…after evaluating pros and cons, it sure looks like I would be friggin' nuts to go to West Point! The bad reasons have it three to one over the good ones.

However, the very first reason in the good column—make a man out of me—carries a lot of weight. At age seventeen with a fragile ego, I'm thinking it might be nice to "walk like a man, talk like a man, walk like a man my son." Manliness: next to Godliness, albeit with humility; smart, suave and slow to anger, but able to exhibit controlled violence when needed for the right cause. A real "man", mild-mannered, soft-spoken, attentive, strong individual, like a Clark Kent, who knows right from wrong, rescues damsels in distress or goes to war against the Nazis and saves the world! A "man" knows the right answers to difficult questions, has the skill to hit a home run on the ball field and the confidence to make love to a woman in such a way that she tells him quietly, breathlessly, "You satisfy me in every single aspect of our life together." A shining guy standing out in a crowd, while everyone around him turns to and comments, "Now *there's a REAL man....*"

The idea of graduating West Point is becoming more appealing to me by the minute. Maybe my folks are right to think I should go there, even if for the wrong reasons! Of course, it means giving up my dream as a touring tennis professional. After this Orange Bowl tourney however, maybe I haven't been realistic about my tennis ambitions. I know I can get to a high level but maybe not high enough to earn a great living or have the unique life I want. It's coming to a point in time where I must make my decision. What should I do?

CHAPTER 16

One of the good reasons for going to West Point was that all expenses were paid. This included the food! So as our Squad followed the Squad Leader single file into the Cadet Mess Hall, that free food was totally on my mind. I was extremely hungry.

We still had our chins slapped in and couldn't look around to see how majestic this Cadet Mess Hall was supposed to be. It accommodated the full Corps of twenty-four hundred Cadets on the main floor and was broken up into four sections. The center section, where I hoped to eventually sit, was reserved for athletes who played varsity and freshman sports. Two wings jutting off the center section were for the two different regiments of Cadets: First Regiment on the left, Second Regiment on the right. In front of the Mess Hall was a high terraced area overlooking the entire ground floor called the Poop Deck, from whence information flowed over a microphone system. There was an eating section up there for guests, senior high-ranking cadet officers, the Commandant and the Superintendent.

Still bracing, we were directed to three different tables, each with space for ten occupants. Eight New Cadets were assigned to a table, sitting four on each side. Seated at the head was an Upperclassman,

Squad Leader rank or above, called the Table Commandant; at the end was another Upperclassman I nicknamed "The Enforcer."

Since we had nine men in our Squad, we were broken up in groups of three around the Platoon and assigned to three different tables. We got to meet new Platoon mates this way and, at the same time, encounter new Upperclassmen. I recognized my Table Commandant, since he was also our Platoon Leader, but I didn't know The Enforcer at the table's other end. Neither of them looked happy.

Once all New Cadets were assigned and our tables were ready to be occupied, the New Cadets stood, still bracing and standing at attention, hands by our sides, until the order came from the Poop Deck to "Take seats." Little did we know that taking seats did not mean we could untuck our necks.

The Table Commandant yelled, "Who ordered all of you to let your necks out, Smackheads?" Eight responses of "No excuse, Sir!" followed. So, we all sat at attention, chins in, gaze directly ahead, hands by our sides, ramrod straight, on the outer quarter section of the seat making our posture even less comfortable

"Cadet Corporal Johns will now demonstrate the proper way to eat at MY table," barked the Table Commandant. "Direct your attention to Cadet Johns now," he said, facing The Enforcer. He directed Cadet Johns to pick up his fork, load some imaginary food with it and bring the loaded fork straight up and level to his mouth, about six inches in front of it. Cadet Johns paused in that position, then moved the fork directly towards his mouth to deposit the food. He withdrew the empty fork back to that six-inch spot in front of his mouth and paused again before returning the fork straight down to his plate.

"Gentlemen, eating like this is called a square meal," said the Table Commandant. "It is called a square meal because, every time you enter these hallowed halls, you will eat enough, sufficient sustenance to keep you squared-away on the field of battle. You will eat exactly like this because you sit at MY table!"

"Cadet Johns," he continued, "Please show our new charges the proper way to drink out of your water glass." The Enforcer grabbed his water glass and, in the same squared-off manner, took a sip of chilled water. His face showed no emotion at all.

"Gentlemen, listen closely: the servers will be bringing out the food in just a moment," the Table Commandant informed us. "You are not to engage in any discussion with the servers, nor will you engage in any discussion with each other. If asked a question by me or Cadet Johns, you will return your fork to your plate and then answer the question properly, keeping your posture straight and your gaze forward. Is that understood?"

"Yes, Sir!" the eight of us responded loudly in unison.

The Table Commandant yelled out, "I can't hear you, ladies! Is that clear?" All eight of us yelled,

"Yes, Sir!"

"Each server will start at one end of the table and hand you a dish containing ten servings of that specific food. You are to respond to the server, only saying 'Thank you' while you take your own portion from the dish and then pass the dish to the individual to your right. You will not eat that food on your plate until the order to eat is given. Is that clear?" "Yes, Sir!"

Almost immediately, over one hundred servers—mostly short Filipinos with rich, dark hair, wearing bright smiles and crisp white aprons or jackets—approached us from the enclosed kitchen, each carrying a separate plate of steaming food: meat, several vegetables, potatoes and gravy, as well as bread, butter and salad dressing. It all smelled divine.

Once all the food was delivered and passed around, the Table Commandant gave the order, "Fall out, eat!" That meant we were allowed to let our necks out to chew and swallow properly. But seconds later, Cadet Johns, The Enforcer, ordered, "Stop eating!" Several of us has already taken bites and were in the process of chewing them.

"All of you pull your chins back in and sit at attention!" Cadet

Johns said. "New Cadet Kantrowich, how is the cow?" He grinned as I tried politely to finish chewing and swallowing the contents of my mouth. Having no clue what my answer should be, I said nothing.

"Where're you from, Kantrowich?" Cadet Johns demanded.

"My momma!" I replied confidently, deflecting his question about the "cow."

"I mean in what state, within this great country, the United States of America, do you live?"

"Florida, Sir!" I snapped.

"Do they have cows in Florida, Kantrowich?" I hesitated. "Well, they must have cows in Florida, right?" He sounded deadly serious. "Yes, Sir!" I replied.

"So...How is the cow?" Once again, I failed to respond to his question. "Kantrowich," Cadet Johns continued, "unless you can tell me how the cow is, you can forget about eating what's on your plate right now!"

"Gentlemen," the Table Commandant chimed in, "You were all given a copy of *Bugle Notes* when you passed through Cadet Supply. That book is to be memorized from cover to cover. There will be times that you will be asked questions on your knowledge gained from *Bugle Notes* and, if you cannot answer the question or give an improper answer, you will forfeit something. In Kantrowich's case he will forfeit his lunch until he comes up with the appropriate answer. Understood?"

Eight New Cadets answered, "Yes, Sir!"

WHOA, I immediately thought in a panic. *I had better come up with an answer if I want to eat.* I yelled out, "Sir, how is the cow? The cow is fine, Sir!"

Both Upperclassmen thought my answer was hilarious. When they finally stopped laughing, they asked each New Cadet at the table a different question.

"What is the definition of leather?" "How many lights in Cullum Hall?" "How many gallons in Lusk Reservoir?" "Who is the Chief of

Staff of the Army?" "How many nights until the 100th Night?" "Sing 'Army Blue!'" "What is the Superintendent's middle name?" And the Upperclassmen's favorite, "How is the cow?"

None of us could answer any of the questions correctly. Our little copies of *Bugle Notes*, received slightly over one hour ago, held all the Plebe Knowledge; they were still stuffed in the bottom of our duffel bags back at the barracks, so no New Cadets at my table got to eat lunch that day.

"Attention to Orders!" came the announcement from the loud-speakers on the Poop Deck. Instantly, it became so quiet in the Cadet Mess Hall, all you could hear was the background hum of the large, revolving fans dangling from the high ceiling.

"All Squad Leaders and all Platoon Leaders will have their personnel prepared and ready for the Swearing-in Ceremony at 1730 hours. The location will be Trophy Point, the uniform will be Dress Gray with white gloves. End of Orders."

The Mess erupted with hundreds of Upperclassmen chattering, cajoling, complaining and barking out orders for their table. Ten minutes later, after dessert was served but not eaten, the dishes were removed; the meal was officially over. We were called to attention and marched out of the Mess Hall. Then, hungry and thirsty, we double-timed back to our Area, shuffling into our barracks.

Our Squad Leader called a Squad meeting in his room directly upon our arrival. We all lined up at his doorway. One Squad member would knock, report and, after the command "Enter," stepped forward through the doorway and into the back of the room, standing at attention, chin in. The next Squad member would repeat the ritual until we were all inside. It wasn't great to be first in line, because you would be under scrutiny the longest by the Squad Leader and his roommate. You never wanted to be last in line either; standing out in the hall the longest, you could be subjected to a multitude of Upper-classmen passing by from different floors who always had something to say or make you do while you waited to enter your Squad Leader's room. Of course, I was the last to arrive.

I knocked and called out "Sir, may I have permission to enter your room?" "Enter," the Squad Leader remarked, and I complied. "Sir, New Cadet Kantrowich reporting to his Squad Leader as ordered, Sir!"

Danford Brite, our Squad Leader, leapt from his desk chair and confronted me, his face in my face. He remarked quietly, "You are the last man reporting, Kantrowich. There is a penalty for that!"

Brite's roommate chimed in, "Oooooh, no! The Last Man! Ooooooh, no!" He appeared to enjoy teasing people to get a rise out of them. I was in no mood for it.

"Kantrowich, give me fifteen pushups for this," Brite continued. "The rest of your Squad mates, give me fifteen pushups as well for Kantrowich being late!"

When all our pushups were completed, Brite said, "Here's the deal, you guys...we have certain things that must be done before any of you get to Trophy Point at 1730 hours. First, you'll have thirty minutes to set up the rest of your gear. There will be an inspection by me and then the Platoon Leader and Company Commander, and then by the Officer-in-Charge. We must be ready and look sharp. Second, we will have 'Clothing Formations' to get you ready for wearing different uniforms properly. Then, finally, the swearing-in ceremony will be held at Trophy Point where we will all march in front of all your parents and guests who dropped you off today. I am sure you'll want everyone to be proud of you as a new West Pointer. Any questions?"

No questions asked, no answers needed. "Move out!" he commanded, and the Squad scrambled to get back to our rooms without slamming the wall too many times. I was determined to meet my roomies and get my gear tidied up and in place in time for the inspection. I was also determined to look at *Bugle Notes*. I needed to eat today! Three whole hours into being a New Cadet, I remembered how much I had wanted to leave this place three hours ago. Why was I still here? Exhausted, parched and starving, I was even more confused than before.

You were allowed to "fall out" once you got to your room. I immediately introduced myself properly to my two other roommates/ Squad mates. Since most of their gear was already laid out nicely and they seemed to know what they were doing, I asked them to help me get ready for the inspection. While polishing their new regulation black leather shoes, they introduced me to the art of spit-shining. Once they'd finished their shoes, they polished their new brass belt buckles to a high golden glow with Brasso metal polish. We all wiped down our M-1 rifles, tidied up our footlockers, put the finishing touches on our individual closets and took a deep breath just as we heard the inspection and turmoil starting in the adjacent room to ours. It was our Squad Leader's inspection.

Our Squad Leader was neither a screamer nor into drama; he was more of a teacher. This bode well for the entire Squad. As he entered our room, one of my roommates yelled, "Room Atten-hut!" We all stood at attention as Squad Leader Brite entered, cruised around and instructed us on what had been done correctly or flat-out poorly so that we could make changes on the spot.

The first time I tried to clean my belt buckle, I wasn't aware of the plastic coating over it and wasted a lot of time and energy polishing without good results. White showed us how to peel the clear plastic coating off before using Brasso. He also taught us to properly fold our white boxer shorts and tee shirts, and how to display our hats on the upper shelf of each closet. He demonstrated how to square off the corners of the sheets and blanket and how to tighten up the appearance of the bed after it had been already made up; you could bounce a quarter off the bed to show how tight it was.

"Not bad," Brite said as he left to supervise the rest of the Squad. The second he was gone, I put my head under the water spigot of the sink to suck up some welcomed hydration, then recleaned the sink before the next inspection.

About ten minutes later, there was a knock on the door. We stood at attention but did not brace.

The Platoon Leader entered the room with the Squad Leader and braced us all for not bracing to begin with. Then he casually looked around the room and asked each of us, "Where are you from?" "Do you have a sister?" Then, "Why does this sink have water drops in the basin?" "Why aren't the towels folded the same length?" "Why aren't the M-1 stocks properly linseed oiled?"

"No excuse Sir" each of us parroted.

He turned to our Squad Leader. "Not bad, Danny, correct these small problems now and I'll bring the Company Commander and the Officer-in-Charge over to your Squad in less than one-half hour."

Our Squad Leader followed the Platoon Leader out the door as he proceeded to the next group's room for inspection. We fell out to correct the small problems noted. My one roommate, Michael, went over to the shoe kit box where the linseed oil was stored to get it ready for use. The other roommate, Charlie, straightened the towels while I recleaned the sink. Michael showed the two of us how to apply linseed oil properly to our rifle stocks, without making a mess.

I asked my two roommates where they hailed from, if they had any siblings and if they played any specific sport. Michael was from the state of Arkansas, Charlie was from the Chicago area; neither had come in by way of an athletic appointment.

They were hollow-eyed and edgy; they both looked exactly as I felt. I asked them how they were handling all this chaos up. I needed verification that I wasn't just imagining all the craziness. They glanced at each other, then directly at me. "You should stop being the reason we have to do all these extra push ups. You should start shaping up. You are bringing all our own personal performance down." *Wow. The truth hurts.* I swallowed the lump in my throat and kept silent.

Once we'd finished our tasks, we stood around looking at each other while we waited for the Company Commander's inspection.

I thanked them for their help thus far and I promised them that I would try harder. The famous "cooperate and graduate" attitude I had heard so much about earlier in the day, preached by the Upperclassmen, was missing in this room? I thought to myself, *I need to get the hell out of here! Even my Squad mates are assholes!*

CHAPTER 17

'm sneaking out of calculus class fifteen minutes early because I must get ready for a tennis match...and I can't concentrate anyway. It's two in the afternoon, the sun is shining brightly outside, but my heart feels like it's leaking blood from the newly ripped hole in it. Trudging down the hallway, *schlepping* my books along with my three racquets, I can think only of Jill and the news she gave me just before class as we passed each other in this same hallway.

"Paul, I can't see you Saturday night...sorry!" No explanation, no empathy in her voice, no nothing. Her girlfriends quickly whisked her away before I could respond. That was the second time this week she cancelled, with the same indifference...leaving me feeling unloved, hollow, as if a big vacuum cleaner was on my head sucking all the life force out of me.

It was only two weeks ago that Jill and I went to the submarine races at Haulover Beach. After an amazing make-out session, there was no doubt in my mind how she felt about me. There had always been a lot of touchy-feely action between us, but this time it was especially hot. I was trying to be a gentleman, even though she gave me the impression it was okay to go further. Honestly, I was too scared and I'm not exactly an expert at this stuff.

I drove her home early that night. She gave me a peck on the cheek in front of her house and murmured "Honey, I don't think you are ready…you think too much!" She sounded extremely frustrated, very annoyed. "Goodnight!" *But…I'm ready, very ready* I wanted to say and didn't, couldn't.

As I waved back at her, her front door opened. Jill's grandmother stuck her head out and waved to me a simple signal: *Hello!* Now I'm wondering, maybe it was *Good-bye?*

The following day Helen meets me at our car, and we ride to the tennis courts. Since it's her turn to have the car all day, she's driving.

"What's the matter with you today? You look like you got run over by a truck. Jill problems?" I wish she couldn't read my mind so clearly, but that's twinship for you. "Mind your own business," I grumble.

"You *are* my business. *And* you're an asshole. Look, I was going to tell you earlier, but I saw Jill last week with a couple of college kids over at Jahn's Ice Cream Parlour…and they weren't just scarfing down ice cream!"

"What do you mean?" I shot back. Deep down, though, I think I already know. "I don't want to have this discussion," I tell her.

But Helen clearly wants to. "I didn't say anything at the time because I know how you get about her…defensive, very defensive." Well, Helen's not wrong about that. "I don't like seeing my brother getting taken for a ride," she continues. "Remember how I told you to be careful about her? That's what I meant. She runs around with older guys."

God damn it! I know Helen is just being caring in her blunt and direct way, but I'm too pissed off to continue this conversation. Helen has never had a sweetheart; clearly, she doesn't get it. How could she possibly understand that Jill is the sunrise and sunset of my existence? I've already picked out the names of our future children. I've mapped out our life together, a house with a white picket fence and a new Snapper lawn mower in the garage.

"Helen," I reply back, "I *said* I don't want to talk about it.

But she will not shut up. "Paul, come on, Jill isn't worth the time of day so stop mooning over her and find someone else. I know that Margaret is wild about you, Janie as well."

"Shut Up! Helen, please!"

That whole afternoon during my high school singles match, I curse on the court if I miss an easy shot, talk to myself like a disturbed person, act like a jerk. For a guy who just won several sportsmanship awards in the last few tournaments, it's out of character. I'm not in my right mind.

Fortunately, it's an easy match against an average player. We don't know each other, but he comes up to me after the match, all worried. "Are you okay? Are you mad at me? Did I do something…give you a bad call?"

"No, no…I'm sorry…just losing my mind along with my heart." *Shit, what a weird thing to say to someone I don't even know.* Shaking his head, the kid says goodbye and leaves. He must think I'm a real dickhead. Can't say I blame him.

The trip home with Helen isn't any more pleasant than it was on the way to the tennis match. "I told you so," she keeps chatting. *Shut up, shut up, shut up!* At home, I run straight to my room, slam the door, throw my racquets down, turn to the wall and punch my right fist through it. Thankfully I don't break my racquest hand. Florida houses are made of cinderblock walls with rectangular spaces in them, so I pierce one of those spaces, making a hole in the wall to match the hole in my heart; my father might put a hole in my head later if he finds out what I just did. I'm not thinking straight as I hang a poster over the hole, so my parents won't see it.

★ ★ ★

It's my time to have the car today, so I'm skipping tennis practice and I'm on my way to confront Jill. I've been driving past her house every chance I get hoping to see her silhouette in her bedroom window. I tell her friends how much I miss her. I doodle hearts on my schoolbook covers with "JD loves PK." At night, I have feverish dreams of her. I can't study, I'm testy with my parents, my tennis game is in the toilet. I'm just a flayed mass of flesh, splayed out on the torture rack we call "life". If that sounds pathetic, so be it. I can't take it any longer. I must see her, talk to her, hold her.

Driving to her neighborhood, I fantasize how Jill will look at me, cry, take me into her room and make sweet love to me. I park down the street from her house and sit in my car for a few minutes. Not five minutes later, a light blue Chevy Bel Air convertible pulls up to the house with some guy driving. Jill's along side him on the bench seat, arm around his shoulder...she can't see me parked nearby. Helen's right...damn it!

I can't hear their conversation but Jill plants a big kiss on this guy's lips before getting out of his car. As he pulls away, leaving tread marks on the gravel driveway, she's waving goodbye with undue enthusiasm. She turns and walks into the house with a huge, ooey-gooey grin on that beautiful face of hers, oblivious to my car nearby.

I'm furious, angrier than I have ever been in my entire life. My world is dissolving. I bang on the front door. Jill's grandmother opens it, after looking through the peephole seeing it's me. She can tell I'm in a panic.

Jill's grandmother has always been extremely kind and warm to me. While I would wait for Jill to get ready to go out, she'd always sit me down, offer me cookies and relate funny stories about herself when she was my age, young and daring. Now that seems like a long time ago.

"Paul...this is a surprise. Jill just got home but she can't see you now." Grandma is looking very uncomfortable. When I don't leave but look at her with such despair on my face, she quietly says "Paul... you should just go home right now...please!"

I'm about ready to fall into this woman's arms and wail like a baby. "She's breaking me into pieces, grandma, I think my heart's going to explode!"

And it finally does shatter when she says, with so much compassion, "Paul, my sweet Paul…you deserve better. Don't be sad! Please go home now Paul…you have always been special to me, let it remain that way!" I truly respected her, so I turn around and walk away.

My sister Helen was right. If I am going to survive this breakup, I need to put myself back into a winning frame of mind, throw myself back into my studies and my tennis.I have no idea how I am going to do that, or if I even want to.

I need to concentrate on the future, forget the past, and hope for some happiness. I can't imagine my life being more horrible than what it is at this moment.

Perhaps I'll give Margaret a call?

CHAPTER 18

have often wondered about my future but never expected to feel the depth of despair as horrible as I was feeling now. Even after my break-up with Jill, which left me empty, I hadn't ever experienced such a growing sense of apprehension until Beast Barracks. My anxiety was now caused by my first room inspection; it culminated in my receiving six demerits: three for improperly shined shoes, three for improperly shined belt buckles. I was still unaware of what a demerit meant!

Captain Forman, who led this inspection group, was one of the Regular Army officers with the responsibility of supervising the cadet cadre. He complimented both senior cadets on the appearance and preparedness of their Squads and Platoons. I thought he was a good man until he released a barrage of disparaging remarks in my direction; something about my poor posture and improper personal preparedness, hence the demerits. I was still unaware of what a demerit meant in terms of punishment.

As Captain Forman finished his room inspections and left the barracks area, our Squad Leader remained. "Gentlemen," he announced, "you are about to embark on a journey into the world of

West Point Fashion," —meaning the Clothing Formation. "Relax a little, get to know each other better, write a letter home to your folks if you want, call your girlfriend and give her my regards, and then return to formation outside suited up in Class "A" uniform with white gloves in five minutes...got it? So, let's get to it!"

For some reason, my roommates always seemed to be one step ahead me no matter what the situation. Within minutes, they bounded out the doorway wearing gray wool trousers, a gray long-sleeved shirt bloused in the back, a black tie tucked into the shirt after the second button, the belt properly positioned with the shiny belt buckle meeting the center seam of the shirt, black socks along with the black shoes. No hats this time. White cotton gloves, held gingerly in the left hand, finished the look. I imitated Michael and Charlie's every move and bounded out the door, slammed the wall three times for three different Upperclassmen and arrived, once again, as the last man in formation...and my Squad Leader again took note.

He proceeded to check each man in his Squad for uniform suitability and appearance. "This is the uniform we will wear when we march to Trophy Point for your induction ceremony at 1730 hours," he said. "You will take the oath of allegiance as a member of the Armed Forces of the United States of America. There, you will pledge your devotion to our great country and to these hallowed halls of The United States Military Academy. At the conclusion of ceremonies, we will march into the Cadet Mess Hall for supper. The next uniform change will be into the parade uniform in eight minutes!"

Squad Leader Brite told us what a parade uniform looked like, which seemed straightforward except for the white belts which were to crisscross over the chest with the shiny breast plate placed in the middle, a different belt buckle intersecting them at our waist. Then there were the parade hats—called "tar buckets"—with their large, felt pom-poms inserted into the front and on top; the cuffs and collar linings for our parade jackets; white cotton pants that required the use of our bayonets to split open since the leg compartments were so heavily starched we couldn't get our legs through; the dress bayonets hanging down our left buttocks; decorative black ammo boxes worn over the coccyx where the jacket tails hung down; M-1 rifles at a 45-degree angle leaning onto our right shoulders.

"Now you've got seven minutes…move out!" he yelled. It took four of those minutes just to get back to our fourth-floor room. With so many Upperclassmen on each floor during uniform formation, all three of us had to slam the wall several times, making sounds like an automatic weapon: POP-POP-POP! That left us less than three minutes to change and report back. Without a complete picture of how to wear this new uniform, all three of us were late, harried into a high state of anxiety. Like nearly everyone else in our group, Michael, Charlie and I arrived improperly attired, missing at least one element of the uniform.

Squad Leader Brite sent us all back to finish making the changes and ordered us to report back in five minutes. Only when every member of our Squad had their new uniforms put together properly could we move on to the next uniform change. Six more uniform changes later, we reassembled for our 1730 hours march to Trophy Point to be sworn in. After that, hopefully, I'd get to consume a decent meal at the Cadet Mess.

If I had only one thought during a quiet moment, it was *Please God, help me get through this day!* But I did have other thoughts racing through the empty corridors of my mind: *Am I going to get food to eat at dinner? With all my mistakes and violations, will they kick me out? After this exhausting ordeal, will I be able to get some sleep tonight?*

In my world of competitive tennis, there had been times I was so exhausted and dehydrated, with feet hurting, muscles cramping and imagination playing tricks on me, that I wanted to quit, but I never did. At those times, if I truly wanted to win, if I wanted to fulfill my potential, I needed to yank out more will-power and courage right then and there, not a minute later; to bolster myself, decide what price I was willing to pay to win, decide if it was worth it and then work harder, get the adrenaline flowing, run faster, swing fuller and sincerely believe more in myself. In tennis, sometimes you need a little luck, but you can't ever count on that. If it came down to simple, sheer willpower to get through and win, I knew I could be victorious.

But that's a tennis match, a game! I told myself. *Nobody dies; it's a sport, not a war. Someone always wins, someone always loses, but there is always another chance tomorrow to succeed. West Point is no game,* I thought. *There's no room for failure.* The disgrace of quitting, to be put on a pedestal by friends, family and teachers and then to fall off...it was inconceivable. My whole world would have collapsed. *If they kick me out after I've done my very best, at least I'll go out fighting.*

But, NO! The voice of my competitive spirit shouted at me over the din. I couldn't allow myself any negative thinking. I just had to believe in myself more.

On the otherhand...why did I denigrate myself? Why did they want to whittle down my spirit to a level where they could control and manipulate me?

I thought teaching leadership could and should be done differently but I was in no position to do anything about it. If I left, I could still go to college, play tennis, live and strive to succeed at something different.

I realized at that moment that it was okay to doubt myself and the circumstances; it wasn't okay, however, to make any judgments or decisions about my future in my present mental and physical condition. Perhaps, with a good meal and some sleep, things would improve. I also truly believed that even God couldn't help me; I had to help myself.

It was now 1720 hours. We formed up by Squad, Platoon, Company and Battalion. Over nine hundred young men marched onto the street, past a large crowd of adoring family members and over to Trophy Point, a beautiful expanse overlooking the Hudson River. There, we raised our right hands and pledged to defend and protect this great country of ours. It was a somber moment as I took that solemn oath: one young man among many, swearing allegiance. I was making a promise…something I never took lightly.

CHAPTER 19

I NEED A TWO-HOUR SHOWER

We about-faced and forward marched to the Cadet Mess Hall for supper. As we passed the sidewalks still crowded with well-wishers and family, a little pride began seeping back into my exhausted mind. As part of a new group of patriots, sworn to uphold our country's foundation of justice and freedom, I had a purpose and a reason to stay at West Point.

The oath we'd just taken provided me with a clearer direction and renewed energy. In my mind's eye, I saw myself dressed as a minuteman, musket at the ready, tricorn hat too large for my head and ammo pouch hanging too low off my hip…with the grim determination to fight for freedom fixed on my face. The image inspired me to try harder at West Point.

It amazed me that, in such a short period of time, particularly after such a harrowing and humiliating afternoon, my attitude had flip-flopped from severely negative to optimistic and positive. It was a similar experience to being down match point against a terrific tennis player, in an important tournament, and pulling the match out; a quietness within where I could safely smile and congratulate myself for a job well done.

My pride then palpably surged even much more intensely than having won a tennis tournament. This was a feeling that encompassed not just myself, but my family, my community and my country as well. I started to remember how good it was to be alive.

As we marched the quarter of a mile back to dinner, no Upperclassmen harassed us; they, too, were affected by the solemn moment we had experienced together. Perhaps the ceremony reminded them of why they had come to West Point, of the oath they themselves had sworn. Maybe this memory pushed aside their desire to break down the New Cadets in their charge, if only for a short while.

Entering the Mess Hall, standing at attention at my seat, chin in, eyes gazing directly ahead, I could feel deep hunger gnawing at my stomach. It made me smile to know that we were about to finally enjoy the good food that would be offered to us.

"Take seats!" came the order. But, before I could do so, the Table Commandant got in my face. "Wipe the smirk off your face, Kantrowich! Why are you so happy? Did you swallow a happy pill returning from Trophy Point? IRP!"

Instantly I replied, "No Sir, no excuse Sir!"

"Kantrowich," he growled, "What is the definition of leather?" That was from the *Bugle Notes* Plebe knowledge again, which I still didn't know. I ad-libbed, "Sir, the definition of leather...it's the skin of an animal, Sir!"

During this exchange, the food had started to be served and passed around the table. As I was engaged in discussion with the Table Commandant, the food passed me by. Cadet Johns, on the other end of the table, also chimed in.

"Wrong, Mister. Let's see...how many lights in Cullum Hall?" Again, I ad-libbed stating "seven hundred and twenty-eight lights in Cullum Hall, Sir!"

Cadet Johns, evidently, was not feeling all that warm and fuzzy about the oath our Class of 1965 had just taken. He kept pummeling me with questions.

"What is the middle name of our Superintendent? Who was the general, in the Civil War, that supervised the supplies sent to the

Union soldiers? How many gallons of water in Lusk Reservoir on a hot day versus a cold day? What year did General MacArthur graduate West Point?

I remained silent, trying to shrink myself into invisibilty. The Table Commandant added, "Kantrowich, give some thought to the questions asked. Until you know all the correct answers, you will remain in place and not eat. Once you do have all the correct answers, you may finish your meal!"

How can I finish a meal I haven't started? I thought.

I was hungry, I needed energy and it was not to be. I wasn't the only New Cadet singled out at the table. More than half the group was included this time, but it sure felt personal to me.

Before long "Attention to Orders" was announced and we were marched from the Mess Hall to report back to our Squad leader's room. Would this nightmare of a day never end?

It was about 2000 hours as the entire Squad continued to brace in Cadet Brite's room. He eventually said, "Fall out!" so we were able to let our necks out.

"Listen up," he said. "It's been a long day, you men are probably tired, you certainly need to shower and clean up, so that's what we will do next. Bedtime will be at Taps or 2200 hours. Between the time Shower Formation is called and Taps, you will be allowed to shower, and, if there is any time left before Taps, you are welcome to return to your room, clean up your gear and study. Shower Formation uniform will be a bathrobe over your birthday suit, clogs on your feet, folded towel draped over your left arm with your bar of soap in your plastic soap dish displayed in your left hand. Your Cadet bathrobe should be tied in front with two knots. You will line up against the wall on the fourth floor when the formation is called. Any questions?"

None was asked, none answered. He continued: "When you are individually excused, proceed down the stairs to the basement which is the location of the latrine and showers. You will proceed to take your shower and then you will move promptly back to your room immediately afterwards. Any questions?"

I did have a question, but thought better of asking it: *Why did we need two hours to take a shower that might typically last from five to fifteen minutes?*

Brite then excused us by standing us at attention and remarking, "Exit gentlemen, exit!" At the appropriate time, our whole Squad was lined up, shoulder-to-shoulder, at attention, chins in, all in the proper uniform on our barrack's fourth floor. The other three Squads of New Cadets from our platoon, housed on different floors were also herded to the fourth floor for this Shower Formation. It was imperative that every one of us run the full "two-hour shower" gauntlet.

Cadet Brite checked each of us in line. "Congratulations, ladies, this is the first time you are one hundred percent on time, in proper uniform and ready to go. Stand tall men...slap those silly necks in, all the way back to the wall, feet together, eyes straight ahead. We will now begin the Shower Formation!"

With that remark he walked away. There was no air conditioning in the barracks, which caused all of us to sweat from the heat as well as the uncertainty of what was in store for us.

Coming up the stairs were four or five Upperclassmen I'd never seen before, each stopping directly in front of our group. Casually dressed in white tee shirts, some in gray shorts, others in khaki or fatigue trousers, they all had something in common; they were pissed off and ready for a fight.

"Slam your dumb head in Cadet! Put your neck against the wall! AGAINST THE WALL, NOW!" Pennies and nickels were produced and pressed between our necks and the wall. The concept was that the sweat produced on our necks, with our chins shoved all the way back, would make the coins stick to the wall. If a coin dropped to the floor, there was more hell to pay.

Bayonet tips, the glowing embers of lighted cigarettes, fingers, pencils and other sharp objects were used to help keep our chins in, coins on the wall. The deal was simple; sweat through your linen shower robe and you would be allowed to go down to the showers. Squads from the other floors were doing the same thing. The problem was that, upon finishing on one floor, we then had to ask permission to pass from the Upperclassmen on the next lower floor. To do that, we had to hit the wall and ask, "Sir, may I have permission to pass?" This usually resulted in getting harassed for asking that question and then being made to go through the whole routine again on that floor. Hazing was flourishing.

Throughout Shower Formation, we were braced hard, screamed at, commanded to hit the floor for repeated pushups, and asked questions about facts from *Bugle Notes*. Occasionally we were physically pushed on the shoulders, chest and rib cages by several Upperclassmen at a time. The intensity of noise from the yelling and hazing by all the Upperclassmen might have reached the decibel level potential of breaking a person's ear drums.

My chin was slightly bleeding from the slice of an errant Upperclassmen's fingernail. I had sweated pennies, nickels and even dimes against the wall so that my bathrobe was completely saturated with perspiration. With ringing ear drums, I finally made it down to the third floor where the whole procedure was repeated. Since I had already sweated through my bathrobe, I was allowed to pass more easily; the same went for the next two floors.

At last, I made it to the latrine in the basement. Hot water and soap had never felt so good! I spent five minutes showering, luxuriating as the suds twirled and cascaded down my torso, until I was forced to exit due to more New Cadets arriving...but not before I peed in the shower.

What a great and glorious release! Such a gleeful, emotional moment as I performed an undetectable infraction against the military establishment! The small act of rebellion soothed my wounded spirit. I planned to enact more such minor transgressions whenever I could get away with them, as to retain some semblance of individuality amid the regimentation; carefully though, because there were always four or five guys in the shower at the same time.

After drying off with my small towel, I was ready to travel back to my room, but the Upperclassmen were lying in wait; getting back to the fourth floor proved to be the same nightmare as going down to the latrine.

My shower was for naught. By the time I reached the fourth floor, two hours after the Shower Formation began, I was sweating profusely again. I was, however, happy to at least be back in my room. It was almost Taps; time to sleep and reflect.

My roommates joined me shortly thereafter. The first thing we did together, as a team, was to scan *Bugle Notes*. We all wanted to be able to eat breakfast.

Finally, I flopped down on my bunk to go to sleep, exhausted as never before. It had been the longest, most physical and completely horrible day of my life. I was fried and miserable but so relieved that this day was over.

But it wasn't over. About ten minutes after Taps, with the lights out, there was a knock on the door.

They had come for me!

CHAPTER 20

Should I, or shouldn't I go to West Point? I know nothing about the Academy. I'd be going in blind. I ought to do some research to be doubly, triply, quadruply sure it's for me, but to be brutally honest, all I care about, at that moment, is winning tennis tournaments and trying to get laid.

I know it's time to get on with my life and to get Jill out of my mind. If I go to West Point, I'll clear my head of my misfortunes, do right by my family and make my parents proud.

I think the decision just made itself. It's simply the right thing to do…I think!

So, I go to Fort Benning, Georgia for a weekend, to complete the entrance requirements. There's a medical exam, a Cadet Fitness Requirement—pushups, situps, pullups, running, no big deal—psychological tests. I just move from one building to another and do whatever they tell me to do. I am doing what they ask of me.

About a week later my folks get a letter stating that I'm to report to the United States Military Academy at West Point on July 5th, 1961, not later than 0900 hours. I've been accepted for admission as a cadet.

★ ★ ★

July approaches. I've been playing as many tennis tournaments as I can before my departure for the Academy. I won the Florida State Doubles title and I placed as a semi-finalist in singles. I got appointed to the Florida Junior Davis Cup as well. It's been so great! I'll be ranked in the top six in singles. Since Florida had the best group of junior boys in the country, if I could have played the summer circuit, I'd probably would be in the top fifteen in the United States.

Helen and I also finished high school! Now she'll be a Gator in Gainesville, living the life, and I'll be starting a whole new life in New York, in a world I still know nothing about. What the hell...? Am I crazy?

Oh well...it's too late to turn back now. And at this point, there's no time to study up on the Academy. I'll learn as I go, I guess. Since they have invited me, I feel confident they will welcome me, show me the ropes and make me feel happy to have joined them.

CHAPTER 21

am dead asleep. Then, a heavy knock on our wooden door shattered the first quiet moment of the whole first day!

We all jumped out of our bunks and stood at attention. My mind, having already taken refuge in rest from the day's turmoil, was now disoriented and confused. The door opened, revealing one of the Upperclassmen I had met earlier while traversing the Area: the one with the slight southern accent. His narrow, angular face now sported a five o'clock shadow.

I didn't remember him at first, nor could I place the three angry men accompanying him. All of them were dressed in tee shirts with various colored trousers or shorts. One wore suspenders over a gray "Triple A" tee shirt: Army Athletic Association, which I had first seen when I met the cadet tennis players in Florida. But those guys all had smiles on their faces; this stranger was scowling at me.

"Kantrowich," the southerner said, "Follow us. The rest of you get back in your bunks and go to sleep." I panicked, knowing strange things can happen at night,

The four Upperclassmen walked me down one flight of stairs to the corner room on the third floor, back section, where it was quiet.

One left the group and positioned himself as a lookout on the first floor, at the door near the stoops of the barracks. I remained in place, sweat soaking my standard-issue white tee shirt and white boxers.

"Start off and give us twenty pushups, Jerkoff!" hissed another Upperclassman. He had a broad barrel chest, a short blond crew-cut and a contorted scowl that, without my glasses, looked like a facial disfigurement.

When I finally got to the twentieth pushup, the young Torquemada slipped a laundry bag over my head, pulled the string taut and yelled, "Give me fifty situps Mister!" I ran out of gas at about number forty-six and moaned.

The three Upperclassmen stood me up and braced me against the wall, took the laundry bag off my head and produced a lit cigarette with a large golden ember on its tip. I smelled it before I saw it's glow in the reduced light. As the burning tip inched closer, I could feel the hairs on my chin start to singe.

The brutes surrounded me, peppering me with questions. "Keep that stupid neck in!" "Where're you from?" "Jam your chin in, But-twipe...and give me your sister's phone number, 'cause I need a blow-job!"

"Miami, Sir!" I reported. I avoided the question about my sister.

"Are you a little pussy, Kantrowich?"

"No, Sir!"

"Are you a momma's boy, Little Paulie?"

"No, Sir!"

"Does your momma make a living on her back?"

"No, Sir!"

"You are not happy here at West Point, are you, Mister?"

"No, Sir!" Tricky question. Someone blew smoke in my face. I perspired and coughed as they continued.

"Ya go to church, Kantrowich?" "No, Sir."

"Everybody here goes to church. Are you going to church"? "No, Sir," I answered, trying not to tremble as I asserted, "But I will go to temple." There was a sudden change in the atmosphere, as if all the air in the confined space had been sucked out.

"Temple? What is a Jew-Boy like you doing here?" another Upperclassman chimed in. "What's the matter, little Hebe, can't take the heat, can't be a man? Maybe you should go back to the desert where you came from."

The anger rose in me like a flame from a fire. "Sir, may I make a statement?" I yelled at the top of my lungs. Three distorted faces glared at me with unbridled rage.

"Kantrowich, shut the fuck up! Shut your stupid Yid mouth or I'll put a sock in it!" said the southerner. "NO! You may not make a statement!"

The men shoved me into a squatting position with an M-1 rifle, its wooden stock and heavy barrel behind my head, my arms slung around and over the weapon to keep it in place. The rough trigger guard pressed into the back of my neck, scraping it. Once again, the laundry bag went over my head, its string pulled taut, as the three of them continued to bombard me with verbal abuse. Someone whacked my back with a flat object; someone else slapped the side of my head with an open hand. I was starting to cramp in both thighs and fell backwards against the wall. I wondered if they could smell my fear, which was escalating at an alarming rate.

Finally, they put me upright. The first Upperclassman, with that Southern accent that seemed to have an edge of sharpened steel to it, said, "Kantrowich, you are always to remember that you, personally, are the lowest form of dog shit that exists on the face of this Earth. I will personally ensure that you will remember that for the rest of your life. We don't want any Jewish dog shit here at West Point!"

Just then, the lookout came bounding up the steps to report that the Cadet Officer-in-Charge was making rounds and entering the building. The bag came off my head, the rifle was put aside, the yelling stopped. I was left bracing the wall as all New Cadets were supposed to, but it was really the wall holding me up.

The charming southern gentleman moved to the doorway and casually stepped out to the hall to greet the Cadet Officer-in-Charge, who had just arrived at the third floor. It was apparent they knew each other. "Hey, Rich," he called to the OIC, "What are you doing here? Why aren't you over at Brigade?"

The OIC replied, "I am doing a favor for someone...looking for a New Cadet. Got a message for him and he's supposed to be on the next floor up."

Could he be looking for me? I coughed loudly from the smoke still filling the room. The OIC stepped inside and saw me.

"Well, look what we have here after Taps," the OIC said. "A little dancing party! Who is the guest of honor?"

"Some fag Jew from Miami who doesn't belong here," replied my friend, the good ole boy. "He was just getting ready to tell us he's quitting and wants to go home to his momma!"

"What's your name, Kid?" asked the OIC. I would find out later his name was Richard Carlson. I choked out something that sounded like "Kan wech," because I was still having trouble breathing.

"That wouldn't be Kantrowich, would it, Son? You must be the New Cadet I am looking for. Glad I found you even if it is at this late hour."

"This guy's a real jerk, an ass-wipe and we don't want him in Beast Barracks or at West Point;" drawled the Leader of the Dog Pack. "He was just about to resign and leave before you walked in."

Carlson smiled, looked at me and asked, "Is this true?"

My body ached and my mind was close to shattered. Here was an opportunity to leave this insane place and try for a normal life on the outside with normal people. Instead, I stated, "Sir, no Sir! I have never quit anything in my life, Sir! I never give up, Sir!"

No one else said a word. Finally, Richard Carlson said quietly, "I guess there has been a small misunderstanding here and it's time to put it behind us. It's late and, since we all agree New Cadet Kantrowich should get some needed sleep, if you'll excuse us, I'll see he gets back to his room."

Cadet Captain Carlson grabbed my elbow and we left together for the fourth floor. When we got to my door, he stood me at attention. "Kid," he said, "You had better try to stay clear of those guys because I won't always be around to save your ass. Don't volunteer information and don't ask any questions right now. You got that? If they haze you, then you are just going to have to take it and be strong, be tough! By the way," he remarked, his eyes seeming to twinkle, "Coach Nordlie asked me to check up on you to see how your first day went. I'm going to report back that you were down a set and a break in serve, but you bounced back to win the match!"

I should have thanked him, but I was at a loss for words. Maybe he could have done more, perhaps reported the men to higher authorities, maybe not. Since I didn't know how the system worked, I trusted that Carlson was doing what he could to extricate me from a difficult situation with those troglodytes by downplaying it.

First Class Cadet Richard Carlson was only four years older than me, but light-years ahead in this world of West Point; a world about which I had no clue. I vowed that if I ever met him again later in the year, I would properly thank him for helping me that evening...but would not let him beat me on the tennis court, if we ever played!

My first official day at West Point had ended. I was a Jew at the Point, at the point of leaving...but there I was, still.

CHAPTER 22

I n my slumber something very beautiful comes to me.

At this moment, I have everything I have ever needed or wanted in my life. People are clapping, cheering, chattering while sunshine twinkles off green palm fronds framed by the azure sky of a beautiful South Florida day. There's a light smattering of puffy, high- altitude clouds. The sun at 2 o'clock in the sky on the north side of the court is at just the right angle to interfere with a left hander's serve. My slightly older and much higher-ranked opponent, Teddy Travis, is a leftie. This gives me an advantage; he might have beaten me otherwise! But he doesn't and I am now the Men's Singles Champion. It's the perfect day and I am revelling in every second of it.

My opponent and I approach the net and, shaking hands meaningfully, he says, "Great match!" With my racquet tucked under my left arm, a huge silly grin on my face, I pump his hand. "Thought you had me, Ted. I was lucky!" You should always leave your opponent a little room to save face. This makes him think you are also a good sport, which I hope, most of the time, I am.

Ted and I part ways at the net and go off in different directions. I'm smiling so hard I might split my face! My girlfriend Jill rushes over to congratulate me, which makes me smile even broader. Not just another day at the office, it's "Championship Day at Office Headquarters!" She kisses me on the cheek. I hope she'll make a promise to me later that could result in another championship moment, if you know what I mean.

Abe, with a big grin forcing his cigar over to the left corner of his mouth, comes over to shake my hand. My sister Helen waves and mouths, "Good job!" She's sitting, as always, with her pal Lenore up in the grandstand, probably plotting their weekend escapes.

Dad is seated up near the back, a cigarette in his hand; his buddy, John Campbell, sits next to him. John is wearing his rose-colored glasses and puffing away as well. It makes dad nervous to see me compete and I don't want his nervousness to become mine. I've had to ask him several times not to fidget so much during my tennis matches and to stay in the background. Luckily, he always honors my request.

I signal "thumbs up" to my father as I leave the court. He is always so kind and generous with everyone, my image of what a real man should be. I'd like to be half the mensch he is. Winning tournaments is one of very few ways I can thank him for his support.

Walking around the grounds, I soak up the thrill of victory in this perfect world. I can still feel the lingering sensation of Jill's lips on my tan, wet cheek. The loud roar from the crowd still reverberates in my ears and....

WHAM, BAM! Piercing sounds shook me from my slumber. I awoke to the blare of an Army bugler playing *Reveille*. It felt as if I had just fallen asleep, but it was already 0550 hours; time for my second day at West Point.

Joints achy, vision blurry, I jerked up and jumped off the upper bunk directly to the floor, slightly rolling my right ankle. A little pain accompanied the wobble as I hit. I shook it off quickly; I had to. Not knowing what to do next, I imitated everything I saw my Squad mates do as we assembled uniforms then raced down the stairs for formation.

Hitting the wall several times enroute delayed our timeliness. Once there, we braced at attention and were swarmed by a cluster of Upperclassmen, all yelling and issuing orders as if war had just broken out. It had rained the night before and the Area reflected beams of sunlight in each small puddle on its cement surface. The beauty of the prismatic colors seemed inappropriate for this second day in Hell.

In a semi-conscious state, way too soon after my night's dream, I didn't understand what the Upperclassmen were yelling. I didn't care, either; I was severely annoyed. My ankle pain reminded me of the emotional pain I had been feeling since leaving the sally port on that first morning of Beast Barracks. *When does this ever end? Does it ever end?*

As oxygen began swirling back through my brain, I realized where I was and what I was supposed to do. *Am I dreaming of THIS nightmare called West Point or still snoozing somewhere else? Now, that would be extremely disturbing!* I wasn't really thinking properly. I labored to wipe the annoyance off my face when, at that moment, the Company Commander walked by, stopped, turned a right face to face me, staring with an unkind intensity. "Kantrowich, step forward!"

I braced harder and stepped forward, embarrassed to be singled out, amazed he remembered my name. Then I recalled it was sewn right above my left pocket in dark letters large enough for a movie marquee.

"You are in the wrong uniform, Smackhead. Did your Squad Leader teach you that?"

"No Sir!"

"Are you sure he didn't teach you to dress that way?"

"No Sir!"

"No, he *didn't* teach you, or no, he *did* teach you?" he snapped back. "Sir," I boldly asked, "May I make a statement? Sir, my Squad Leader did NOT teach me to dress this way."

"Then who taught you to dress this way, Smackhead?"

There didn't seem to be enough oxygen in my brain yet to supply a reasonable answer to the Company Commander's question.

Scrambling for something that would lay no blame on my Squad Leader, I said loudly, "I taught myself to dress this way, Sir!"

The Company Commander called over the Squad Leader. "Danny, did you teach Kantrowich to dress this way?"

"Negative, Sir!" he answered. Meanwhile I was thinking... thinking...*how do I get out of this predicament?*

The Cadet Commander turned again to me and asked, "Why would you teach yourself to dress this way when everyone else is dressed in proper uniform, but you are not? Why are you the only one?"

Aware now that there was no correct answer to his question, I replied, "No excuse, Sir!"

"I'm not looking for an excuse, Kantrowich," he said. "I'm trying to figure out why YOU would teach yourself to dress this way. Are you different from everyone else?"

"Yes, Sir!" I replied. Then I realized my mistake. "I mean, no, Sir!"

"Step back in line, Kantrowich," the Cadet Commander ordered. "Everyone else take one step forward. Now everyone hit it for fifteen pushups except Kantrowich. He can watch, since he is different from everyone else! From now on Kantrowich," he continued, "I, personally, would like to see you dress in the proper uniform called for, just like every one of your classmates does. Understand? Got it?"

"Yes, Sir!" I replied sheepishly, as I heard some of my classmates grunting from the punishment awarded them on my behalf. It was going to be a very long, difficult, second day in Beast Barracks. I knew I would have to suffer my Squad mates' dislike for me once again. Adding that to the gnawing hunger in my stomach, it was distressing; my fuel tank was running dangerously low.

I also had to control my temper, as it was wont to erupt over the simplest provocations. This wasn't the time nor the place to lose it. I was at a point where it was important to learn this aspect of myself quickly.

CHAPTER 23

The day became drab and overcast quickly. The rising sun still hadn't broken through the dark alleys of the barracks area when the Reveille formation was finally dismissed. We raced back to our rooms to get into the uniform appropriate for breakfast then lined up in our Squad Leader's room for a brief discussion of the day's events. Immediately after breakfast we were to be trained in how to properly clean an M-1 rifle, practice marching for the afternoon parade, and have uniform formations to ensure we had on the proper uniform when called for. We were also to do calisthenics; prepare for the cadet obstacle course; get ready for a room inspection and a fingernail inspection; line up for a shot formation; attend a class on the Honor Code; have lunch and dinner; and finally, another shower formation for a nightcap. It promised to be a busy day, but I was too starved to think about anything but food.

As we re-formed into breakfast formation, I knew that I had not memorized enough "poop" from *Bugle Notes*. There was a lot to know and no time to study, particularly after my little "After-Taps Soiree" the night before. I remembered a couple of worthless paragraphs about leather, lights and gallons, but that was only the beginning of the knowledge I was required to learn. My optimism about eating breakfast was deflating rapidly as we moved to our assigned table.

At the head of my table was a new Table Commandant, Cadet Evers: a short, blond, crew-cut, ruddy-faced, bulky-shouldered, smiling Platoon Leader somewhere in the Company. The same "Enforcer," Cadet Johns, was at the other end. Johns had starved me the night before and I had every reason to believe he would try to do it again.

Clean, gleaming dishes, white linen table napkins and glistening silverware graced our table. My growling stomach pain was further exacerbated by the aroma of strong coffee and the sight of juice, milk, bread, butter and jam already in place. We were ten hungry men at the table, eight of whom were New Cadets hungrier than alley cats trolling garbage cans.

"Take Seats!" came the order. I was placed adjacent to Johns at his left, requiring him to pass food to me that I was then to pass to my left, clockwise, with military efficiency. As we sat, Cadet Johns asked, "Kantrowich, what is the definition of leather?"

Our new Table Leader chuckled and said, "Fall out, eat up! We all have a busy day today and you are going to need all your energy." As everyone started passing trays of hot breakfast treats, I prayed a silent prayer of thanksgiving: "The definition of leather" was one of the few excerpts from *Bugle Notes* that I had memorized previously but I thought it would be rude to interrupt the table food chain to answer the question, figuring Johns wouldn't mind waiting, per the rules of decorum. But as my tablemates began shoveling chow into their hungry mouths, Cadet Johns, irritated that I had kept him waiting, screeched over the already boisterous noise level of the Cadet Mess Hall: "IRP!"

"Sir," I loudly proclaimed, "The definition of leather: 'If the fresh skin of an animal, cleaned and divested of all hair, fat and other extraneous matter be immersed in a dilute solution of tannic acid, a chemical combination ensues; the gelatinous tissue of the skin is converted into a non-putrescible substance, impervious to and insoluble in water; this, Sir, is leather.'"

I ended my speech with unbridled enthusiasm, proud of myself. The Enforcer smiled and chuckled, "Didn't think you had it in you, Kantrowich! You may be eating now, but I will be around the next time you screw up at the table. Go ahead...enjoy your meal."

The pancakes, eggs, sausage, hash browns, juice, milk and little cheese Danishes were the sweetest, chewiest, most succulent food I had ever put to my tongue. Energy flowed through my body as I felt my competitive spirit returning. As the meal ended, the Table Commandant complimented me on my knowledge of the proper poop. I saw one of my Squad mates wink a "congratulations" at me.

The air seemed infused with more oxygen as the turbulence in my mind subsided. I screwed my chin back in, pulled my shoulders back and started to smirk feeling joy from just the aroma of such good food. Maybe today would be a better day after all.

As we formed up to march away, Cadet Johns reminded me that, while I had been allowed to have breakfast, lunch and supper might be a different story. The smirk vanished from my face as I realized he had been one of the late-night cadre trying to run me out of Beast Barracks. Shocked I didn't recognize him from before, I needed to tread very lightly around him. How had I not recognized him as part of the vigilante group?

We reported back to Squad Leader Brite's room, where he lectured on the art and science of cleaning our own personal M-1 rifles. He reminded us of the eight pounds of weight, the linseed-oiled stock, the carbon-steel housing and trigger guard, and the semi-automatic function. The thick, brown leather strap could be used to sling the weapon over our shoulder and for a multitude of other tasks as well.

We used our Army-issued rifle cleaning kit to remove any trace of oxidation or lint outside on the rifle and inside the rifle bore. Brite mentioned we would be going to the firing range later next week to fire our weapons, so they had to be always immaculate. We had none of the 7.62x33mm NATO rounds of ammunition to seat into the housing yet. That would come later when we were at the firing range. The training session underscored the fact that I was now a soldier, whether I liked it or not. My weapon would be a lifeline while in battle and I had to keep it clean, close and safe.

Next, we formed up as a Squad in the Area and marched with our rifles on our right shoulders. We were instructed on the proper way to "port arms"—stand at attention with our rifles by our sides, shift them back up to our right shoulders with a certain rhythm, in unison. We learned to "fix bayonets" by taking the chrome, decorative bayonet from its sheath and attaching it to the barrel of the M-1; and how to position the rifle as a salute in "present arms." We would be doing all these maneuvers later as we marched in our very first parade for the public.

After practice-marching for a short period, we re-formed, having changed into our proper gym uniform—gray shorts with a black stripe on the sides and an elastic waistband, white short-sleeved USMA collarless gym shirt with black circlets around the neck and lower edge of the sleeves framing our biceps, white socks and black high-top sneakers. To complete the ensemble, we also wore a USMA-approved jock strap with an intricate woven design cup. The shirt with its helmet, shield and sword of the logo imprinted over the heart gave us a professional look while the floppy socks and Keds high-tops reminded us we were still amateurs. I felt as if I were back at gym class in junior high.

Next, we double-timed over to another grassy area adjacent to the Plain and performed an hour of high energy calisthenics: jumping jacks, pushups, situps, stretching, bending and squatting, all to the cadence of the commands of the Upperclassman cadet instructor who stood atop a four-foot high, sixty-four square-foot wooden platform. First, he would demonstrate the proper way to perform the exercise; then the whole Platoon repeated it. Every exercise was coordinated and performed as a drill with at least ten repetitions. This type of physical exercise was slightly rejuvenating for me and a good stress reliever. It was also fun to do them in a group.

Tall, well-muscled and confident, the cadet instructor projected an attitude of authority and leadership. As we were counting out the number of repetitions we were up to, he constantly complained, "Come on, ladies, I can't HEAR YOU!" although apparently, he had no hearing issues. He too was being evaluated on his performance.

Supervising Upperclassmen circulated through our ranks, ensuring we were doing the exercises correctly and with proper enthusiasm. They pulled out slackers from our group to do some added work in the form of additional individual pushups, some with an Upperclassman's boot on their backside to make it more difficult.

Afterwards we double-timed back to our rooms, where we were allowed a two-minute shower. We cleaned up as best we could and reported to our Squad Leader's room, where he brought us back outside to double-time over to another area on the Plain. It was time for the much-heralded "Honor Code" lecture, held outdoors on a cool, dark green grassy area surrounded by lush foliage and a beautifully scenic view looking back at the statuesque structures of the Cadet Mess Hall and barracks. The large Cadet Protestant Chapel loomed in the backdrop high atop an overlook, casting a religious presence onto Academy grounds; it was the perfect setting for this consequential lecture.

We were seated as a full Company en masse, quiet and ready to learn about this sacred and hallowed part of being a West Point cadet. The Upperclass Cadet Honor Representative approached a podium, stood tall and somberly started his oration, in an imperative and moving matter. Up until this point in my life, I had no idea what the word "honor" truly meant. I decided to give the Honor Code lecture my full attention.

CHAPTER 24

"DUTY, HONOR, COUNTRY": THE "HONOR" PART

"There are only three rules a Cadet must follow, always," reported the Cadet Honor Representative. "These rules are simple, easy to understand and pure. These rules, however, carry with them great significance and consequence." He paused for dramatic effect.

"A Cadet will not lie. A Cadet will not cheat... and... a Cadet will not steal!" he continued. "The basic premise is that if a man does a dishonorable act, he will do the same dishonorable act on the battlefield, which may cause significant loss of life. Also, we live in a society based upon the rule of law. Those laws protect the individual but also the society itself from varieties of lawlessness. Men—especially men living in close quarters—must have a basic trust and belief in each other to fulfill whatever their mission is. This Honor Code helps build that trust and belief in each other. It's that trust, as a leader, that you must possess and utilize for yourself, your men, your family and your country."

Sitting on the grass, cloudless sky above, trees swaying, people milling around on the sidewalks, seeing these tall, dark statues of heroes framing the entire scene, I had to think, are they truly standing and protecting society? Some of the most famous individuals in the history of our nation, first bronzed, then situated, now standing and providing protection...a reminder of sacrifices needed to obtain and retain freedom. No cheating, no stealing, no lying...it simply made sense. Developing trust and belief in each other to get the job done... again, I saw no reason to question this.

"Furthermore," continued the Cadet Honor Representative, "You are just as guilty of violating our Honor Code if you see or even have reason to believe you saw or heard someone lying, cheating or stealing and did nothing about it." He went on to say that anyone who wanted to report an honor violation should do so privately, at an appropriate time, reporting to his room at Company D-1 while Beast Barracks was in session. Later, when we were assigned to a regular Cadet Company to start the academic year, each Company would have its own individual Honor Representative.

The lecture went on for thirty more minutes, after which the Cadet Honor Representative opened the floor up for discussion. A lot of difficult questions and examples were asked or projected. I continued to listen carefully. At the end of the discussion, he stated, "I will be available for prayers and other discussion after the supper meal if any New Cadet feels the need or duty to talk".

We reassembled together as a Company, double-timing back to the barracks for parade uniform inspection with shoes shined, brass polished, wearing our uniforms complete with crossed white belts, tar bucket hat and M-1 rifle. Squad Leader Danny Brite instructed and assisted us—as opposed to bitching and yelling at us—so that the whole Squad would look "strac"—sharp and ready for anything. This was not for nothing because Upperclassmen Cadre were also evaluated on their participation and performance for leading and training their men. Our successful display meant Danny would shine on his performance report.

Following the uniform training, we went through a room inspection by both the Battalion and Company Commanders just before lunch. The Platoon and Squad Leaders tagged along. Any inspector who could squeeze into the room did so, awarding as many demerits as they could for any and all infractions: dust on shoes, misaligned handkerchiefs, rust on rifle, lint on floor, water spots on sink or faucet, condensation on mirror, bed improperly made, belt buckle/breast plate improperly shined, closet clothes not properly aligned, boots/shoes improperly shined, dust on windowsill, smelly laundry in laundry bag, and improper shave or haircut, just to name a few. The list seemed endless and as the demerits added up, there was more difficulty for my Squad Mates and myself; I envisioned a tidal wave of trouble cresting.

I received a lot of demerits during the inspection. Nothing I shined was shiny enough, my bed wasn't tight enough, my closet wasn't properly aligned, and there was lint in my rifle barrel. The inspecting Officers departed, leaving our Squad and Platoon Leaders upset with us. Their anger indicated that lunch in the Mess Hall would be trying at best.

I was still very tired from my first day and first evening in Beast Barracks. Now, into the second day, even after a decent breakfast and the motivational speech by the Honor Representative, I still felt a little empty and somewhat lost: empty because I needed rest and fuel, lost because I knew I was in the wrong world, although I was still trying very hard to convince myself I belonged here. A disheartening wave of anxiety still passed through me since leaving that original sally port the day before. Honor, as explained by the Honor Rep, was an interesting and moving way of looking at goodness and righteousness and taking those concepts to a higher level. I should just put more thought into being honorable and push aside my anxiety.

The Squad lined up in formation and got a quick chewing out by our Squad Leader for being selfish and totally unprepared for inspection. We had created difficulty for him in the chain of command, Danny told us. We all had to do better in the future for ourselves and for him. The "or else" was left unsaid.

Double-timing to lunch, bracing at our table awaiting orders from the poop deck and then taking seats, there was an ozone odor of frustration orbiting above my table, a black cloud waiting to erupt. Fall out instructions were not given and Cadet Johns, still in place at the foot of our table, started in with hostile questions.

"How many elephants did Genghis Khan use in his front line of battle? How many 105mm Howitzer rounds accompany each tube during transport?" He fired one question after another at us; questions that none of us could answer. None of his questions came from Bugle Notes so where did he learn this crap from?

Not one New Cadet at our table ate lunch, but I took little comfort in knowing I wasn't the only screw-up in our group. Beautiful food, served steaming hot on stainless steel trays, was all removed from the table by our servers once the two Upperclassmen had taken their share. Succulent Swiss steak, creamy mashed potatoes, cooked corn and sliced whole grain bread vanished while tantalizing aromas remained to torture the hungry. Eight delectable servings of chocolate pudding—a food I basically grew up on as a youngster because I was such a picky eater—were also removed. Cadet Johns clearly was enjoying his power trip immensely while eight devastated New Cadet stomachs growled.

When lunch was over, we double-timed back to the North Area to assemble for a shot formation. A more appropriate title for this gathering would be "Inoculation Formation." It was a simple, easy activity we were not allowed to miss.

There were two parallel rows of four healthcare professionals on each side. The doctors, nurses and medics in each row all had inoculation guns in their hands. We were directed to roll up our sleeves on both arms and proceed down the center between the two rows.

I moved slowly, received a shot from two people—one in each arm—then stepped forward. The process was repeated three more times. I'd always been afraid of needles, so this shock of eight at once was almost too much for me. When the first Squadmate had finished, he dropped down and knocked out ten pushups to show how tough he was, while I kept my eyes closed the entire time, trying not to pass out. I made a mighty effort just to stay with the group in an upright position.

The order came to form up and we immediately double-timed back to the barracks for more training; this time, "how to build a military backpack," for those future New Cadet hikes we would undertake. Not having eaten lunch wasn't helping matters and left me lightheaded. I needed to eat something, anything...please! I was trying to learn, experience and grow in order to do my duty to my country. Why did I have to do it all on an empty stomach? Where was there any honor in withholding food as punishment?!

CHAPTER 25

MY SECOND DAY CONTINUES

Our Squad Leader gave us all a half-hour of down-time before we had to work on our backpacks and gear in preparation of our future field activities. Returning to my room with my Squad mates, I was determined to memorize as much of *Bugle Notes*, the "Cadet Bible," as I could. With more knowledge, perhaps I might get the chance to eat supper. I had been extremely lucky never to have experienced this kind of hunger before in my life; I felt badly for all those around the world who had.

I learned as much as I could in the free time allotted and said a silent prayer to God for help. Studying Torah is the entry requirement for Jews to be considered adults at the tender age of thirteen. Since I had failed to achieve that rite of passage as a Bar Mitzvah, if studying and memorizing *Bugle Notes* at age seventeen would allow me entry into yet another hallowed category of manhood—as a West Pointer—I had no decent excuse not to redeem myself.

The logic didn't add up, however. Why would I want to use manhood and being a member of the Long Gray Line as barter for the privilege of eating a lousy burger and fries? My enthusiasm was waning exponentially as my hunger and anger built.

During the following hour and a half, we learned how to set up and assemble our backpacks, field belts and helmets, properly blouse our boots, affix our ponchos to the packs and our entrenching tools so that they wouldn't fall off or scrape our backs on long hikes. It was explained that our final hike, at the end of Beast Barracks, would be about twenty-five miles long while toting about eighty pounds of equipment, completed in under six hours, so the equipment had to be tightly secured. The idea of hiking that distance was unsettling, particularly on such a low-calorie diet.

It was time to get into parade uniform, be inspected and form up outside the barracks. From the barracks stoops we would move, by Company, to the assembly area on the outer ring of the stone buildings and archways of the Academy, for public viewing. From that new assembly point we would march as a full brigade of New Cadets onto the public street and proceed toward and onto the Plain.

Our M-1 rifles with attached chrome bayonets were positioned on our right shoulders and, with the U.S. Army Band (permanently stationed at West Point) playing a vibrant John Philip Sousa march, the entire new brigade stepped forward, left feet first and proceeded to march off for our very first public parade in full parade regalia. The crowd loved to see this spectacle. For us, however, it wasn't comfortable to march with our chins smacked back to our necks in a bracing position.

Once on the Plain and formed up by Company again, we stopped, listened to "Attention to Orders" and then were ordered to "pass in review"—meaning we would march past the reviewing stand where the Superintendent and the Commandant of the Academy were positioned along with all the VIPs and their guests. As we passed the center of the stands, we were ordered to "Eyes Right" while the Company Commander and Platoon Leaders saluted the reviewing stands with their erect sabers. As the distinguished group saluted us back, I began to feel the return of some personal pride. I saw the jutting jaw and blazing eyes of our Superintendent, Major General William C. Westmoreland looking daggers in my direction as we passed by. I imagined he and the other officers were sternly glaring directly at me. Was I becoming paranoid?

Thinking about it…that specific thought unsettled me! I questioned why West Point wanted to reshape me into someone different than myself? What was wrong with who I am?

The answer dawned on me: *because they want that type of person who does well under the circumstances of adverse conflict: WAR!* That is the type of man they wanted at West Point. There was no room for proud individuality. This hard realization hit me as the parade tailed off back towards the Quadrangle. *Who wants to be involved in war anyway, especially war created by faulty politics and greedy, stupid human beings? What individual wants to have his personality shaped by avaricious people? What person in their right mind anyway? Not me! NO…NO…NOT ME!*

After the parade, we were to scramble back, get into our dinner uniform, and head for the Mess Hall. As we marched to supper, my competitive spirit was trying to jack me up, get me thinking smarter, adopt a more positive attitude. I knew that after our evening meal, we had a shower formation, only after which it would be possible to rest and relax. The prospect of a little quiet time was exciting.

Supper turned out to be less of an ordeal than I'd anticipated. I had some of the answers to questions they asked me from *Bugle Notes*, so the spotlight was less focused on me. I got to eat a little. Roast beef, spud potatoes, salad and custard crème pie for dessert never tasted so delicious.

I was now viewing the shower formation as a two-act comedy and, bolstered by some nutrition, I knew I could get through it unscathed…and I did, although the verbal and light physical abuse I had to endure was still both punishing and mystifying.

Soon it was 10PM or 2200 hours military time. Taps were played and we settled in for the second night of Beast Barracks. It was wonderful to lay down on my bunk and close my eyes.

I was immediately asleep at 2201 hours.

CHAPTER 26

MY SECOND GO-AROUND

I was dead asleep at 2215 hours when they came for me again.

"I've had enough crap from you, Kantrowich," drawled the Cadet Upperclassman, Mr. Southern Comfort, who was anything but comforting. Three men stood behind him and we were now down in the basement latrine.

"Tonight, you resign and leave this place," the southern Upperclassman said. "You got that? Do you understand?"

"No, Sir!" I replied.

"Smart-ass jerk-off," one of the accompanying men replied. The southern gent continued, "The correct answer is 'Yes, Sir!' Kantrowich, pull your head out of your ass and answer correctly right now! You got that? IRP!"

I remained silent. If I replied "Yes, Sir," I wouldn't be telling the truth. If I planned to quit West Point, it would be on my own terms, not because of these vigilantes. I hadn't made any decisions yet. Although terrorized, I still tried to invoke the rule I had adopted from tennis: when you are losing it's easy to quit; a real champion works through hardship and difficulties to win.

A new routine began: How many times can we hit a New Cadet in the stomach before he crumples? They started poking me in the gut, first with one finger, then two, then a fist to my solar plexus. I was winded immediately and fell, groaning, laying curled up on the damp, cement floor. A minute later, I was doing a handstand against the wall for thirty seconds until both arms gave out and I collapsed. A minute later, one of the larger men wanted a pony ride. He straddled my back, sitting heavily; I collapsed after one lap around the john. Pushups and situps followed with the laundry bag in place over my head; then there was sweating coins against the wall with either a lit cigarette or sharp bayonet two millimeters from my chin. All the while, the four snakes hissed derogatory remarks about my family, my mother, my sisters, my religion, my face and the size and appearance of various parts of my body. They were totally obsessed with my Jewish nose, my circumcised *schlong* and that I was a "beanie boy" who didn't wear a yarmulke on my head. Even if I could have protested and lived to tell the tale, I was too breathless with exhaustion and fear to speak.

One of this group said, "Tomorrow you will resign after breakfast, Shithead. If you don't then tomorrow night and every night thereafter, we'll keep having the same type of party until you do!" They left amid a chorus of jeers and more insults.

I wasn't feeling strong nor spry as I gripped the bannister of the stairs tightly and pulled myself up, one step at a time, to get to my fourth-floor room. Passing out on my bunk, I dreamed again of being in South Florida, winning tennis tournaments and basking in the adoration of the people around me; people who didn't treat me like dog shit.

After what seemed like five minutes, I awoke with a jolt from the Reveille bugle. My entire body, hands and face were covered with beet-red, itchy, blotchy, angry lesions. Now I had a medical reason to leave West Point without being a quitter. Maybe it was time for my New Cadet misery to end.

Cadet Johns was at the breakfast table. He looked at me as if he'd never expected to see me again…which would have made the both of us happy. My Squad Leader ordered me to go on sick call right after a breakfast of little food and a lot of bracing and torment.

Soon I lined up in the sick call formation and an Upperclassman marched us to the hospital. Approximately twenty-five New Cadets went for sick call that day; none, however, appeared to have as serious a problem as I did. I reflected on what I would do after I left the Academy. *First, I'll find a restaurant in Highland Falls that serves steak. This steak must be a big, juicy T-bone, medium rare. After devouring it, then, and only then, will I call mom and dad....*

"Kantrowich!" the doctor called. Breaking me out of my reverie. I walked into his cubicle. "Why are you on sick call?" he asked. I explained that I was dying of an unknown skin disease.

The doctor looked at me skeptically, then whipped out his stethoscope and listened to my heart, took my blood pressure and asked me to look in the mirror and point out the skin disorder I had reported. The mirror reflected the haggard-looking face and downward-cast eyes I was feeling. But... there were no marks on my face at all; nothing!

I rolled up my uniform sleeves: no marks. I opened my uniform blouse, no marks here either. The doctor started laughing.

"Son...you had an allergic reaction to stress called 'hives.' That's what you saw at first. Now all the hives have dissipated and are gone. You are a perfectly healthy New Cadet. Get out of here!" he chuckled, then yelled out the name of the next patient in line.

Disheartened, defeated, I marched back with the other New Cadets. I decided I would turn myself in on an honor violation, which would immediately end my West Point experience for sure. Perhaps I had lied about something during a vicious confrontation with a member of the cadre? Accidental, but still a lie. The more I thought about it, the need to leave increased exponentially.

I didn't want it to end this way, but since I couldn't get a medical discharge, it seemed my only way out. After supper, I would report to the Honor Rep over at D-1, turn myself in and then move on, back to the civilian universe...hopefully back to my world of tennis.

I was about to learn that a New Cadet should never, ever report on sick call during Beast Barracks. When I finally returned to the day's activities, I was way behind on the learning curve. The cadre regarded sick call simply as an excuse to miss training and they made sure I understood this. My welcome back to the Squad was twenty pushups and a recitation of passages from *Bugle Notes* in my Squad Leader's room. Everyone else got some down time to rest and relax.

Throughout the remainder of the day's arduous activities, I kept reviewing my feelings about this West Point adventure. I had been hazed severely, starved inappropriately, criticized unmercifully, and beaten down emotionally. There were few moments in the last fifty or so hours at the Academy that weren't filled with some unfair act, ridiculous policy or silly tradition. They could take this beautiful environment, with its majestic stone buildings, green, grassy parade field, adoring admirers, Spirit of the Long Gray Line, oath of allegiance to protect and defend...and shove it all where the sun doesn't shine. I had never quit anything in my life; never even thought about the possibility of failure in any endeavor I'd undertaken. It went against my very nature. However, there had to be a first time for everything. I was pretty sure I wanted out of this crazy place.

CHAPTER 27

THE HONOR REPRESENTATIVE

When supper formation discharged, I was supposed to report to my Squad Leader's room. Instead, I did a swift sidestep and left the barracks, slipped over to Company D-1 where I reported to the Honor Representative. It was time to end my stay at West Point. I couldn't see any reason to remain and undergo the training they had in mind. Looking for truth and honesty within myself, I realized West Point wasn't where I should ever have chosen to be. I needed to get away...not by quitting though...but by whatever other reason possible.

It was hard to admit I'd made such a huge mistake. I had passed every single requirement, obstacle, roadblock and minefield placed before me, as all the other New Cadets have done over the decades, just to get to this moment of realizing that I'd made a terrible decision. I didn't belong here. One had to have a fire in the belly, a calling of sorts, in order to accept and carry on the traditions of the Academy and military life afterwards. Without that kind of passion, as in any vocation or avocation, there's no way to excel and stand out. It would be a waste of time and energy for me to continue at the Academy with my one and only God-given life. I didn't have West Point in my heart and soul.

I wasn't leaving because of the four yokels hazing me at night;

they were ignorant men, not worthy of the uniforms they wore; hating them would only have depleted my spirit. No: I wanted to leave because the Academy didn't fulfill my needs or reinforce my values. It was perhaps selfish of me to feel that way. However, I wouldn't quit. They had to throw me out. Reviewing statements, I had made to the cadre previously, perhaps there was some ambiguity I could use against myself. An easy way out was to report to the Honor Committee, tell the truth and leave on a high note.

Easy or not, I hadn't committed any intentional lies nor felonies. At age seventeen, I wasn't devious, had no guile, no Machiavellian tendencies. I just wanted to leave this miserable place and do the right thing for myself. I had to have faith that my family would understand.

I knocked on the Honor Rep's door and reported, "Sir, New Cadet Kantrowich reports to the Honor Representative to make a statement, Sir!"

Cadet Patrick Egan, his captain's stripes on the shoulders of his unzipped uniform, opened the door and gazed at me with a gentle smile. "Come in," he said. A soft aura of light framed parts of his face, which radiated calm and peace. I was able to relax as he welcomed me inside, saying, "Please let your neck out and sit down in that chair over there."

I sat down.

"I would appreciate it, Mister, if you would start with your full name and a little background about yourself before we get into the exact reason you are here." Egan then pulled out a well-used yellow legal pad and a sharpened number-two pencil to take notes.

I went through the whole rigmarole of my name, where I was from, what Squad I was in, what sport I played, how the weather was in Miami and so on before he asked me directly, "Why are you here right now?"

"Sir," I answered, "I am turning myself in on two honor violations!"

"Two," he acknowledged with an accompanying grimace. "Okay, let's just start with the first violation. Please report."

I explained that during the first day of Beast Barracks, while several Upperclassmen were yelling at me, another Upperclassman asked me how tall I was, guessing about six feet. I replied, "Yes, Sir," knowing full well I was shorter at five feet eleven and one-half inches tall.

"I lied about my height, Sir!" Cadet Egan stopped his note taking immediately, pulled his chair a little closer to me.

"What about the second honor violation, Paul?" His voice was quiet and understanding.

I explained the situation that happened with a candy bar in my room. During our first full room inspection I had forgotten that I had hidden a candy bar in my shoeshine cleaning box. I knew we weren't supposed to have candy in our room, but it was my only food group lately and I was starving.

Cadet Egan stopped me in my tracks. "Didn't you know every cadet stashes candy in their shoe cleaning box? Every room inspector believes it would be too stupid for a New Cadet to leave candy in a shoebox during an inspection, because that is the first place the inspector would look...so they don't look! They will simply ask." He chuckled. "Excuse me, please...go on."

Staring directly into the Honor Rep's eyes I continued, "When the inspector did ask if there was any candy hidden in the shoebox, my roommates yelled 'No, Sir!' but I refrained from answering the question. I'd momentarily forgotten that I'd hidden candy in the shoebox and my roommates didn't have a clue it was there. But before I could answer "Yes, Sir!" the room inspector was satisfied with my roommates' answers and moved on to inspect another room.

It had started to bother me later that, since I hadn't answered the question verbally, I might have given the impression that there weren't any candy bars in the shoebox when I knew damn well that there was one. I believed, therefore, that I had made a false statement to the inspector. It was a form of quibbling, which had been explained in class as "being in concert with the act itself." Still looking directly at Cadet Egan after making my declaration, I barely held off tears as I resigned myself to leaving West Point. I felt calmer, but deeply disappointed in myself.

When I finished my report, Cadet Egan took furious notes on his yellow pad for quite some time, with his head buried in his work. He eventually looked up asking me "How tall are you, Paul, in your stocking feet?"

"Five feet, eleven-and one-half inches tall, Sir!" I replied.

"How thick is the heel on your cadet shoe?"

"About one-half to one inch thick, Sir!"

"How tall do you think you would be if you were wearing your shoes and not in your stocking feet"

I answered quickly, "Over six feet, Sir". The Honor Rep continued, "You admit that you were wearing your shoes at the time the Upperclassman asked you how tall you were. You also admit that, with your shoes on, you were over six feet. Ergo, you did not lie!"

I guessed I hadn't. Why, then, was I not happy to hear it?

Cadet Egan then asked me about the candy in the shoebox. "Kantrowich, you admitted you knew there was candy in the shoebox but, momentarily, forgot about it."

"Yes, Sir!"

"And in this moment of forgetfulness, when asked if 'anyone' knew if there was candy in the shoebox, you didn't say 'No.' You weren't sure if you remembered candy being placed there and, since you weren't sure about it, you couldn't say yes or no. If you said 'No,' you would have lied. But you didn't say 'No' at all."

"Correct, Sir," I replied trying to understand where he was going with this.

"You didn't say yes either!" Egan said. "You didn't lie, Kantrowich. If anything, we would describe it as 'quibbling.' When asked the truth indirectly to the entire group, you responded indirectly by not responding. This double-negative suggests a cancelling out of the cause and effect that the answer would have created. Furthermore," he continued, "There was no cause to lie. You had forgotten about the candy bar being where it was and there was no effect because you personally did not give an answer either way. The cause and effect created by your roommates' answer didn't involve you because they were the individuals that answered, and you didn't. Also, the Inspecting Officer was, apparently, completely satisfied with the answers given or, in your case, not given and he moved on. Your momentary forgetfulness saved you from telling a lie and it was your honesty that allowed you to remain quiet. All in all," Egan said, "I would say it's a standoff. No lie was intended, no lie spoken. Therefore, there was no lie. This might be a good case of 'quibbling by exclusion' and let's leave it at that. If I brought both these incidents to the full Honor Committee for a hearing, they would all agree with me as well. Case closed!"

The Honor Rep then paused and asked me, "What's really bothering you, son?" Overwhelmed with emotion, I considered my options: open up to a complete stranger, or stoically hold it all in?

CHAPTER 28

EXODUS REPLACED BY RESURRECTION

opted to open my heart. My feelings had to come out, to scream out! It was the only way to return to my authentic self, not the man I thought I was supposed to be. I considered myself no better or worse than those fellows with whom I was trying to survive Beast Barracks. I just needed to be who I was, and I wanted to be heard.

I explained to Cadet Egan about my lack of preparation prior to Beast Barracks. My energies had gone mostly into tournament tennis before coming to West Point. I was recruited for tennis and squash, so, since the Academy wanted me, I thought they would tell me what they wanted from me when they wanted me to know. This indoctrination through Beast Barracks was ridiculous in my mind.

My assumption had been a cataclysmic error; I should have come to West Point with a much better understanding of what was required, what to expect and what preparations I needed to make before arrival. I was paying the price for my nonchalance, emotionally and physically.

A long litany of complaints formed in my mind. I blurted out some of them: *Why do young men have to be treated like dog shit in order to teach them to subjugate themselves to the group's needs rather than act out of personal desires? Some Upperclassmen's attitudes are pure harassment! Obedience should be taught through positive leadership, not* negative agitation. I was singled out for my mistakes and my Squad mates were punished for them. My punishment was my humiliation at being singled out and the scorn I received from them for the punishment they received on my behalf. That's a very poor teaching technique.

When asking us simple questions, why berate those who haven't yet learned the simple answers? We should be directed and taught, not yelled at for our shortcomings. For example: Why during the first couple of days at Beast Barracks wasn't I allowed to eat when I didn't know the answers to Bugle Notes? The first 48 hours didn't allow a reasonable time period to study and learn hundreds of pages.

Punishing me by withholding food made me physically weak and taught me nothing of value. Yes, I learned the need to memorize the damn book! But the build-up of resentment that occurred made me want to throw the damn book in the garbage.

Why is yelling or screaming at someone even necessary? Wouldn't a sincere exchange of words, said quietly, be more meaningful? It would allow that person to retain his own dignity. What about leadership through sensible communication? Communication needs to flow both ways.

And if you don't like the shape of a person's nose, does that give you the right to humiliate him in front of his peers...or in front of anyone else for that matter? Bigotry in all sizes, shapes and forms should never be tolerated, especially if a unit is to remain cohesive. Would you expect a man to attack a machine gun position under your command when all he has heard out of your mouth is that he's a subhuman with a nose that is too big? Leadership develops the installation of loyalty, not the buildup of anxiety and hatred.

Since we took an oath to serve, protect and defend...why do I have to defend and protect myself from others... while surrounded by others that took the same oath? Why are those same people now trying to hurt me? If you are going to defend and protect, that means all people, right? At night, I have been physically brutalized by men who have sworn to protect the American public...of which I am a member!

Why does a person have to answer a stupid question with a stupid answer? A perfect example of that would be when I've been asked, "Why are you an idiot?" I don't believe West Point would have opened their doors to me if I were an idiot; maybe the individual asking that question should be considered the idiot for asking it?

Why is "No Excuse" given as an answer to serious questions? Wouldn't a reasonable person want to know what that other person is thinking in order to teach and train him to succeed? A lot of incidents have mitigation that needs to be brought to the surface and worked through.

I realized that obedience and subjugation were necessary in order to build a cohesive unit. Harassment and bigotry, however, were unacceptable anywhere. It seemed to be here at West Point, in abundance!

I stopped, looked directly up at Honor Rep Egan's face and told him about an incident that had happened to me only a few months before. This story, I said, typified who and what I was:

I was playing Richie Peters, the recent National 16 and Under Boys Champion, in a high school match on my home courts in North Miami Beach in the spring of 1961. We were on a court out of the way of most activity going on in the park. High school tennis wasn't so important back then, since most of the better juniors played the Florida circuit for state rankings, where the real competition was.

I played the 18 and Under junior boys when Richie won his National Championship Crown of the 16's. In the hierarchy of Florida tennis, I should have defeated him in a match, since I was a year older, with more experience. But Richie was murdering me on the court.

Ahead at 6-0, 5-0, 40-Love, triple match point, he was serving. If he won any of the next three points, he'd win the match: an upsetting and humiliating loss for me. No one in their right mind ever wants to ever be humiliated, so I dug deeper into myself than ever before, concentrating so powerfully I could see the seams of the tennis ball

The Corps of Cadets March:
(WEST POINT ARCHIVES, PHOTOGRAPHER UNKNOWN)

Paul & Jacqueline

(PERSONAL COLLECTION)

New Cadets First Day

(WEST POINT HOWITZER 1962)

Maurice (Dad) on left. Abe Revman on right

(PERSONAL COLLECTION)

Bad Day
(WEST POINT HOWITZER 1965)

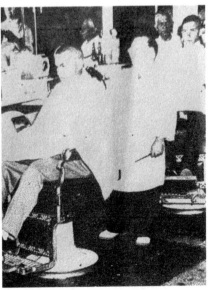

New Cadets marching
(WEST POINT HOWITZER 1962)

Cadet Barber Shop
(WEST POINT HOWITZER 1962)

"Shower Formation"
(WEST POINT HOWITZER 1962)

"Clothing formation "
(WEST POINT HOWITZER 1962)

Beast Barracks Exercise Hour
(WEST POINT HOWITZER 1965)

Plebe Hike "Pass in Review"
(WEST POINT HOWITZER 1965)

Cadet Jewish Choir
(West Point Howitzer 1962)

Jewish Chapel
(West Point Howitzer 1962)

Old Jewish Chapel
(West Point Howitzer 1962)

Colonel Harvey R. Fraser

(WEST POINT HOWITZER 1965)

Major General William C. Westmoreland

Superintendent

(West Point Howitzer 1963)

As recipient of the Fifth Annual Sylvanus Thayer Award, presented each year to a citizen with accomplishments in the national interest. General Mac-

Coach Leif Nordlie &

Captain Jim Peterson

(WEST POINT HOWITZER 1962)

Douglas MacArthur

(WEST POINT HOWITZER 1962)

Reorganization Day
(West Point Howitzer 1962)

Trophy Point
(West Point Howitzer assorted years)

Paul

(Personal Collection 1965)

Walter Oehrlein & Paul

(USMA Staff 1965,

photographer unknown)

Tennis Team

(West Point Howitzer 1965)

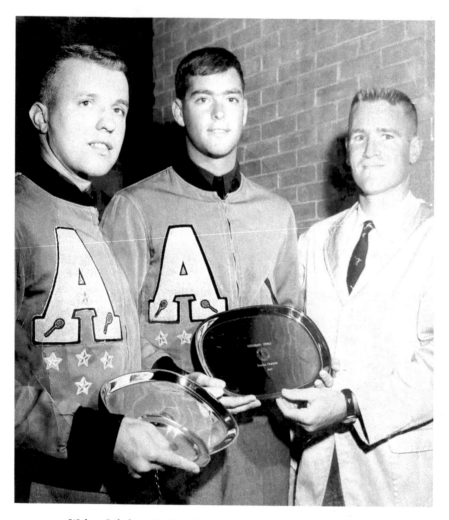

Walter Oehrlein, Paul and West Point Tennis Coach Bill Cullen
(USMA ARCHIVES 1965 PHOTOGRAPHER UNKNOWN)

Personal Collection	Graduation Yearbook Photo
(PHOTOGRAPHER UNKNOWN 1965)	(WEST POINT HOWITZER 1965)

PAUL JULES KANTROWICH   L-1
Kantro

The man with the golden tan and the sky-blue contact lenses — "the Florida flash" has vowed that he would not let the pressure of regimentation affect his carefree life. Having achieved this goal with minor exceptions, he devoted his charm and talent to becoming the Academy's finest and most popular tennis-squash player combination. His tremendous popularity with both sexes will readily assure that success, in any field he chooses, will be Paul's future.

Tennis 4, 3, 2, 1, Numerals 4; Major A 3, 2, 1; Squash 4, 3, 2, 1, Numerals 4, Major A 2, 1; Jewish Chapel Choir 4, 3, 2, 1.

Graduation Yearbook Entry

(WEST POINT HOWITZER 1965 FILES)

WRITTEN BY JAMES WOOD, CLASS '65, PAUL'S ROOMMATE IN COMPANY L-1

Personal Collection
(PHOTOGRAPHER UNKNOWN 1968)

while it spun at high speed, skid marks on its white, fuzzy surface. I relaxed my body, my spine and stooped shoulders, my cramping toes, my tense fingers from holding too tightly on my grip. I envisioned myself hitting the ball freely and joyously, the way I normally played. I realized I had to unleash my forehand and let it just flow.

I won the next point and the point after that…then the game, the set and, finally, the match. It was an impossible scenario: but I never gave up…ever! "That's who Paul Kantrowich is," I told Honor Rep Egan.

We both were silent for several minutes. Then Cadet Egan asked a remarkable question: "If you never give up, why are you giving up here, giving up now?"

Such a simple question. I had no answer.

"Get some sleep, think it over" he gently advised. He told me to contact him the next day if I still wished to pursue my claims against myself.

There was no simple answer to his question. Physical and emotional pain, sleep deprivation and lack of food can all make a person act contrary to their true nature. Survival is a word no one can understand until they *must* survive. Hearing myself spill my guts to Cadet Egan had made me realize I had let circumstances spiral out-of-control and result in a defeatist attitude.

Perhaps it was time to dig deeper, be stronger and make a more heart-felt commitment to West Point. Perhaps it was time to concentrate on my purpose in coming to the Academy rather than dwell on all the negatives. After a more sincere effort and soul-searching, if I still wanted to leave, it would be with a solid understanding of why I felt compelled to pursue a different path.

If the Honor Committee decided my transgressions were not in violation of the Honor Code, I would take that as a positive sign—a blessing—and work harder to get through Beast Barracks. Egan had read me like a book, leaving me with the impression that I was over-thinking the situation and had built a faulty case against myself just to get myself booted out rather than just quit.

I decided then and there that I would remain in Beast Barracks and endure whatever they threw at me...good, bad or whatever! I wasn't going to quit. I was once again Paul Kantrowich, the never-give-up Jewish guy who had been resurrected.

I'm still at the Point.

CHAPTER 29

A NEW MATCH, A NEW ATTITUDE

The bugle blasted Reveille and I woke up with resolve and determination, calmer and more relaxed than I had felt since arriving at West Point. I jumped down from my bunk, ready to face the day. I planned to contact Cadet Egan and ask if I could withdraw my complaint against myself. While I was as far down emotionally over the last three days as I had ever been in my life, today I knew I was heading in the right direction. It was time to be my authentic self again.

At the morning formation, my Squad Leader directed me to report to his room as soon as the fall out order was given. My optimism dampened a bit. *What next?*

I bounded up the stairs, knocked on the door and reported. Danny Brite told me to fall out. "Kantrowich," he began, "You are presently last in performance in my Squad, with more demerits than anyone, late to formation more than anyone and lacking in poop knowledge and uniform assembly more than most. What am I going to do about you?"

"No excuse, Sir!" I responded, not out of weariness but with vigor.

"Listen Paul...you have got to start performing better and be on top of the situation rather than letting the situation control you. But I can only help you so much. I must apply myself equally to all my men. I'm just giving you a heads-up that West Point wants and needs more from you. I am not the only person evaluating you and my report only goes so far."

I had no response to give to his honest remarks.

"The Honor Rep called me last night," Danny said.

What?! I had thought that meeting was confidential.

"Cadet Egan is not pursuing any violations of honor concerning you; he said the Honor Board would only laugh at the situation and throw the complaints out." *Whew.* "He feels you are a good man and have a good heart," Danny continued. "Having a good heart and surviving Beast Barracks, however, are two different things...and I can only help you so much. You have to help yourself!"

I was wondering how I could respond to Danny when I realized he wasn't really looking for an answer from me. This was his way of giving me a pep talk. His sincerity and concern showed me his humanity.

"What do you think of what I just said, Kantrowich?" he asked.

"Sir, may I make a statement?" I asked.

"IRP!" he replied.

"Sir, everything you said was correct. I can and will do better, starting now." Of course, proving my intention over the next seven weeks would be extremely difficult, almost improbable, but not impossible. However, I had done the impossible before, so....

"Okay, great," Danny said, "You are excused." He had done his job and gotten through to me. That he didn't harp on a lot of issues in detail was encouraging.

Racing back to my room I reasoned that I could help myself the most by studying *Bugle Notes*, because I had to start eating regularly. My lack of energy was depleting my performance; the only way things would improve was to memorize the damn book.

I told my roommates I needed to speak with them. I explained my new attitude as quickly as I could. They listened, heard me, then went back to their own world of survival and mayhem. I shouldn't have expected anything much from them; they had their own problems. Since I had some of my confidence back, I felt ready to play and win. As a singles player, I was used to being on my own anyway.

The next few days were relatively routine: hard times, lots of sweat, but manageable with effort and a good attitude. At the Mess Hall, my spouting of poop knowledge wouldn't have dazzled anyone, but I now knew enough to get to eat regularly. Fortunately for me, Cadet Johns had moved on to another table. The new table "Enforcer" was a nicer human being who preferred that New Cadets eat sufficiently while still squaring off the meal. I even had chocolate pudding for dessert one night, manna from heaven.

Table Commandants came and went also. Most were reasonable, even friendly. At one supper meal, our Table Commandant confided he had just received a 'Dear John' letter from one of his female admirers, breaking off their affair. He had been afraid, he said, that if his main girlfriend—the one with whom he was supposedly in a serious relationship—found out about his girlfriend on the side, he would have gotten in big trouble with her family, whom he knew very well. So, the breakup was a cause for celebration. That was the meal where we had the chocolate pudding for dessert.

Back in our rooms after dinner, we had a little peaceful time to clean quipment, spit-shine shoes and study *Bugle Notes*. We were given an order to write letters home to our parents. This would be my first correspondence with them since I had left home. I made it very brief and to the point:

Dear Mom and Dad,
 Having the worst time of my life...but...I am taking it one day at a time. Hope all is well at home. Love, your only son,
 Paul

At 2200 hours, Taps played, and lights went out.
At 2210 hours, they came for me again!

CHAPTER 30

THE STONE WALL

n a tennis match, if you are losing, you must change tactics and try to reverse the situation in order to seek out victory. There was no question I was slowly losing to these after-Taps vigilantes. When they came for me this time, even though I hadn't expected them, they didn't realize who they were dealing with. I had a new attitude.

I remembered when Rich Carlson broke up my first night of hazing, advising me to suck it up and deal. I was resolved to do more than that. In my mind, I became a stone wall...made of the same rock as the massive buildings of the Academy: granite. I would be silent, emotionless...a barrier of strength, durability, sustainability. The "New" New Cadet Paul Kantrowich was hard and impenetrable.

After about twenty minutes of hazing, I knew the night was still young for Mr. Southern Comfort and his stormtroopers. Most of the tricks they had me perform I had done before. I wasn't surprised or intimidated by them anymore and, with some of my physical strength back, because I had eaten, the hazing seemed more annoying than difficult.

"Kantrowich," they heckled, "Why don't you resign? We don't want you here...you are worthless!"

I didn't respond. I'd decided their comments and actions would simply rebound off me. They weren't worth the energy it took for me to talk to them.

"Smackhead, your nose has gotten bigger since Wednesday! You need a shave, you need a haircut, you need to go home to momma and poppa. We could have you on a bus to the airport tomorrow morning and you could be home by afternoon. You could sleep in your own bed with your own teddy bear by tomorrow night. How about it?"

The stone wall didn't answer.

"Tell us how the cow is tonight!" one of the men taunted, trying to be a tough guy. I finally did know how the friggin' cow was tonight! I decided to break my determined silence and quoted *Bugle Notes* loudly and with enthusiam.

"'Sir, she walks, she talks, she full of chalk, the lacteal fluid extracted from the female of the bovine species is highly prolific to the nth degree.'"

Taken aback by this change in me, my assailants began to punish me, this time for *having* knowledge. Once again, I had to hold out an M-1 rifle at arm's length. This was difficult and, after about two minutes, my arms started shaking.

"Are you scared, little boy? Your arms are shaking," said one genius.

"Poor, little, momma's boy, can't take the heat" yelled another tough guy.

Next, they made me squat and hold the rifle over my head. They put a laundry bag over my head and made me squat with the rifle in front all over again. The stone wall still would not be moved.

Word came from their lookout: the OIC was entering the adjacent barracks. Getting caught hazing a New Cadet would be a major problem for the Cadre. They decided to leave. Mr. Southern Comfort growled, "I'm not finished with you, Kantrowich; be seeing you again sometime. Don't ever forget I'm around and I don't like you. We still have unfinished business together," he added, walking away.

I went back to my room, but before going to sleep, I reviewed what had transpired. The vigilantes had gone through their usual routine of menacing, taunts, anti-Semitic remarks and physical punishment; but I had reacted differently. My stone wall demeanor made them feel awkward and puzzled, whereas, in our previous encounters, they had been more confident.

I went to sleep knowing a positive change had taken place within me. That night I dreamt about crashing waves of the ocean, swaying palm trees and sunshine. The brisk breeze off the surf helped me to sleep very well indeed.

CHAPTER 31

SUNDAY SERVICES

When the first Sunday of Beast Barracks rolled around, it was time for all New Cadets to attend worship services. Attendance was mandatory, no ifs, ands or buts. Most New Cadets really wanted to go and pray to their God either to lighten their load or strike down all the Upperclassmen who were pricks. I had similar requests and a few more, too.

Both Christian houses of worship were architecturally and aesthetically beautiful. The largest congregation among cadets was Protestant; their beautiful Chapel rose majestically above the Academy grounds on a sloping hillside, proudly on view to all denizens of the reservation and visitors alike. The magnificent, ornate Catholic Chapel was situated a little higher up and held a panoramic vista of everything West Point. Situated behind the gymnasium and up another hill, it was reached by walking up stone steps or around the paved road curling off the main artery.

I was to attend the Jewish Chapel with ten other New Cadets who were Jewish. There was one other Jewish New Cadet in my Platoon, Benny Goldberg from Brooklyn, New York, to whom I had nodded, in recognition of a fellow tribesman, during the first few days of Beast Barracks. We were both labeled "fuck-ups" by the Upperclassmen, but for different reasons. Benny was hard to miss, because he sported a dark five o'clock shadow by 0900 hours, which only got worse as the day went on. Upperclassmen were always on his case for being unshaven. I guess in the Army that was a major criminal offense.

We were formed up into a single line and marched to the Jewish Chapel by an Upperclass cadet who was probably not Jewish; I guessed this because he wasn't very friendly to us and, from what I heard, there were only eleven other Jewish Cadets in the next three Upperclasses. That made a total Jewish population of twenty-four at the Academy or one percent of the twenty-four hundred cadets in the entire Corps.

Six in my group were athletes, with three of them hoping to join the football team. Mike Berdy, Mike Leibowitz and Gary Kadetz were all big guys and would probably make the team. Leibowitz and Berdy were affable and funny, each with an air of frivolity. Kadetz seemed to be the most serious and astute of the three. Jim Scheiner and I were tennis players while Bob Wolff was a gymnast. I could sense, by the way Jim carried himself, that he wasn't going to be a factor on the tennis court, although he did have an intellectual intensity. Bob, the shortest of the group, was built like a fireplug and could probably have kicked all our asses combined.

As we marched out of the Area, we passed the parade grounds and the beautiful overlook of Trophy Point, where we had been sworn in. We marched by the Superintendent's house and the Commandant's house, passed the gorgeous Protestant Chapel and the big hill where we had five mile runs up and over; then continued around the bend past a lot of the officers' quarters or houses. Looking to our right, we passed the field house and the outdoor track facility and kept on marching on the main road; not quite the Bataan Death March, but it seemed endless.

Finally, we arrived at a small, dark, baroque structure positioned in the middle of a large circular drive area, with eight large, white doric columns protecting the entrance. Surrounding the building was the West Point cemetery, dotted with grave markers of all types, from statues and headstones to simple embossed foot stones. The view there was pretty darn depressing.

We entered the chapel, past the columns through heavy oxidized brass and wooden doors that opened into a small sanctuary, where we were seated on wooden pews with red cloth covers designating seating sections. The pulpit was squared away in the center of the front of the chapel, with a large brass Catholic cross positioned near it. On the front part of the ceiling and wall behind what would serve as our *bimah*, there was a large, semicircular, colorful mosaic depicting a man, some women and an eagle. The inscription read, "Righteousness exalteth a nation but sin is a reproach to any people." This sanctuary became the Jewish Chapel when the Jewish Chaplain or Rabbi removed the cross; out of sight, out of mind, I guess.

The Chaplain welcomed us in English and in Hebrew and introduced himself as Rabbi Steinberg. Since it was Sunday and the Jews' main worship days are Friday nights and Saturday mornings, it was obvious that the United States Military Academy at West Point had hired a "Rent-a-Rabbi" to satisfy the criteria that all cadets go to services on Sunday. Furthermore, because the Jewish cadet population was miniscule, it warranted only a makeshift temple. I later learned that our Jewish Chaplain was a celebrated spiritual leader from a very large and wealthy congregation south of the Academy. If he was schlepping all the way up to moonlight at West Point, either he wasn't compensated enough by his *shul*, or he was seriously interested in saving Jewish souls.

Rabbi Steinberg began by asking each of the eleven of us which tribe of Israel we belonged to. Not being a Bar Mitzvah boy nor a regular attendee at Friday night services—actually, I went as infrequently as possible—I had no idea what he was talking about. He went on to describe the three major groups and tribes back during the time of Moses, Abraham and Joseph: The Kohains or Kohanim were the priests, the Levites performed all the duties and roles around temple activity and the Israelites or Yisraelim were the local yokels and members of ten of the other twelve tribes.

Steinberg was seriously interested in our individual heritage. He asked us to raise our hands if we were Kohans, Levites or Yisraelim. I had an uncle named George Cohen who was married to my Aunt Miriam, my father's sister; the same Aunt Miriam who drove my mom and me up to West Point for my first day. Since I was related to a Cohen by marriage and it sounded like Kohan, I raised my hand when the rabbi asked if there were any Kohanim in the group.

I was the only one. The Rabbi made a big deal about me being a Kohan, asking me questions about my religious background, religious training and so forth, but he quieted down when he realized I didn't know a damn thing about any of it. He proceeded to provide a short service, shook each of our hands and quickly left to go back to his suburban *shtetl*.

We lined up and marched for what seemed to be about two miles back to the Area for a short period of quiet time before lunch. As I had before, I was feeling inadequate as a Jew. Every sunday thereafter, I would carry with me that same feeling of inadequacy.

CHAPTER 32

THE GOLDBERG DEBACLE

I'd sat next to Benny Goldberg during our service at the Jewish Chapel. He seemed like a very nice guy. Benny was short, slightly built, with a dark head of hair to match his infamous five o'clock shadow. The ever-present stubble, against his pale complexion, made him look somewhat unkept, like Richard Nixon during his television debate with John Kennedy. We had briefly chatted while the Rabbi had his back to his "congregation." Benny wanted to go to West Point to prove to himself and his family that he was a real man. He planned to make the U.S. Army his career, no doubts about it. This was the opposite of what I had planned for myself, so he intrigued me.

Benny mentioned to me he was a good student with a very high SAT score over 1550 (1600 was the max). He had been offered scholarships to some Ivy League colleges, but West Point was his first choice. While he wasn't an athlete *per se,* he felt he could handle any physical tasks required of him. He had been doing okay so far during Beast Barracks, but his damn heavy beard was causing him severe difficulties; the Upperclassmen claimed he wasn't getting "close enough to his razor" and the demerits were piling up.

I asked Benny why he was having so much trouble shaving and what method he used. He mentioned he had a Remington electric shaver and shaved in the morning and at night, but he couldn't get a close enough shave with it; his facial hair grew like wildfire. He had no solution to the problem and was frustrated and nervous about it. Benny was constantly harassed for his appearence, hence the demerits.

I had been shaving since I was sixteen and considered myself an expert on the subject at seventeen. I honestly thought I could help Benny get a closer shave and eliminate, from his life, all the extraneous crap the Upperclass cadre of creeps were throwing at him. Also, since he was a fellow Platoon mate and a fellow Jew, I believed it was a *mitzvah,* or good deed to help him. I always liked to help people, anyway; making them feel good made me feel good too.

So, I convinced Benny to meet me in the latrine early in the morning before Reveille the next day, where I would show him how I got a nice clean-shaven face that lasted me all day. Perhaps it would work for him as well and would get the cadre off his back.

That Monday morning, I met Benny at 0515 hours and introduced him to my Gillette double-bladed, hand razor. I demonstrated how to wash his face and beard with soap and water first, to loosen the hair follicles and open the pores of his skin; next, how to properly insert the double-edged steel blade and clamp it down by screwing the handle around, closing the top where the blade was inserted; and how I lathered up my face with Barbasol shaving cream.

"Make it nice and thick and wait a couple of minutes or so. That way the foam will continue to plump up your facial hair and you'll get a closer shave," I rambled on. Benny hung onto my every word, as if I were the "Oracle of Personal Grooming".

I showed Benny how to apply the razor against the skin and slowly draw it up or down, depending on how the grain of the skin and hair combination felt. "Don't pull the razor across your face too quickly or too hard," I instructed him, like the teaching tennis professional I had never wanted to be. "You'll have to get a feel for how the blade is cutting and adjust your stroke accordingly. Just slide the razor about one-half inch at a time to retain the feel. You can also change the angle or pitch of the blade for a stronger or weaker feel. Just go slowly at first, stroking the razor smoothly, letting it glide across."

Once I completed my own face, Benny started using the procedure himself. It worked! Benny was amazed at what a good shave he was getting on his first try. Again, I explained how important it was to moisten his face before starting to move the razor across it, especially with his fair and delicate skin. I had learned the hard way since, when I first began shaving, I got plenty of nicks. Only one year prior, rushing to catch the school bus, I would leave my house many times with dabs of toilet paper staunching the bloody cuts on my face. With his type of skin, I emphasized the importance of having a decent blade in the razor, that it was only good for so many shaves. "You can feel it pulling the facial hairs, not shaving them, as the blade gets dull. Benny," I reiterated, "Always remember to moisten your skin properly before you start!"

I went over the steps with him one more time before we had to run to the Reveille formation. Benny had every intention of going to the Cadet Store, when he could, to buy the necessary shaving equipment. I was quite cheerful knowing I had done a good deed; that feeling lasted me all day long.

Life continued frantically for the next few days. We had started getting ready for field operations by first preparing our equipment and carrying it on short hikes of three to five miles over the reservation terrain. I had no physical problems doing this, except I never could get my backpack to ride high enough on my shoulders to be comfortable. This became an issue as the hikes increased in duration. My Squad Leader saw what was happening as we trudged up and down the forested areas; he helped me reposition my straps to make it easier.

At the next Sunday Chapel formation, Benny Goldberg had gone missing. I asked around, but no one seemed to know where he was. Since he was in another Squad of my Platoon, it wasn't easy to inquire about his status. When he was absent from the following two days of formations and activities, I was concerned; but I had to wait until the next Sunday Chapel formation to learn the truth about Benny.

Shortly after our shaving lesson, Benny had gone to the Cadet Store to get the gear we had talked about. The following morning, he attempted his second Gillette safety-razor shave on his own. The next morning after that, he went on sick call and was never seen again.

I subsequently found out the doctor made a medical diagnosis of "Impetigo of the lower jaw and extremities." Benny's entire jaw was badly infected from improper shaving. He wound up being admitted to the Academy infirmary, but his recovery was very slow, he missed too much Beast barracks training time, and they washed him out of West Point on a medical discharge shortly after that.

I went over the instructions I'd given Benny many times in my mind over the next few days; many, many times. I was sure I had explained the importance of softening up his face before starting to shave. Rumor had it that Benny was in such a hurry to get a clean shave before the Reveille formation, he didn't bother soaping up with warm water to begin with, nor did he use shaving cream.

He had dry shaved! OUCH!! The thought of fur-faced Benny using a Gillette safety-razor with a double-edged blade without lubricating his beard made me wince. Alas, the intense emotional pressure of Beast Barracks caused intelligent men to do very stupid things.

The following sunday in Jewish Chapel, I prayed that Benny would forgive me. I also prayed to God to continue giving me the strength to maintain a strong, positive attitude at West Point. Benny's plight caused me great distress and my enthusiasm for the Academy was badly slipping again. I knew Benny would probably wind up being alright in his life because he was a bright man; I still felt terrible he wouldn't achieve his life's goal of being a West Pointer.

It wasn't wartime; West Point lost a good and devoted New Cadet, a possible terrific, future Army officer and a sincere patriot over…a friggin' five o'clock shadow.

CHAPTER 33

THE TRYOUT

Several days had passed and I was still trying to shake off my sadness about Benny. I sincerely hoped he would wind up in a good place. Meanwhile, I dismally struggled to lift my dwindling motivation again while the bullshit level of Beast Barracks increased exponentially. My intense competitive spirit was all that was keeping me in this game.

I was down to one hundred twenty-eight pounds; all muscle, but my endurance was starting to wane. My Squad Leader put me on the "diet table" because of my weight loss and haggard appearance. The diet table accomplished two different tasks, depending on where you were assigned. My diet table was for underweight New Cadets who needed to eat more and bulk up. The other diet table was for New Cadets who needed to lose weight.

At my table, if you finished your assigned portion of food, you were allowed to ask for a second portion. If you wanted more steak, you got it! More potatoes, more chocolate pudding? You got it!

It sounded great to be at a Mess Hall table where the Upperclassmen would allow me to eat without harassment. The problem was that you were not allowed to pass a dish to another New Cadet without taking one's own portion first. I was required to take every dish offered and then eat it all. The day I passed the creamed spinach was a day I'll remember the rest of my life. It happened to be my very first day on the diet table.

"Hold onto that dish, Kantrowich!" stated the Table Commandant. "I noticed you were given a dish by our server to take your portion and pass it around. Why did you not take your rightful portion? Why did you try to pass it on without indulging in this delicious food group? Don't you like creamed spinach?"

We were all sitting in the fall-out position at the table so, as New Cadets, we could eat in a relaxed manner and digest our food properly. That allowed us leeway to look around a little as well. I looked directly at the Table Commandant and said "No, Sir!"

"All of you New Cadets listen up," the Table Commandant continued. "You are here to gain weight, which means you must eat a proper diet. The meal today has been especially prepared for all of you. It has an unsurpassed nutritional content and is also aesthetically appealing. You must all eat your fair share."

He called over our Filipino server and asked him for another serving dish containing another ten portions of creamed spinach while making sure I was still sitting, holding the original dish of the stuff in my hands. Within a minute, the extra plate arrived, and the Table Commandant announced it should be passed around to everyone but me. I was to keep the original dish I was holding.

"New Cadet Kantrowich has his own portion of creamed spinach in his hands right now. He will not leave this table until his dish of creamed spinach is completely empty. All of you, please, EAT!"

I was stunned. I couldn't move. I kept holding the platter of food without taking one portion, much less ten. Always a very picky eater to begin with, the one dish I found most distasteful, the one I couldn't stand to look at or smell, was creamed spinach!

I glanced up at the Table Commandant pathetically and asked, "Sir, may I make a statement?" "No," he replied quietly. "Eat your creamed spinach!" I placed the dish down over my plate, grabbed a spoon, closed my eyes, scarfed down all ten portions and prayed I wouldn't gag and throw up.

At that very moment an announcement came over the loudspeaker from the Poop Deck, "Attention to orders. At 1330 hours, all New Cadets trying out for Plebe Corps Squad teams will line up by the sign that indicates your sport and march over to that sport's intended assembly area."

In my distressed gastronomic state, I almost missed that announcement. Sick to my stomach, I was now confused by it. Why did I have to try out for a sport that they brought me here to play? I became even more nervous because I hadn't hit a tennis ball in over three weeks and wasn't even sure I had enough rhythm to stroke the ball well. My forehand was a weapon that needed to be tuned and calibrated almost daily...but I really wasn't expecting a tryout!

I had been eagerly awaiting the day I could see Coach Nordlie and cry on his shoulder about what was happening to me in Beast Barracks. *Now that I'll finally have that chance, I thought, I'll probably throw up creamed spinach all over him.* Anxiety coursed through me and, upon returning to the barracks, I ran to the latrine and vomited up the entire meal. I vowed never to pass another plate in the Mess Hall without taking my allotted portion.

Hustling to my next formation took my mind off the distressing experience I'd just had. I was living hour by hour in survival mode, not projecting into the future. I went where I was ordered to go, I followed my roommates wherever they were going, did what they did just to get through the day, each day.

The nights were a different story. Mr. Southern Comfort and his goons still paid surprise visits to me after hours; not as much as before, but they always showed up again when I thought they had finally stopped. The night before had been a particularly distressing session. The upchuck special for lunch certainly didn't help matters; I was exhausted. How was I supposed to show everyone what a great tennis player I was? In Florida I had never gone more than one day without practicing and playing. If it rained and I couldn't play, I would literally lose my feel for the ball so when I was back on the courts, I'd have to work extra hard to compensate. I'd squeegee the courts as fast as I could and sometimes played with puddles, dogging around or jumping over them, sacrificing my natural gut strings, just to get in a few more hits.

I lined up at the sign marked "Tennis" with about twenty other guys and we marched to the Library tennis courts. There were six reddish, granular-clay courts lined up in a row adjacent to the main road curving around the Plain. They were laid out properly with the vertical axis of the courts running north and south. Court number one was adjacent to the main street, with the remainder of the courts running eastward towards the Officer's Club.

I had first spied the courts when marching past them during my first parade. They were directly across from the Cadet Library, hence the name. There was a large statue of General George Patton gracing the grounds adjacent to courts three and four facing southward, a viewing grandstand looking out at court number one facing east.

As we marched to the tennis courts, I tried to observe the men in our group. They all appeared as haggard as I felt. None of us looked like we were ready to compete properly, except for one taller guy who carried himself with an air of confidence, his head up and with a smile of great expectations on his face.

Since I had been recruited by the coach, I expected to make the freshman team easily. In 1961, college players were not allowed to compete on the varsity team until their second year of college. I continued to wonder why I had to try out to make a team I had been hired to play on.

Arriving at the courts, I didn't see either Coach Nordlie or MSGT Milliken. An Upperclassman handed each of us a Davis Imperial racquet strung at about fifty-six to fifty-eight pounds of pressure. He split us up into groups of four and we went onto the courts to knock balls around for awhile. Back home, George Shuert, a nemesis of mine, used Davis Imperials. They were heavy in the head, very rigid in the throat, with no whip in the shaft. I hated them. Also, I liked my racquet strung between sixty-four and sixty-five pounds, a lot tighter than the one in my hand now.

The first four or five balls I hit cleared the fence by a couple of feet...the fence, not the net. Not a very impressive start! It was right about the time my last shot cleared the fence that I saw Coach Nordlie. He made a beeline for me, came to the chained-link barrier, called me over and asked, "How are you doing, Paul!"

I replied, almost crying, "Coach...they are killing me here. They really ARE trying to kill me...to get rid of me."

Coach Lief Nordlie had been coaching tennis and squash at the Academy for over fifteen years; he probably had seen and heard almost everything from his players. He must have heard the statement I'd anxiously blurted out many times before from a whole group of New Cadets. He just looked at me through the fence and told me to come out through the gate and talk to him.

Now at his side, Coach put his arm around me. "Paul," he said, "You've got to hang in there. It's going to get better. You are a fighter and I know you can make it through. I'm counting on you, Paul, I need you on the team. We are going to do good things together. You are my guy that's going to help lift West Point tennis to the national level." The man clearly knew how to motivate people.

"Come over here Paul, I want you to meet someone really special." Coach gently guided me over to the court where that tall New Cadet I had seen before was fluidly stroking the ball, moving gracefully and with ease. He certainly looked, to me, to be a better player than I in most aspects of the game.

"Paul...meet Walter Oehrlein from New Jersey. His brother Richie is a Yearling"—a second-year student—and number one on the varsity. I hope the three of you will become friends. I consider both you and Walt to be great additions to our tennis team here at West Point. Terrific things are going to happen for Army tennis!"

I mumbled something to Walter quickly, asking Coach if I could speak to him privately away from all the others again. We walked over to a bench near General Patton and sat down. The general observed us quietly.

"Coach," I said, "I wasn't prepared for what is going on here in Beast Barracks. At the end of the day there is a group of Upperclassmen that usually comes around and tortures me after hours. They are trying to get me to resign and go home and I think about it all the time. Strong comments have been made about me being a Jew, a weak individual, a total screw-up. I'm very unhappy. One reason I am still here is because of you and because I have never quit anything in my life. I don't want to let you down but...I hate it here!"

What I remembered about Coach Nordlie, after meeting him in Miami, was his calm demeanor, his fatherly image, his sincerity and kindness. He spoke softly to me now. "Paul, I personally know you have the heart of a champion. Everyone I've ever spoken to about you have confirmed it, many times over. I believe in you, and I know you can get through Beast Barracks training." He continued, "I'm going to ask some Upperclass cadets to step up and help you from time to time, when and if it's possible, BUT you are still going to have to fight mostly on your own. Please don't lose heart!" He smiled, patted me on the shoulder and repeated, "Don't lose heart!"

I took a deep breath, knowing Coach Nordlie was a genuine mentor who was absolutely on my side. I replied with the deepest of emotion, "Coach Nordlie, it's not my heart I'm worried about, it's my mind!"

Upon hearing that, Coach just chuckled! Then he laughed out loud and said, "West Point owns your mind right now, Paul; don't let them control your heart as well."

We walked back to the tennis courts together. He still had his arm around me until I opened the gate and went back onto my assigned court. The reddish granules of the clay felt more comforting under my feet, the sound of the racquets striking tennis balls seemed more familiar, the humid warmth of the air reminiscent of a South Florida summer day.

But...I still felt alone...again. My racquet was too heavy, the strings too loose; the court was too slow, the balls too fuzzy; I didn't have a sweatlet to catch the perspiration pouring out of me; my timing was way off; my "world famous" forehand continued to fly over the fence; and coach's pep talk had put even more pressure on me not to let him down.

After the tryout, marching back to my room, I descended into a dark, ugly, angry, mood. Without tennis I was nothing.

CHAPTER 34

MY "POP-UP" TENNIS BUDDIES

The tennis tryout proved how tenuous my game really was. Having the opportunity to talk to Coach Nordlie had a somewhat calming effect on me but seeing how my forehand had deteriorated was very alarming.

I was upset when I returned to my room to prepare for the dinner formation. My two roommates stayed away from me, as they usually did. I thought about Upperclassman Cadet Rich Carlson, who had helped me out of that big jam my first day at the Academy. Where was he now when I needed him again? I wondered about the mysterious statement by Coach Nordlie, intimating he would ask some Upperclass cadets to lend a hand.

My dick-head roommates had their own agendas in Beast Barracks. When they learned that every New Cadet was being evaluated for leadership qualities and performance, they both went into serious operational "stardom" mode, looking to gain an upper hand in the Class of 1965 hierarchy. Their shoes and brass were shinier, their uniforms looked more professional; their answers to New Cadet poop were sharper, more exact. They were always rushing to be the first in line at formations and their attitudes towards me were, "don't bring ME down, loser!" I can't blame them for trying for a better future. Oh well; I was a singles player anyway. To hell with them!

Marching into the Mess Hall for dinner, I began thinking about my conversation with Coach Nordlie. I felt I could trust him; his fatherly approach toward me was very comforting and I didn't want to let him down. Another part of me wanted to leave on the first wagon train heading south! Talk about being conflicted!

While I was seated at the supper table that night, an Upperclass Cadet Lieutenant approached the Table Commandant, looking for me. He introduced himself as Cadet DiDi Voss and asked me how I was doing. Not knowing what to say, or who he was, I replied, "Fine, Sir!"

Cadet Voss turned to the Table Commandant then, scanning other tables, and in a commanding voice stated, "Kantrowich is an outstanding tennis player, and we are lucky to have him here. Let's make sure we give him as much support as we can. We need him badly on our team!" He shook my hand, said, "See you on the tennis courts in September," and waltzed away. WOW! Another guardian angel had dropped down from the sky to lend a helping hand.

After supper, we had more training to prepare for the future Cadet hikes. Squad Leader Brite told us we would do a few short hikes to start. When hiking, we would need to check our feet before and after to make sure we didn't get blisters. To keep our feet dry, we needed always to have a backup pair of socks in our backpacks. He went over a few other items and was about to dismiss the Squad when there was a knock on his door; a smiling Upperclassman, with a lot of stripes on his shoulders, appeared.

"Is there a New Cadet Kantrowich in your Squad, Danny?"

"Oh, hey Jim," Danny said. "Yeah, he is."

"Mind if I borrow him for a few minutes?" Jim asked. My Squad Leader nodded.

The decorated Upperclassman took me out into the Area and told me to fall out. "I'm Jim Peterson, Paul. I'm Captain of the Corps Squad tennis team and I want to know how I can help you? Coach Nordlie asked me to check up on you."

Another "pop-up tennis buddy" sent from Heaven! Thank you, God and thank you Coach Nordlie!

"The team wanted you to know we are behind you," Jim Peterson said. "We're glad you are still here working hard and making a supreme effort to get through Beast Barracks."

"Sir, may I make a statement?" I asked.

"Of course," he answered, "But let your chin out and relax!"

"Sir", I said, "I can handle most things here but the 'after-Taps activities' are killing me!"

He asked what I meant by that. It was my first opportunity to fully talk to someone about Mr. Southern Comfort and his posse. I told him that Rich Carlson had interrupted the first session, but there had been two or three sessions a week, after hours, since that first incident.

Jim Peterson had an infectious smile. He quietly said, "I'll get this squared away, but you've got to continue doing your absolute best to keep trying to fit into the system, to hang in there. Coach told me you were special, you can do this!"

I reiterated my mantra: "Jim, I never give up, but some of the methods here called 'training' are very abusive and stupid. That is what really gets me down."

Peterson grinned. "We've all gone through this training they call Beast Barracks. It's tough, difficult, a lot of times nonsensical, but you'll make it through by just keeping your competitive spirit strong and resolute. Keep your eyes on the ball!" He wished me good luck and we went back to my Squad Leader's room. He asked Brite to step out in the hall for a minute while I rejoined my Squad. Because they went down the hall to talk, I couldn't hear their conversation. When my Squad Leader returned alone, he dismissed the Squad to prepare for shower formation. He seemed very uneasy and distracted; I could tell he was upset.

I didn't normally worry about what would happen next during Beast Barracks. That night, however, I had built up a dread of the

Shower Formation because we were also getting a "Fingernail" inspection for the first time…and I had a chronic nail-biting problem.

"Paulie…stop biting your fingernails," my mother would constantly carry on. "Honestly, I don't know why you are so stubborn, with your fingers in your mouth all the time. Your nails are disgusting, they are chewed down into little nubs and they're bleeding! It's such a filthy habit, you should be ashamed of yourself!"

I would think to myself, *yes, mom, and you are one of the reasons why I bite them like I do.* I didn't mention to her that my toenails received the same attention; I spared them no mercy either. The ridiculous contortions I put my body through to get at my toenails was amazing…and comical too! I had tried over the years to stop but something would always arise causing anxiety; that anxiety would turn to self-mutilation.

If my Squad Leader had ever taken a good look at my hands and the state and condition of all ten of my fingernails, demerits would have flowed. I had made my best efforts ever in my life not to chew, grind or pick at my nails, especially during all the stress of Beast Barracks; but, to no avail. Now I was going to have another person, other than my mother, pointing out to me what a disgusting habit I had. At least that night I only needed to be concerned about my fingernails; we wore bath clogs that covered our toes.

The shower formation that evening was especially difficult. It was longer than usual, with more pennies and nickels plastered against the wall, the glow of more cigarette tips, more perspiration expelled and a greater amount of reverberating, boisterous noise, and hazing. Then came the dreaded fingernail inspection conducted by the Squad Leader.

"Prepare for inspection," Brite ordered. "Eyes front, hands up parallel to the ground with palms facing down, fingers together, hands shoulder width apart." He swaggered down the line, saying, "Good, Hennessee; excellent, Arnall; very nice, Brown; looking good, Koleszar!" Then he got to me.

Scowling and with disgust in his voice, my Squad Leader grunted, "Yuck, ugh, disgusting, Kantrowich. Does your mother know you bite your nails?"

By then I had completely sweated through my bathrobe, my face was dripping, my chin so far back to my neck it hurt. "Yuck," he said again, "That's three demerits, Kantrowich," he barked before moving on to the next New Cadet, "And three demerits every week until you can grow better fingernails."

My spirits instantaneously lifted, and my anxiety abated. I could certainly deal with three puny demerits; I had worried about this damn fingernail inspection for no good reason at all. At that moment, I realized something about myself; I tended to become very anxious about things over which I had absolutely no control over. All my life, I had been making myself crazy for nothing…and I had the shredded fingers and toes to prove it!

I felt grateful and extremely lucky that Jim Peterson and all my pop-up tennis buddies were providing strong support. *Perhaps,* I thought, *it's time to grow up and only concern myself with matters that I CAN control.* So simple, but such a huge epiphany.

CHAPTER 35

MY HERO

When Taps was over, my roommates and I hit the sack. I felt an ominous vibration in the atmosphere around the barracks area; something seemed off, but I was too tired to pay attention. That day, like every other day at Beast Barracks, had been exhausting. The minute my head hit my pillow I fell asleep.

A few moments later our door shook from the banging on it. The air rippled with danger. Mr. Southern Comfort and his group came to roust me from sleep once again, to escort me to the quiet of the latrine area. The usual escapades ensued, starting with pushups, situps and sweating the penny, as I just had done an hour before at shower formation. Then it got mean, rough and nasty.

"Kantrowich, this is it," yelled Mr. Southern Comfort, as another of the group punched me in the stomach. "We want you gone, out, now!" he continued. "This has gone on too long. Quit and go home!"

One of the guys smacked the side of my head. That ear began to ring. Another pulled out a sharpened field bayonet and pressed it against my chin as I braced against the wall. Two men, one on either side of my ears, screamed obscenities; their spit dribbled down each side of my face. The hazing has escalated to real physical abuse.

"This is it!" yelled Mr. Southern Comfort again, with the ugliest voice I'd ever heard in my life. "Your nose is too big; you have a Yid accent, and nobody wants you here. GO HOME!"

Them's fightin words. My fear switched quickly to extreme anger. It was time to defend myself against these bastards. Yes, I was a stone wall but, tonight, for some reason, the wall was collapsing. I was about to take a swing at the southerner's snarling mouth when my Squad Leader walked into the latrine. The lookout man was near the front stoops of the barracks gazing outward, so Danny Brite had passed by him inside the barracks without being seen. Apparently, he had been alerted by Jim Peterson, who stated his concern about my after-Taps extracurricular activities. Jim must have impressed Danny with the futility of my situation. Or perhaps God had answered my prayers?

"Hello, boys," Danny greeted the gang, grinning like the Cheshire Cat. "Looks like you've got a little problem here. Everyone...notice...I didn't say WE...I said YOU!"

The torment had stopped immediately. The group backed off from me. Danny said to Mr. Southern Comfort—apparently, he knew him—and continued the conversation. "Jack...you know better than this! If you don't like my New Cadet, if you don't enjoy his company, if you think he's got a problem, then you come to me. I'm his Squad Leader. He is MY man, MY problem! You will keep your hands off MY man now and forever."

"Danny," Jack replied, "This guy is a complete fuck-up and he's a Jew. We don't want his kind here!" The other men took another step back. If there had been a hole nearby, they would have crawled into it.

A one-sided conversation ensued. Danny spoke loudly and with firm conviction.

"This bullshit is over right NOW...got that Jack? That goes for the rest of you assholes. Stop now and walk away, and this will be the end of it. Continue hazing Kantrowich and I'll report all of you to the damn Tac Department, and you know what will happen then, don't you? This guy may be a giant screw-up, but he is MY giant screw-up to deal with. Why are all of you demonstrating such childish and bigoted behavior? Get the hell out of here NOW!"

As the sweat poured off me and my addled brain started to clear, I realized how lucky I was. My Squad Leader had come through for me in a big-time leadership capacity. Coach Nordlie and Jim Peterson had both protected me in their own quiet way. Now it was Danny stepping up to quell the storm.

The group left quickly. As I was about to thank my Squad Leader, he suddenly braced me hard. He was pissed off.

"If anyone is going to haze you, Kantrowich, it's going to be me. You don't get a free ride around here because you can hit a little white ball with a little racquet. You must toe the line, learn, compete and succeed at everything West Point needs from you. If you can't do that, I'll personally escort you out the reservation gate myself. You got that?"

"Yes, Sir!" I said feeling quite self-satisfied.

"Wipe the damn smirk off your face, Kantrowich. I'm warning you, someday I won't be around to help like this. An officer in the U.S. Army is responsible for his men, to guide, teach, protect and lead. That's why I am here at West Point. I accept and intend to fulfill that mission. Why are you here?"

I did not say what I was thinking: *I'm here to play tennis, Sir!* That would have been idiotic. However, I couldn't come up with a decent or honest answer. Until this moment, my attitude had been changing like the direction of the wind, moment by moment, event by event. I was torturing myself trying to understand the full range of my emotions. I hated the Academy at this juncture. I didn't like the way people were treated, but I was still there. I didn't have the same value system or the passion everyone around me seemed to have for this "Long Gray Line". Still, I was there. The rah-rah Army bullshit was wearing thin, yet, once again, I was still there.

I still had so many more questions than answers about life, sex, politics, parents, career and about West Point. I wished I could talk to my older sister Wilma, or my twin sister Helen, right then...or my buddy Donnie. My concentration level was transient, my stamina nearly depleted, my emotional state in the toilet.

The one thing in my life I had ever been fully confident about was my love of tennis. The blood flowing in my veins when I competed, the sound of the ball smacking the center of my racquet strings, the spin of my forehand jumping wildly when it impacted the court surface. Another surety was I wouldn't let people like Mr. Southern Comfort beat me down…no way!

I wasn't sure about wanting to be a West Pointer.

Thinking about Coach Nordlie, Rich Carlson, Jim Peterson, Didi Voss, my dad, Coach Abe and now my Squad Leader—all of them supporting my effort, trying to protect me, trying to help me succeed—should have helped screw my head on properly. It should have enabled me to think clearly and be able to answer my Squad Leader's sincere question in a responsible and sensible manner.

Still, I had nothing good to say. I looked at Danny and said, finally, "No Excuse, Sir!" He shook his head sadly.

Why am I here? Knowing the answer would allow me to rest easy.

CHAPTER 36

THE RIFLEMAN

In the days following my Squad Leader's intervention in the latrine, life in Beast Barracks continued to be as hectic and stressful as ever. I now felt, however, a ten-ton load had been lifted off my back; a different melody played in my head. We had started training in military activities that drew my interest, somewhat. Taking Beast Barracks one day at a time, instead of hour by hour, was extremely helpful. My anxiety level was at its lowest level since the beginning of Beast Barracks, I felt less tense although I also kept biting my nails continuously.

I was still earning a lot of demerits for the usual reasons: room inspections, lateness to formation, shoes not spit-shined enough, brass streaked or not shiny, hair too long, fingernails (of course!), and other mundane crap—but it didn't weigh as heavily on me as the physical hazing had. Demerits weren't physical abuse, at least. However, they were still piling up and could lead to expulsion. I had to be wary of that.

I had since gained a little weight so now they took me off the diet table; that meant regular Bugle Notes torture during meals again. I was trying to learn the proper chain of command so I could eat once more: Commander-in-Chief John F. Kennedy, President of the United States; Secretary of Defense Robert McNamara; Secretary of the

Army Elvis Stahr, Jr. I kept getting hung up on the Chairman of the Joint Chiefs General Lyman Lemnitzer! What possessed his parents to name their son Lyman, for God's sake! At least the name Elvis was unique as it had some flare.

We had started a new routine of trucking out a few miles to the USMA Rifle Range to fire our M-1s. These were not just display guns but working weapons that had to be cleaned several times a week, particularly before inspection. Prior to each parade, we underwent a rifle inspection, in place, at "port arms" position.

Since it had been raining, our M-1s were placed over our shoulders in the downward position, the rifle barrels pointed toward the ground to keep the water out. We were wearing ponchos which, theoretically, kept our field uniforms dry. It was so humid, however, that the hot air trapped underneath the thick ponchos soaked our shirts. Wearing our metal helmets with their shell inserts in place, the whole Platoon looked like a large pack of drowned rats with hats on.

The rifle range was strategically laid out so that no one would be in front of you while you were lying in a pre-dug, shallow foxhole looking at targets downrange from fifty to two hundred and fifty yards away. Our foxholes had turned to mud that day. There was a berm area behind the foxholes which was laid out on a horizontal line, targets separated by about eight to ten feet. Another berm was situated behind the targets so that ricocheting bullets were absorbed by it rather than flying into the wooded area beyond. There was a wooden observation tower in the middle, towards the back of the range, where the Range Master could supervise the firing of weapons and training of the New Cadets under the comfort of a slanted roof canopy that kept out the rain or the bright sunshine. There was no sunshine today at the range or in my heart.

With all the shooters in place the Range Master would yell, "Ready on the left, ready on the right, ready on the firing line…commence fire," and all the M-1 rifles would bark and pop out seven point six two-millimeter NATO bullets at six-foot-high enemy cut-out figures located at various distances away. Upperclassmen and Regular Army sargeants got down on bended knees, smacked the top of our helmets so we would cease fire; then they'd correct our technique. The rules were simple:

1. Never point your weapon at anything other than to shoot it.
2. Keep your weapon pointed, down range, at all times.
3. Remember your weapon is your best friend and treat it accordingly.

Before it was my turn to flop down and take position to fire, I flashed back to when I was ten years old. We were living each summer at Schroon Lake in the Adirondacks. I was carrying my father's twenty-two caliber rifle on my shoulder, looking for red squirrels to shoot. The State of New York had placed a bounty on the little scavengers, since they were very destructive to the locals' property.

My dad trusted me with the rifle; I was a pretty good shot. Our black and white springer spaniel, Peppie, always accompanied me. He would spot the squirrel in the tree, bark for me to come over, and I would shoot the little critter down. Peppie would go pick up the squirrel in his mouth and run to place it on the burn pile. There were never any people in the general area; dad would never have let me take the rifle out if there had been.

On this day, the squirrels were lying low; they must have sensed I was hunting them. Bored since there was no action, I walked to the edge of the lake and followed the shoreline a little way, foolishly thinking I might shoot a big fish, but I couldn't find any of them swimming in the shallow, clear, fresh water amid the lily pads.

Farther along the shore, I spied a little bird about fifty yards away who was scanning the water's edge looking for any grubs or worms that might have washed up. That would be its lunch. It had soft brown feathers with a white underbelly. There was the muffled sound of an outdoor motorboat one-half mile away on the water, but it was very peaceful at the lake today. I positioned my rifle on my right shoulder, took aim, then blasted the little bird dead.

Peppie didn't rush to get it. He just stayed in place. The sound of the shot reverberated off the trees and foliage with a sharp "CRACK!" I congratulated myself on being such a good marksman, fancying myself a hunter providing food for my family.

I walked over and towered above the tiny dead bird, its feathers and innards splattered all over the sand. This wasn't some nasty red squirrel with a bounty on its head, but an innocent creature. It's death and destruction were my fault. Sick to my stomach, I ran crying back to our house realising I had done something stupid and heartless. I then put my dad's rifle away in the closet and never touched it again.

Now, seven years later, I had in my hands a bona-fide United States Army-issued M-1 rifle with tremendous killing power. "Ready on the right, ready on the left, ready on the firing line, commence fire!" yelled the Range Master. In my mind's eye, I kept seeing images of that tiny bird sprawled out dead on the beach.

A member of the cadre smacked the top of my helmet, yelling, "Why aren't you firing?" There was too much noise and smoke to explain to him about the little bird; not that this soldier would have understood my feelings anyway. I was at the firing range to learn how to handle a soldier's basic offensive/defensive tool. Not some other day, but today...now!

Pretending the target was Mr. Southern Comfort, I shouldered my rifle, ripping off six quick shots that formed a little cluster of holes in the target's groin area. The shooting instructor was angry at me; we were training to hit the enemy in the heart, not his balls! Once again, I had violated military instruction.

That evening after supper, my roommates and I broke down our weapons and cleaned them properly. I was thinking, *Could I ever kill another human being if I had to, if my life was on the line in combat, even as they were trying to kill me?* Even to contemplate taking a life made me want to vomit; not a good sign for a guy going into the U.S.

Army to defend and protect.

Then, when I began thinking of the stupidity, insensitivity and bigotry of people like Mr. Southern Comfort, I was shocked to realize that I *could* kill someone like that but there would be no satisfaction or joy in my actions.

I would have to have been pretty pissed off to do it, though. It had to be a lawful and righteous act as well. Feeling that I was too young to have to make decisions like this, my mind drifted back to an incident which caused great concern in my life as well. An incident where I felt real fear.

CHAPTER 37

AN OBSTACLE OF SORTS

Early one Saturday morning in the spring of 1959, five of us teenagers were riding north up the Florida State Turnpike with my tennis coach, Nick Bollettieri, in his brand-spanking new, white 1959 Oldsmobile convertible. With the top down, we were speeding along at over one hundred miles per hour, Nick showing off what his hot new automobile could do. I think he won enough money to buy it by betting tourists at the local Miami Beach bars that he could do one hundred pushups with his right arm, then when he'd win, he doubled his money by challenging them with his left.

An ex-Marine, Nick was in remarkable physical shape, but sometimes his ego got in the way of better judgment. The five of us in his car were scared shitless, since this was one of those times when Nick's ego won out. Seat belts had not yet been invented. I was sitting next to Nick and could see the speedometer needle clearly, petrified as it kept inching higher and higher: one hundred-five, one hundred-ten miles per hour. He was yelling, "Wow, this baby can fly!" The Florida State Police were not around to verify this. I really thought I was going to piss in my white tennis shorts.

That was one of the few incidents in my life where I felt abject terror. I remembered and relived it in a dream the night before our Squad had to take the dreaded New Cadet obstacle course. We had heard a lot of different tales about the difficulty of the course, the length of it, the stamina needed, the climbing heights, the cajoling to get through it and, of course, the injuries. My fear of this upcoming event was as extreme as the fear I had felt in 1959 while my friends and I rumbled up the turnpike at reckless speed, Nick oblivious to our emotions.

Not only did we have to complete the entire obstacle course, but we had to pass a time trial as well. Rushing through anything had always caused me difficulty; rushing through a tennis match, for example, meant a guaranteed loss. Losing a game was bad, but the thought of getting seriously injured petrified me. I could keep up with all the day's New Cadet activities even if I was whipped by the end of the day. I knew that injury was a distinct possibility if I had to run the course while exhausted so I would have to pace myself and err on the side of caution rather than go for speed.

Lately we had been doing a lot of calisthenics, running and conditioning to get ready for the course as well as for the upcoming Plebe Hike. A big to-do was made about the obstacle course because—we were led to believe—completing it was a requirement to move on through the rest of Beast Barracks. I had added back a few pounds of muscle on my body and was more in flow with New Cadet life, but I was still concerned I wouldn't complete the course. Washing out of West Point because of my failure to achieve an athletic requirement when athletics had brought me there? I wasn't going to let that happen, but I was still nervous.

That morning, we all trucked out to the hills outside Newburgh, New York. It was hot and humid, a typical Beast Barracks Day. Luckily, our Platoon would be going through the exercise as a group, so we knew there would be camaraderie, joking and friendly competitiveness to ease the tension and help our performances,

The morning dew had made things slippery, the wooded hills, slick leaves underfoot. A central staging area was where Upperclassmen were already bellowing orders and insults. From there we could see what was in store for us. There were obstacles with thick ropes, wooden slats, round logs, high mesh, over water, over mud, under barbed wire. Some towered sky-high, other obstacles were low to the ground. Some required strength, some agility; some speed, others just sheer dogged determination and willpower.

Both sides of the narrow course were lined by the cadre of Upperclassmen and Regular Army. Some men shouted encouragement, others jeered, but most screamed insults. Nothing like the Army to continue to provide a certain type of positive motivation!

"What are you, a pussy? Where are your diapers, little baby? Pull up harder Mister, your arms look like twigs! Hey buddy, got two left feet? WHOA, Mister, what planet do YOU come from, Uranus?"

Noise, sweat, grunts, shortness of breath and grimy tee shirts pervaded the atmosphere. Some New Cadets glided through the obstacle course with ease, others labored tenaciously, while still others made it through yelling and urging themselves to keep pushing in the exercise and succeed. You could sense the desperation of some, the physical prowess and confidence of others. Very few of my Platoon mates lacked athletic ability; most were physically quick and strong and relatively agile. The one characteristic we all shared was determination. Class of '65, "Strength and Drive!"

With all the wild stories bandied about, warning of the extreme difficulty of the obstacle course, my tendency to go negative was off the charts, making me crazy with fear. Worse, I knew I was making myself nuts; why did I always do this to myself? When would I learn not to anticipate the worst scenario about everything, always?

To my great relief, I had no problems with this challenge; I even helped a few guys who had trouble getting over the wall as the Upperclassmen bitched at me, "No help allowed!" My worries dissipated with each obstacle I conquered, and I finished the course without difficulty. I hadn't felt that jubilant since I won the City of Miami Singles Championship three months prior, beating my nemesis, George Shuert, to boot.

All my Platoon mates finished the course. Some had to repeat the process a second time in order to pass but, thankfully, we all overcame one of the most mysterious and dreaded roadblocks in Beast Barracks. This was a "one and done" affair. Our full attention now could be directed toward the upcoming Plebe Hike. Our Squad Leader Brite was so ecstatic about his Squad's achievement and success, he rewarded us that evening with a quick and easy shower formation.

During the long ride back to the barracks, I remembered I had an unopened letter from dad waiting on my desk. He'd written me a note or a card every single day since I left home. His letters were always short but encouraging, optimistic about my circumstances and, occasionally, very funny. Sometimes he would enclose a dollar bill, with which, he hoped, I would buy candy. Sometimes he wrote about tennis. Occasionally, he would mention what my twin sister Helen was up to as she was getting ready to become a Gator. He talked about Wilma being pregnant and his excitement about his future first grandchild. Every day, I looked forward to hearing from my father, since few people ever wrote to me. His letters always bolstered my spirits, even on the worst of days.

Today, however, was a triumphant one for me, my first great day at Beast Barracks. Waiting in my room, upon my return, was my dad's unopened letter which made this day even sweeter!

CHAPTER 38

URINE FOR A SURPRISE, SIR!

E ven though life near the end of Beast Barracks was getting a little easier, it still strained me to my emotional limit. My dad's letters kept urging me, "Let's give it one more week, just one more week," to keep me from jumping on an airplane home. Dad was living his life vicariously through me and, since I never wanted to be a big disappointment to him, my whole family or myself, I kept giving his mantra of "one more week" continued effort. Especially since my sister Helen had made such a big deal around high school and the florida tennis community about my being at the Academy, quitting would be a failure of immense proportions.

The Plebe Hike, touted as the culmination of our training and the end of Beast Barracks for New Cadets, was only days away. Afterwards we were to be moved up into the category of Plebe. Reorganization Day was next, with the entire Corps of Cadets back on the reservation. New Companies would be formed, the academic year would begin and a whole new experience of harassment would occur.

I thought it would be far better to be a Plebe than a New Cadet. With Beast Barracks behind me, Corps Squad sports would soon start. Being a Plebe on a Corps Squad team also meant I didn't have to sit at Company tables in the Mess Hall once the academic year began. Each sport had its own table in the center section of the Mess

Hall. Plebes on the freshman team would sit with members of the varsity, fall out and eat a relaxed and generous meal instead of being on a Company table where it was like Beast Barracks all over again. I would be able to sit with Rich Carlson, Jim Peterson and Didi Voss, and feel wanted rather than bitched at and starved. This would be a tremendous burden off my back, three times a day, every day!

Once academics started, Plebes would have extra free time on the weekend, following the Saturday room inspection, after Saturday morning classes. Being on a Corps Squad team also excused us from most parade formations, since we were expected to be at practice during that period; another burden lifted. However, the academic year also meant being confined to my room on weekends after all the other activities were completed. This was due to all the demerits I had racked up.

I had found out that each demerit represented a one-hour tour marching the Area on the weekend with our rifle on our shoulder or a period of confinement lasting one-half or one full day in my room, depending on the day.

Preparing for the Plebe Hike wasn't anything special. We had done a lot of marching, running, hiking and equipment checks up until then, so most New Cadets were in decent physical shape. Knowing I could start playing tennis again, when the academic year began, had eased my mind significantly about all other upcoming events, the Plebe Hike among them. Being me, however, I was still nervous about it.

I banged on the frame of Danny Brite's door to announce I had arrived for the pre-hike meeting. "Sir," I shouted, "New Cadet Kantro…."

He interrupted me quickly. "Stop banging on the Goddamn door, Kantrowich, and come in. I know who you are by now and you are the last to arrive, as always!" He looked at me for a moment and turned to the group, "Squad, listen up…there will be no more banging on my door from now on. Also, when you enter my room, you are to let your chins out and stand at parade rest. You got that?"

"Yes, Sir!"

"The Plebe Hike is tomorrow. Let's go over the 'rules of engagement' and how this will pan out. Listen closely because I am only going over this one time." He reminded us to take the extra pair of socks he had always harped on. He further instructed, "Make sure your poncho is rolled exceedingly tight and secured safely to the top of your backpack. During the five-minute breaks, every hour, remove your boots and check for blisters or extraneous matter that may have found its way in by accident. Make sure you keep the man in front of you close, but not too close, don't straggle behind. There will be no straggling from my Squad, got it?"

In unison the Squad answered with a loud, "Yes, Sir!"

He continued, "And when we have to double-time or run to make up some lost time, I don't want to hear any of you breathing too hard, grunting from extra effort or falling behind! You are all in excellent shape at this point in your training, so I don't anticipate any problems from any of you. Do any of you have any doubts about this? Do any of you have any questions?"

The lighter atmosphere in the room was comforting. Even our Squad Leader's roommate was smiling and humming to himself.

"Brite's going to take a hike!" he cheerfully chuckled.

"Sir, I have a question!" chirped one of my roommates. "What happens if a New Cadet injures himself or fails to complete the entire hike?"

"Stragglers get picked up by a truck, treated as walking wounded and bussed back to the Quadrangle," Brite answered. "Medical care will be provided, if needed, at the base hospital. After treatment is given, that New Cadet will then be given a bus ticket and told to go home!

Listen up men: all MY New Cadets will make it through this Plebe Hike and be strac when we march past the Supe's house. Nobody in MY Squad drops out, even if I must insert my size eleven combat boot up that person's ass the whole way or sling him over my shoulder and carry him the last two miles. No one drops out, got it? GOT IT?"

"Yes, Sir!"

Danny's roommate started to applaud with loud, sporadic claps. Sounding a bit like Little Richard, he sang out, "Don't make a fuss or you'll be on the bus, don't drop out or my roommate will pout!" Our Squad Leader's roommate always had something humorous to add and this time Danny added "Damn straight guys!" with a huge grin on his freckled face.

Since the meeting occurred shortly after an abbreviated shower formation, it was time to hit the sack. The next day was to be a big one for all of us. Parched, I drank two glasses of water from the sink in our room and hopped into bed, only to toss and turn for the next twenty or thirty minutes. I was questioning my ability to take another nine months of military bullshit, even "one more week at a time." I pictured Helen having a blast on the University of Florida campus and felt a little jealous before thinking, *Good for you!*

Lying in my bunk, suddenly I had a tremendous urge to pee and couldn't wait any longer; a couple of droplets had already leaked out. Getting to the latrine in time from the fourth floor wasn't going to happen. Using the Upperclassmen's latrine on the fourth floor would have resulted in instantaneous annihilation if I were caught.

Seizing the moment, I grabbed my roommate's water glass— since it was closest to my outstretched arm—and let loose a stream of steaming urine directly into it. *Ohhhh,* I moaned inwardly, *Man, does that feel good!* That it happened to be Charlie's drinking vessel made my release doubly exquisite; he was the biggest jerk in the room. When I finished, I debated what to do with the warm contents of the glass. I didn't think it would be proper to pour piss down the drain of the sink where we brushed our teeth.

The window was open, beckoning me. I launched my pee outside without thinking much about it; no one would know. Gingerly rinsing out Charlie's glass, I put it back in place on the ledge above the sink and jumped back into my bunk. I had completely forgotten that the small, tiled section of roof beneath the window was tilted on a forty-five degrees angle towards the cemented quadrangle area below. Rainwater sluiced off it efficiently. So did my urine.

The Duty Officer, accompanied by the Cadet Duty Officer, was making his rounds outside my barracks exactly as the projectile of warm urine dripped from the roof. It rained down on the Duty Officer's neat and tidy green uniform and hat, causing him to exclaim loudly and angrily, "What the Hell?!" *Shit!* Hearing this disgruntled yell from outside I slipped down further under my covers and pretended to be asleep.

There was a clatter of feet on the barracks stairs, a muffle of profanity and a thundering of footsteps as the Duty Officer and the Cadet Duty Officer approached my room, knocked, and threw open the door. They peered inside, but all they saw were the inhabitants asleep in their beds, dead to the world. I was on the top bunk behind the door and the least visible.

The Duty Officer muttered, "Wrong room," and closed our door before banging on the door of the next room, which also faced the quadrangle. Afterwards, I could hear him loudly muttering from the stairwell, "If I ever catch that son-of-a-bitch, I'll nail his ass to the wall!" The two men left without ever solving the mystery of *whodunnit!* I didn't move a muscle for five more minutes, then enjoyed one of the best nights of sleep I'd ever had in Beast Barracks.

CHAPTER 39

SPIZZERINCTUM AND ALL THAT CRAP

Backpacks had been stuffed, boots laced up, C-rations stored, our M-1 and field bayonets slung, canteens filled, our entrenching tools in place. The Squad, Platoon, Company and Battalions of New Cadets found the sun ablaze and hot on the morning of the Plebe Hike as we all climbed aboard the back of the deuce-and-a-half trucks to move out. We were to be trucked out far enough to accomplish a roughly twenty-five-mile hike back to the Plain on Academy grounds. It took over an hour to get to our point of departure. On the sixty-first minute of this escapade, it began to rain.

Our equipment totalled about eighty pounds per man. Lugging that amount of weight in the rain made us sweat like pigs under the ponchos we had to wear. A kink in my neck started ten minutes into the hike. Pain radiated from it through my right shoulder blade, curving around my upper back. At the beginning of our first five-minute break, removing my backpack was a welcome relief. We'd only gone slightly over four miles by then.

During our break, Superintendent of the Academy Major General William C. Westmoreland, or "Westy"—the nickname he'd adopted and liked to see used in the newspapers or on television—stopped in front of my section of the march column and started over in my direction, his prominent chin out, a swagger stick tucked under his left arm. As we hiked, he and his command staff of officers had been walking up and down the line of New Cadets showing us their toughness and grit, demonstrating to the cadre of Upperclassmen, as well, the comportment expected of an elite officer in the U.S. Army.

Westy stopped right in front of me. My nametag was hidden beneath my poncho. "What's your name, Son?" he asked. "Where are you from?"

"Kantrowich, Sir, florida," I panted.

"You look like you are hurting, Kantrowich; are you okay?" The General showed genuine concern. I caught my breath. My bravado got the better of me. "No problem, Sir...piece of cake!"

"That's the spirit, Kantrowich...spizzerinctum!" he barked. Westmoreland claimed the word "Spizzerinctum" was his invention. He'd first used it from the Poop Deck in the Cadet Mess Hall a few weeks before, without an explicit definition. We understood it to mean guts, backbone, determination, ardor and zeal. It was intended to inject energy and excitement, strength and drive into the hearts and minds of West Point's Cadet Class of 1965. In fact, that was our class motto: "65, Strength and Drive!" My very first impression was that the word "Spizzerinctum" should also remind us of Westmoreland himself, standing tall and gazing out into the future, resolute, in command, tough.

"Hey," Westmoreland remarked with a sly grin, "Aren't you that hot-shot tennis player we brought in to beef up our team?"

"Yes, Sir!" I replied.

"Well," he said, "We've got to get a little more meat on those bones of yours. Then we'll play tennis together sometime. That's the spirit. Spizzerinctum," he repeated as he left double-timing along the line, bringing U.S. Army and West Point *esprit de corps* wherever he stopped and chatted.

As a tennis player I thought I could determine how good another tennis player was by the way he walked or talked or carried his racquets and the way he handled himself around other people. I would read players like a poker player looking for a "tell" that showed if the other guy was bluffing. After meeting the general on the hike, my impression of him and his spizzerinctum was that he had a spizzer up his rinctum! I didn't care for the man and I reckoned he'd be lousy at tennis also, a ball-basher lacking finesse.

The line of march of the hike continued into the second hour, then the third hour, without much excitement. The sky was still overcast and the rain a slight mist. Most of my classmates were hanging in and getting the job done. The kink in my neck intensified, but I was determined to dog it out; that was because I must have had spizzerinctum in my system!

With a few guys starting to struggle ahead of us, we had to double-time to take up the slack and make up time. With all the gear we had on, it was tough. Even tougher were the C-rations we had to break out and attempt to eat during a break after the third hour. We had a foot check for blisters, a few swallows of water from our metal canteens slung off our webb belts, and that quick meal of cold C-rations. The chocolate bar and Chicklets tasted great, whereas the lima beans and ham weren't worthy of the effort to open the can. Our Squad Leader, Platoon Leader and Company Commander all trooped the line of march to check how the men were doing. No one had dropped out yet, so they had little to say or report. That second pair of socks Danny Brite had bitched about for over a week came in handy.

The worst part of the hike was having to wear the rain ponchos. Body heat got trapped inside, created a sweatbox effect and no evaporation to relieve it. Dehydration became an issue. Several of us asked if we could remove our ponchos to alleviate this problem, but the cadet cadre did not want to violate the uniform called for. So, we marched on stoically, drenched in perspiration and all of us very thirsty.

Some drama occurred into the fifth hour. A few guys were hobbling due to blisters. One man in our Platoon vomited; another was getting severely dehydrated and on the verge of passing out. Our

Platoon Leader dropped by with some band-aids for the blisters and to tend to the nauseated cadet, who admitted he was stupid enough to scarf down his C-rations in total. He felt better almost immediately once the delicacies had been expunged from his system. We all shared our canteen water with the dehydrated cadet and the troop trudged on…and on.

At the end of the sixth hour, during our five-minute break, our Squad Leader formed us up in a small circle. He seemed to be getting revved up and excited, now that the hike was almost over. "When we get to within fifteen minutes of General Sheridan's statute on the northwest corner of The Plain and opposite the Supe's house," Danny Brite informed us, "we are going to stop, remove our ponchos, tighten up our gear, close ranks and look strac. We'll all be graded on how strong and proud we look and how we've performed as a Squad. We'll march as a Company unit when we hit the West Gate, in formation with the rest of the Battalion, then troop past the Commandant's and the Supe's houses in this formation. With our colors flying, our heads held high, our backs straight, a skip in our steps, smiles on our faces, we will show everyone how proud we are to be who we are, West Pointers and leaders of our great country, the United States of America!"

I felt like applauding when our Squad Leader was finished. His passion, energy and pride were meaningful to the haggard, sweaty bunch of young men in his charge. Danny took this hike and the situation seriously and we had absorbed some of that exhilaration. For me it was a strange feeling, as a singles player, to finally feel part of a team.

Fifteen minutes from the end of the hike, we stopped, removed our ponchos and tidied up as ordered. As we formed up again, the atmosphere was filled with an excitement akin to the glory of soldiers returning victorious from war. We finally marched past the Supe's and Comm's houses with pride and precision, heads held high, countenances exhibiting determination.

Our cadet leaders shared salutes with the most senior superior officers at the Academy, who had all lined up as a group to greet us. A bigger surprise was the U.S. Army Marching Band playing the rousing and emotional "West Point Army Fight Song." The song felt like a bolt of lightning surging through my body. I felt an inkling of belonging to something larger than myself as well as a swell of pride in having completed a challenging task. I had held up my end of responsibilities. I hadn't let my Squad or Platoon mates down. It was the first time in eight weeks that I felt there was a chance I was becoming a man.

CHAPTER 40

RECOGNITION AND REORGANIZATION

We were all in Danny Brite's room for our last Squad meeting. With the Plebe Hike behind us, the next day would be the end of Beast Barracks and perhaps the end of a nightmare. Our Squad Leader was in a very relaxed and cheerful mood. An atmosphere of excitement and expectation filtered through our barracks area.

"A job well done today, men," Brite said. "All of you came through like I knew you would. Everyone associated with West Point, from superior Officers to admin clerks, knows these eight weeks of orientation and training are very tough for New Cadets... that's exactly why it's called Beast Barracks! Now I want to go over activities for tomorrow," he continued, turning mysterious. "Just as your very first day of Beast Barracks was memorable, your last day will be unbelievably crazy and memorable as well. Expect it...and embrace it! Make sure your rifles are clean as a whistle after all the rain and mud from the hike, and make sure that you have all your gear ready to be packed up to move out. Tomorrow we will be in full dress parade uniform and after the parade, we'll form up in the Central Area Quadrangle for Recognition Ceremonies. It'll be a formation that will remind you of the minute you had stepped out of the sally port and into Beast Barracks...BUT, it'll be better, I promise!"

Brite waved off questions and added, "After Recognition, you'll get packed up, check the nearest sally port for your new company assignments and move to that location, where you will report to your new Company Commander and be assigned a new Squad Leader. That will be your new home for the next nine months. Officially you will all become Plebes and, on Monday, academic life and your life as a West Point cadet will begin; a new chapter in your future will ensue."

"Most of you have done extremely well this summer," Brite continued, "And you should be commended on your performance. Some of you"—he added, gazing at me—"are still lucky to be here." He shifted his eyes back.

"Once Recognition ceremonies start, you'll stand in line with your Squad and those Upperclassmen that want to recognize you will come over to you. They will brace you, then tell you to fall out. After that, they will extend their hands to shake yours, congratulate you and discuss anything they want to with you. After the formation is over, you'll move on to those activities I previously discussed. Any questions?"

None were asked.

Without a shower formation that evening, we were allowed to clean up and rest, start packing our gear and prepare for our last day of Beast Barracks. I really wasn't expecting anyone to "recognize" me, so I wasn't excited about that. I was nervous, however, about the reorganization and moving into a new type of existence, starting life as an actual cadet. I would have to reaffirm my commitment to stay at the Academy and follow through. I was still going "one week at a time," but my continued discontent had to be put on the back burner. The promise of new and better conditions, academic endeavors and the chance to start playing tennis regularly again was enticing, to say the least.

Thankfully, the prior eight torturous weeks were behind me. The all-consuming, energy-sapping worry, the constant fear and the persistent desire to leave the Academy were slowly eroding away. The end of Beast Barracks promised a better future as a Plebe. Since I had plenty of opportunity to leave West Point and did not, perhaps it was time to devote all my emotions and energy into being more successful while I was still here and stop the damn complaining about it. Shut up Paul and just do as you are told!

I had trouble sleeping that night as disturbing visions occupied my dreams. I saw little white sheep jumping through fiery hoops as men hit them with sticks. There were a couple of black sheep trying to run away while another sheep, wearing a yarmulke and shivering behind a tree, tried to hide, but the tree wasn't wide enough. This scene was replaced by a group of toy soldiers woodenly marching over a hill that was really a cliff and they all disappeared. In another scene, my Squad mates and I were all flying and learning to parachute out of a plane. When it was my turn and the Jumpmaster ordered me to jump, I realized I had no chute on my back. At that exact moment, he pushed me out of the airplane. I woke up in a cold sweat, choking on the fear of falling a long way down.

Later that day we formed up for the parade, marched, saluted the dignitaries with an "eyes right" and marched back into the Quadrangle for the anticipated Recognition Ceremony; different than I thought it would be, it was a lot of fun until near the end.

Prior to the formation breaking up, Rich Carlson and Jim Peterson both came over, braced me a little with "Kantrowich...smack that chin in...now fall out and shake our hands!" They congratulated me and told me I would eventually be sitting at their table in the Corps Squad area of the Mess Hall. What a relief to hear that! I thanked them as much as I could for protecting me.

Danny Brite came over to me grinning, shook my hand and said, "I sure hope you play tennis as well as they tell me you do! Best of luck!"

Near the end of the session, just as I'd begun to feel that everything was going to work out, Mr. Southern Comfort sauntered over with a couple of his goons, braced me hard, but told me to fall out and offered me his hand. I kept both my hands by my sides.

He ignored the slight. "Kantrowich, you have a lot of guts. I like that! You also have a lot of friends, so I wanted to apologize to you and recognize you! My name is Jack!"

I stared at "Jack" for a moment, then asked him point blank, "Does that mean all the water between us is under the bridge, we are going to let bygones be bygones?" He replied with a smile. "Sure!"

I paused for a moment, then replied with a sneer, "Good. FUCK YOU, Jack!"

With a confused look on his face, my new buddy Jack left while his goon squad peeled off out of his way. I double-timed to my room with my neck slammed back in to start the rest of Reorganization Day. I had a huge smirk on my face.

★ ★ ★

All twenty-four hundred cadets were back at West Point that afternoon, swarming and buzzing around looking for their newly assigned companies and rooms as if someone kicked over a hornet's nest of gray-and-white uniformed insects. Some Firsties—seniors—and Cows—juniors—were returning from vacation, or from European assignments as third lieutenants, or some leftover cadre from Beast Barracks. The Yearlings—sophomores—were back from the end of their summer training at Camp Buckner, the dangerous "Recondo" exercise happily behind them. Recondo was a week-long field exercise of training, patrolling and mock enemy engagement, with little rest, a shortage of food and lots of military scenarios including emotional and physical harassment. It culminated with holding a t-bar, clipped to a cable above the head, and flying down a torturous zip-line high above the water, crashing into a lake and then swimming to the shore.

All the Plebes were double-timing (that hadn't changed) with our chins in (that hadn't changed either) while looking for our new assignments. There was a hum and a ripple of high expectations in the air. Upperclassmen were still stopping Plebes and bracing and barking at them. Most of the Yearlings were just trying out their new authority as Upperclassmen. Most had already forgotten how mistreated they were as Plebes...or they were innately pricks themselves.

The wheels of the Corps of Cadets were starting to grind up into full gear. For the First Classmen, it would be their last year at the Academy, with increased cadet responsibilities and the need to decide their own futures after graduation. The Second Classmen were positioning themselves for greater leadership responsibilities. Third Classmen were still pumped up from the difficult summer training, enjoying the freedom of not being a Plebe. Plebes, as always, were just trying to survive the system and find their new assignments. Controlled confusion seemed to be the rhythm and melody of the day. The chaos was lively but friendly and was enhanced by the cool, fresh air that had moved into the area signalling the possibility of an early autumn.

Finally, arriving at the correct sally port to get my assignment, I found it, higher up, under a glass encasement. I was to report to "A" Company, First Regiment known as A-1. There were about one hundred men in each Company, twelve Companies grouping into three Battalions in each of two Regiments: approximately twelve hundred cadets in each regiment with about four hundred men in each Battalion. The remaining men occupied Battalion, Regimental and Brigade Staff positions. The First Captain was the Number One cadet at the Academy leading the Corps. Each Cadet Company had a Tac Officer who was a Regular U.S. Army captain or major supervising their operations, training and disciplinary matters. The Cadet First Captain was like a God to Plebes.

The Company A-1 Tac Officer was Captain Forman, that straitlaced, stern-faced, fair and level-headed man. My new Squad Leader, Matt Stanley, was a man who—unlike other Squad Leaders in the Company—wasn't wrapped up in sweating the small stuff: do your job, pass inspection, stay out of harm's way, cooperate and graduate.

My roommates were Frank Arnall, Larry Smith and Charlie Sotwell. Arnall, I later discovered, was the only real human being of the three of them. Smith always seemed to have a stick up his ass and stars in his eyes, while Sotwell had an ulterior motive for everything. I really wasn't looking for any of them to be my pals. Arnall was pleasant and kind and we did strike up a meaningful friendship.

Company A-1 was known as the flanker company because there were a lot of tall men in it. It was also known as the jock company because of the preponderance of athletes from a broad spectrum of all the various sports. Most of the guys were somewhat loose and reasonable in dealing with Plebes, but there were a few pricks to avoid.

Matt Stanley was one hell of a nice guy who played football, lacrosse and baseball. He was a devout Christian. Our first Squad meeting was relaxed; with our necks out, we took notes about what he expected from us, what our schedules would be, what and where we could go during what little free time we had and how classes would be handled. I was surprised to hear Plebes weren't allowed off the reservation until the end of Plebe Year; even during the Christmas Holidays, the entire Upperclasses would go home, but Plebes remained at West Point. I asked my Squad Leader, "How about Hanukkah?"

"And Hanukkah to you, too!" he retorted, chuckled at what he thought was a hilarious response to a stupid question.

Our schedules repeated every week: Reveille at 0550 hours, breakfast formation, classes starting at 0715 hours six days a week; lunch formation at noon and classes until 1430 hours. Sports dominated the afternoons and, if you weren't on a Corps Squad team, you were required to play intramurals on a Company team four days a week. Plebe (freshman)and Corps Squad (varsity) sports were practiced every day. Supper formation at 1800 hours was followed by study, with lights out at 2200 hours. Wednesdays and saturdays were parade days, unless you were playing Corps Squad sports which meant—*Thank you, God*—very few parades for me.

There were big room inspections after classes on saturday morning and before parade or Corps Squad events. Pop-up room inspections also occurred throughout the week. Plebes had additional duties to perform like mail delivery, laundry delivery and "calling the minutes," which was announcing the time prior to each formation, the dress uniform, and other information at one-minute intervals counting down from five minutes to zero. "Sir...there are five minutes until breakfast formation, the uniform is class A under raincoats, the date today is September 10, 1961, the movie this week is 'Westside Story,' Beat Navy Sir," for example. Screw up on the minutes and Plebe year would be an extraordinarily long year for you.

Grades and academic classes were posted in the sally port on long lists, first alphabetically and then, eventually, by numerical student ranking within the subject of study. We were graded in every class, every day, both for verbal and written performance. The average class load per semester was over twenty-five semester hours, every semester until graduation...a heavy load for sure. There were no elective courses until senior year, when we could choose one or two subjects. The only other elective we could select as a Plebe was a foreign language. I chose french, since I'd had two years in High School, and I thought it would give me a competitive edge.

Classrooms with thirteen or fourteen seats were usually situated in windowless buildings. Our chairs and individual desks were arranged six feet from three of the four walls of the classroom, butting up against each other to form a square horseshoe configuration. Large green chalkboards lined the walls behind the desks. The instructor for each class—usually an Army officer specializing in that subject—sat at a desk situated in the center of the fourth wall. It was a sterile classroom without plants, extraneous books, pictures, posters or apples on the teacher's desk. The Plebe sitting in the first chair of this arrangement was responsible for reporting, "Class all ready and accounted for, Sir!" while we stood at attention until "Take Seats" was ordered. If someone was absent, that cadet's name was noted, since normally there were no excused absences.

After the first four-week grading period, each class was rotated into a pecking order. The first section consisted of fourteen cadets who ranked the highest in the class in that subject. The next thirteen or fourteen in ranking went into the second section. In the first chair of each section was the cadet with the highest grades in that group. The last section, obviously, was occupied by cadets who were having academic problems in that subject; with a verbal and a written grade for each class, it required impeccable preparation and hard work to keep up with these academics.

The maximum grade in each course was 3.0; the minimum passing grade was 2.0. Failing a course meant the end of one's cadet career. We were allowed one makeup exam and tutors would be assigned, if necessary, but flunking it resulted in expulsion from the Academy. We were on a very short leash when it came to performance.

Friday night is the start of the Jewish sabbath, but at West Point, Friday nights were the start of preparation for Saturday room inspections; Jewish Chapel had to wait until Sunday morning. Room inspections were difficult at best because the inspectors, whether the Tac Officer or the Company Commander or both together, just loved to find mistakes. Demerits—especially for Plebes—flowed like water leaking from a garden hose. Inspectors weren't prejudiced, distributing demerits to all races, colors, creeds, religious and cultural backgrounds alike.

Sunday Jewish chapel included the full complement of Jewish men at the Academy marching the distance to the Old Chapel to find our rent-a-Rabbi presiding. There were no orthodox Jews in our group; most of us were of the reform Jewish persuasion, with a couple of conservatives thrown into the mix. Not surprising; what religious Jewish family would ever think of sending their sons to West Point?!

All of us *yidlach* in uniform comprised the not-so-celebrated West Point Jewish choir; however, in my case, because I sang so poorly and so out of tune, the senior cadet of the group politely asked me to mouth the words and lip synch. I wasn't offended at all. I thought back to my high school days when I had formed a band and tried to sing along with the lousy music we played; that band certainly didn't last long and broke up shortly after that. No, I wasn't offended when I was asked not to sing but remain in the Jewish Choir and mouth the words instead!

The atmosphere in A-1 wasn't as difficult as Beast Barracks. If mistakes were made, however—if the minutes weren't called properly, if an Upperclassman was having a bad day, if someone's shoes weren't perfectly shined or their hair too long, or the room, upon inspection, had flaws—life became anxious and frustrating. The only salvation was being able to eat meals in the Corps Squad area of the Mess Hall, with tennis teammates who enjoyed my company and I, theirs. I loved interacting with the Oehrlein brothers, Steve Darrah, Ross Wollen, Bo Forrest, Fred Laughlin, and a host of other guys. Tennis players always seemed to be interesting and smart.

Overall, life in A-1 could have been worse, but I was still living one day at a time. A huge part of my dissatisfaction came from realizing, during tennis practice, that my game wasn't living up to my own personal standard of play. We weren't practicing enough for me to get my groove back, I had too much junk banging around in my head to be able to concentrate fully, I wasn't in love with the racquets we were using, I was getting headaches almost every day and I was lonely for life in South Florida. The weather was getting cooler, wetter, windier and uncomfortable. When the season started in the spring, Walt Oehrlein would be number one on our Plebe team and I would be number two. I kept thinking I was a better player than Walt, but he was too solid off the ground for me to beat him. Every aspect of his game was stronger than mine, except for his forehand; the confidence with which he played was outstanding and I admired that the most about him. I felt his understanding of the game of tennis matched mine. I liked and respected Walt and I hoped we would become good friends.

There were a lot of nice classmates on the team. Ross Wollen was fast on the court and easy to talk to, Bo Forrest was from the South and had a bubbly personality, John Shuford, another Southerner was easy going while Steve Darrah, with his broad shoulders, seemed to be a daredevil and rambucous in a fun way! Fred Laughlin, Jim Scheiner and Terry Carlson rounded out a group of good guys who were all pleasant and a pleasure to share time with.

Nevertheless, despite being around these teammates, my frustration mounted with each practice; I couldn't get my rhythm back no matter how hard I tried. I wasn't the tennis player I knew I could be. I was overwhelmed with the bullshit of everyday cadet life and couldn't free my mind enough to relax enough to swing freely.

It felt as if I had lived several lifetimes during those early months at West Point. I was still only seventeen years of age, but I felt older, worn out and not any more mature nor intelligent than when I had left home. Learning to become a "man" wasn't easy that's for sure!

CHAPTER 41

TENNIS AGAIN

When we started to play tennis again, practice was five days a week. I also practiced on the weekends if I had free time. We only played among our teammates as there would be no organized college matches until the spring. West Point had no indoor tennis facilities so, when it rained, we were shuffled to the indoor hockey rink with its slick concrete. I had learned that by the end of October, when the weather turned cooler and windy, we'd move indoors and play squash. This sport was new to me, but I expected to excel at it, since it required a racquet and a ball. The Academy had ten lovely, white-painted, red-striped, high-walled wooden squash courts with a viewing balcony high above the backcourt. The squash area was isolated from the rest of the gymnasium but within the same building. It seemed like it would be a haven safe from all the other cadet activities.

Now, however, my agenda was to concentrate on tennis. Whacking the ball around outdoors, after academic classes every day, being away from the barracks, my roommates and the pesky Upperclassmen, was very therapeutic for me. For a couple of hours each day, I could let my body's muscle memory take over.

Because of our level of play, Walt Oehrlein and I were allowed to practice with the varsity players. We both struggled to regain some form, but Walter had an easier time of it than I did; his ground-strokes were more fluid than mine. Neither of us were playing even close to our highest potential, as Beast Barracks had interfered with our rhythm and timing. While it was so great to be back on the court, my frustrations mounted over my poor quality of play.

The number one player on the varsity was Richie Oehrlein, Walt's older brother by one year and a Yearling at the Academy. He was too steady for me, although Walt had a little stronger serve and ended up at the number one slot our remaining years. I had no patience and no groove to rally more than three or four shots in a point with either of the Oehrlein brothers, but I enjoyed playing with them. Richie had a great personality, always positive and a pleasure to be around. Walt was more subdued; he let his racquet do the talking.

Another transplanted floridian and Yearling, John Leyerzaph, had an outstanding tennis game and solid credentials, but, unlike the Oehrlein brothers, while still a nice person, he was slightly aloof so I didn't feel close to him. Walt and I practiced a lot together, but my game was still far off. The Davis racquets didn't have a good feel for me; their uneven balance resulted in my having to play with 'tennis elbow.' Desperate to regain my form, I was always impatient, and the damn racquets were a big drawback to feeling confident in my strokes. My upper body had also changed over the summer. All those pushups had enhanced my chest and biceps at the expense of whatever fluid rhythm I previously had on my groundstrokes. I was stronger but needed to adjust my 'feel' for the ball.

I was angry at myself each time Walt beat me. We had totally different type games and he was far more consistent than I. That always seemed to make a difference in our match at the end. Even when I changed my normal style of play, he had good recognition and would adapt. I didn't want to change my style, however; I just needed to regain my groove.

Coach Nordlie approached me on the very first day of practice, his handsome nordic face slightly unshaven, strong grip to his handshake, an effusive enthusiasm in his voice. "Great to see you, Paul. I knew you'd make it through Beast!" His beaming smile was infectious. What he said seemed liked a joke to me since I never thought I would be making it through Beast Barracks. It seemed whatever sense of humor I had left was evaporating as rapidly as my florida tan. Walking off demerits on the Area or sitting in confinement in my room over the weekend further exacerbated my emotional distress.

Coach sensed this and he always tried his best to alleviate my depression with kind words or a motivational comment. I loved this man. That day, I finally had the chance to tell him, "Thank you for sending the guardian angels to intervene in my troubles during Beast. They saved my life! I would have been long gone without their help."

Coach grinned. "When you're back in shape," he said, "please let some of the varsity players win a set once in awhile. That way they can get an ego boost and build up their confidence on the courts... they all need it!"

"If any of them can beat me, except Walt and Richie," I said with bravado, "I'll kiss their butts on the Plain during the parade. I'm playing very poorly right now, but them even taking a set off from me is never going to happen!" Good; some of my displaced and sorely needed confidence was returning.

I mentioned my concern about the Davis Imperials. Coach said they were the best he could do with his budgetary restraints, laughed a little and was still chuckling as he moved to the next court. It never dawned on me to ask my dad to send my old racquets from home. My Spaulding Pancho Gonzales models would have done the trick for sure.

Coach Nordlie made leadership an art form. He wasn't a West Pointer, but he was a man who had carved out his own life based on dignity, sincerity and genuine concern for others. He did it all in a low-key, quiet, unassuming manner. My respect for him was unwavering.

After tennis practice we'd all head for the showers at the gym; race back to the barracks for dinner formation; eat excellent meals on the Tennis Corps Squad tables; and be back to our rooms by 1900 hours. With lights out at 2200 hours, we had only three hours to study and perform assorted Plebe duties—spit-shining our shoes, polishing our belt buckles, cleaning the room, studying *Bugle Notes*—all of which usually occupied at least half of that "downtime." Writing letters home and studying seemed an afterthought in the beginning of the academic year but studying became much more important when I began flunking several of my classes.

I eagerly awaited my daily letter from dad, the only family member who wrote regularly. Jill had ditched me long ago back in high school, so I was without any female contact or communication except nightly in my dreams. Too busy to lust after women and with no opportunity to have done so during Beast Barracks, seeing other cadets with female companionship on the weekends frustrated and tantalized me. With lights off, the moon high over the Hudson River, train whistles sounding in the distance from Metro North and the warmth of my "Brown Boy" comforter, sleepiness rapidly enveloped me after such a hectic day. Before my eyes closed, however, my thoughts always seemed to turn to the dejection I was experiencing or the sexual activity I certainly was not. One night during a bout of depression, I composed a brief poem which accurately depicted my frame of mind:

Roses are Red
Violets are Blue
I'm getting crazy
And so am I!

With Beast Barracks in the past and Plebe year in full swing, the trials of West Point life were slightly easing but always present and they continually eroded my spirit. Calling the minutes, delivering the mail and the laundry from the orderly room to the Upperclassmen's rooms, Squad meetings, hitting the wall to let Upperclassmen pass us in the barracks, unannounced room inspections...the pressure from each activity added up, keeping me off-balance, on edge and anxious all the time. Corps Squad tables and tennis practice provided a huge release, but not enough to offset my isolation from family, friends, and home. The loneliness, lack of feminine touch and fear of failure were ever-present. It wasn't long into the academic year before I felt myself slipping badly into a morass of self-pity.

And...I excelled at this emotion! I never failed to accept what small joys would pop-up from time-to-time like a kind word from a classmate, a funny joke by my Squad Leader or a passing grade on a test I thought I had flunked. It was rare that I would look back on the day and say "that was a pleasant day in my life" or look ahead and think the best was yet to come, and God, how I would have liked to have spent fifteen minutes talking to my buddy Donnie.

CHAPTER 42

FOOTBALL AND HARVEY

September in college means football, and Army football is always exciting and fun. Michie Stadium was our small, intimate football arena, up and over the hill near Lusk Reservoir. How many gallons in Lusk Reservoir? "Seventy-eight million gallons, Sir, when the water is flowing over the spillway!" This simple answer to that stupid question from *Bugle Notes* allowed a Plebe to eat his meal. Walking up near the Stadium, however, no one cared how many freaking gallons of H2O were in the reservoir.

The football stadium was cushioned on all sides by a lush landscape of assorted trees, displaying a fabulous array of changing colors in the fall. Within the stadium itself, one could almost hear faint cheers for the Army football heroes long gone: the dynamic duo of Doc Blanchard and Glenn Davis, Mr. Inside and Mr. Outside of the 1940s; Pete Dawkins, All-American Football, Cadet First Captain, Rhodes Scholar of the 1950s; and, of course, the great Earl "Red" Blaik, football coach extraordinaire and molder of real men. The legacies of these heroes all lent a certain aura to Michie, this field of friendly strife, where opponents came to do battle.

The ghost of George Patton and his aggressive leadership style rumbled through every nook and cranny of West Point during football week. We had pep rallies on Friday nights in the Mess Hall, where sometimes the Supe or the Comm would give inspirational "Go Get 'Em" speeches. In order to win, controlled aggression was a must on the battlefield as well as on the playing field and in the stands.

We had to learn all the songs, cheers and whistles and had to exhibit the right amount of enthusiasm at the games. You were considered a traitor to the cause if an Upperclassman spied you not singing or cheering loudly enough. Once, when we were losing 31-8 to Michigan, I stopped cheering because of a sore throat. I received three demerits for "lacking enthusiasm at a sporting event." Even the officers and their wives had a pecking order: those officers ranked higher judged the sincerity of efforts to cheer exhibited by the lower-ranked officers and their spouses. Gossip traveled fast on a military post.

The Army black-and-gold colors flew high and flapped in the wind on game day. The Army Mule and Cadet Cheerleaders were fabulous as they ran up and down the field eliciting enthusiasm and genuine spirit. Cadets didn't need tickets to go to the game; just wearing the dress gray uniform gained us admission. We could always attend, if we weren't walking punishments tours in the Area or in room confinement. When there was a road game, occasionally we would load up in buses or take a special train.

The Army-Navy game in Philadelphia was the cornerstone of the season, the epitome of youthful rivalry between the two service Academies. The Air Force Academy always took a backseat in our minds, since it had only recently been established and didn't have a lot of history behind it. Coaches' careers flourished or died with a victory or loss over the Naval Academy. A win over Navy resulted in a gold star for a cadet Major "A" lettermen's gray jacket.

When Army played Navy crowds were abundant, cheering was boisterous and the excitement palpable. "Go Army, Beat Navy" was the mantra of the day. Big, zesty and raucous rallies led up to the event. The outcome of the Army-Navy game determined whether the whole Academy would walk around in a state of depression for the remainder of the semester. But Plebe Rocco McGurk, my classmate, had the ability to change all of that. When Rocco stood up to lead a cheer, suddenly everything in the world of West Point seemed magnificent and righteous.

Rocco had taken it upon himself to be a one-man cheer facilitator, the inspirational leader of Academy Hoopla! He was "the man" when it came to establishing *esprit de corps* during football season. When he entered a room, the sun would come out and people buzzed with joy, laughing and friendly. He also may have been one of few men at West Point with a sense of humor. You had to admire a guy who could get everybody, including the officers, smiling and cheering... himself fully aware, all the while, that the underlying foundation of this rah-rah stuff was pure and total bullshit. Even with all the crap he and the rest of us Plebes were going through, Rocco could rise above the normal level of insanity and horse-hockey of cadet life and bring us to a state of gleeful pandemonium, if only for a few moments.

I had hoped Rocco would bring his enthusiasm out to our tennis matches in the springtime, but that never happened. By spring, he would be walking off punishment tours in the Area for all the demerits he had racked up that previous fall! The Tac Department never cut anyone any slack, not even Rocco.

Another bright light in the grim landscape was Harvey Fraser. Harvey was a Yearling in A-1 when I joined the Company. He was the son of the great Colonel "Hot Body" Fraser, a Mechanics Instructor who taught the most highly attended, spectacular lecture at the Academy during Cow year: "Mechanics and Structural Integrity of the Bra."

Harvey befriended me when I joined A-1 and was always there for me. He was a sweet and affable guy, a lot different from many of the men around me. Even though he was an "Army Brat" with a famous father, he was low key, thoughtful of others and great to talk with. Harvey and I once attended a football game together and I would hit squash balls with him occassionally.

Harvey was also a font of insider information. When we attended that game, he would point out all the different officers on the academic and tactical staff whom I needed to avoid, due to their rigidity and demanding personalities. Since the Corps of Cadets was considered the twelfth man on the football team—meaning the spirit of Army football—we were required to cheer with enthusiasm. Harvey's ramblings made the game more fun and interesting while the football team was getting slaughtered by the likes of Michigan or Oklahoma.

During the fall semester at West Point, football season was the premier highlight starting with the Friday Night Mess Hall rallies starring Rocco…watching all the colors and flash of the crowd in the stands…then culminating in the long trudge back from the stadium. Football Saturdays usually began with morning classes, room inspection, parade, and then some freedom until supper and Taps… that is, of course, if you weren't sitting in confinement most of the time like I was. Still, it was a reasonably cheerful day compared to the rest of the week.

A contented West Point cadet usually feels he is a part of something much bigger than himself. When it came to Army-Navy football, each cadet pictured himself as the starting quarterback leading his "Knights on the Hudson" to victory. This time of year, did add excitement and levity to a cadet's existence, but for me, well, I just had a hard time accepting those moments of frivolity and brief sparks of enjoyment because of the shroud of self-pity I encased myself in.

CHAPTER 43

THE CHICKEN

Coach Nordlie was true to his word in trying to help me during the difficult times of Plebe life. His wife worked in the EENT clinic of the West Point Hospital as a receptionist. Her boss was Dr. Herman (Hank) Gensler, staff Optometrist; a smart, gentle man. She had an inkling that she should introduce me to Dr. Gensler and his family through the West Point "Plebe Pop" program. It was a great idea; Hank and his Mary Travers look-a-like wife, Rhoda, virtually adopted me!

In the Plebe Pop program, officers kept tabs on a single cadet, occasionally had him in their homes for dinner; were available to discuss important issues and became surrogate parents. Hank and Rhoda were both brilliant, political, well-read and outspoken. Their two beautiful kids, Pam and Matthew, ages 8 and 6, were animated, highly inquisitive and unique. They both had sky-high IQs. Never having had younger siblings, I enjoyed being around the two of them. That the Genslers were Jewish was not so important to me, but it added an additional commonality. I fell in love with the whole family twenty-three seconds after meeting them. You could easily tell Pam was going to be a knock-out beauty when she got older; Matt had the studious air of an Ivy-Leaguer even though he was only a child.

Hank fit me with experimental contact lenses, spurring my interest in the medical profession and clearing a path to a future I hadn't imagined but would later pursue. Rhoda showed me there could be joy and beauty in life everywhere, even on the reservation at West Point. A woman of impeccable taste, she was something of a pariah within military wives' circles. Most couldn't deal with her intellect, energy and self-assertiveness. Only the Supe's wife, Kitsy, was a match for her. Both were remarkable individuals.

After my first dinner at the Genslers' home, I realized there was a world around West Point that I was unaware of: a life of people, outside interests and community. The Genslers were always gracious and generous with me. When I sent them a thank-you note for that first dinner, Rhoda told me not to send notes anymore. She already knew how much she and the entire family meant to me; no need for thank-yous.

One Saturday night, the Genslers had a mandatory social engagement and their babysitter had fallen ill; could I help with the kids? Rhoda said dinner had been prepared so all I had to do was watch over things after we chowed down. Since I wasn't in confinement that evening, of course I agreed; I would have done anything for them.

As they were hurrying out the door, Rhoda checked the stove to discover that the dinner she thought was all prepared wasn't—she'd forgotten to turn the stove on! There was a beautiful, but raw, chicken sitting forlornly and uncooked in the pan. She fell over herself apologizing, but I told her not to worry, I had it covered! I assured Hank and Rhoda of my competency and finally they left, believing they were leaving their family in capable hands.

Back home, we ate chicken two or three times a week. It was the one dish my mom served us that wasn't dry, overcooked or tasteless. I loved to pick up the hot, juicy pieces with my fingers and eat them right off the bone…yummy! I would watch in famished anticipation as mom put the bird in the pan, basted it with butter and roasted it until the skin was golden brown and crispy. I had seen her make this delicious meal many times over the years. How difficult could it be?

As soon as the Genslers left the house I parked the kids in front of the TV and we played a game I had just invented called, "If you move, I'll kill you." They loved the idea, especially since I had two shiny quarters in my trouser pocket as a reward if they won. I then got on the telephone and dialed "O" for the telephone operator. In 1961, if you didn't have a direct number, there were live operators going through switchboards to help.

When the operator answered, I introduced myself, told her I was a Plebe doing baby sitting duty and really needed her help. She chuckled out loud. "Okay...tell me what you need, sweetheart," she said in a voice that would melt the ice off a Russian tank in the middle of a rough Crimean winter.

I said, "I have a real emergency here. I have to cook a chicken and need to know at what temperature and for how long should I cook it." She giggled in the background. "How big is your bird, honey?" I told her, "About a foot long!"

Once the operator stopped her laughing, she asked me if I was serious or just joking. I told her I was serious and really needed her advice. "Okay," she said, "Usually you broil a chicken for ten minutes a pound at 400°. Make sure you take the drippings and baste it every ten minutes. It sounds like it's about six pounds, so one hour should do it. When the skin is brown and crispy, you are done!" All the while she was talking, her words were interspersed with giggling and downright guffawing. I thanked her profusely for her help.

"Cadet Kantrowich"—she was nearly choking on her words— "When you get to be a Firstie, give me a call and I'll let you cook a chicken for me; I promise you a very special dessert!" The line died as I heard the operator's laughter in the background amongst a chorus of whoops and chuckles.

The chicken turned out great and the kids went to bed with smiles on their faces and a shiny quarter each in their hand. My stomach was happily bulging. Hank and Rhoda returned home, having had a terrific time, so all was well with the world. Rhoda looked at the leftover chicken carcass in the refrigerator, took a taste, smiled and nodded her approval. Within twenty-four hours the entire reservation—almost every occupant at West Point—knew about the Plebe who cooks chicken. I didn't know whether Rhoda was a big gossip, or the telephone operator just couldn't keep a secret.

Three years later, as the operator had asked me to do, I dialed "O," looking for her. She had sounded so young and sweet on the telephone the first time I spoke with her, and I wanted to keep my promise about cooking her that chicken. I was also interested in that "special dessert" she had planned.

Another operator on the switchboard told me that my operator had eloped the year before with a chef from a local restaurant and had left the area. Since this new operator sounded extremely cute and perky, I asked her for a date. She was married, however, and didn't think her husband would approve.

CHAPTER 44

COLORS GALORE, TURKEY, FOOTBALL AND MOOD SWINGS

Fall in upstate New York was a kaleidoscope of magnificent colors. The woods surrounding the Academy glowed with red Maples and vibrant Purple Ash, with shades of gold, orange, yellow, russet, bronze and copper; mesmerizing and tantalizing the artist in all of us. Having lived in South Florida for so long, I had never witnessed such a celebration and saturation of hue and tone. I wasn't happy, however, about the frost-tipped dew clinging to the blades of grass on the Plain, the dropping temperature at Taps, or the replacement of outdoor tennis with indoor squash.

I was barely surviving Plebe year, hanging on by the coating of Brasso on our uniform's gold buttons, by the one-micron layer of black wax on the toes of my spit-shined shoes. Academics were extremely challenging, and I wasn't putting in enough time studying. My mind was in bondage to daily routines, numb from loneliness, sad about losing tennis, moody and morose. My thoughts had drifted back and forth over the previous five months between my breakup with Jill in high school, my poor performance as a Cadet, longing for the warmth of the Florida sun, missing my sisters and wondering about their lives. Scattered, dark, thoughts without conclusions reeked of negativity and radiated despair. A lot of my thoughts revolved around the lack of love.

Jill: my first love who filled me with such unrestrained happiness, joy and excitement. I could remember the flow of energy—of life—pulsating through my body; the newness of intense sexual frustration; the high expectations of close physical and emotional bonding. My joy had arrived so early and clearly when we first met but escaped so rapidly, so catastrophically when we broke up. I was shattered by the rejection.

My sisters: not being a part of either of their lives, not hearing from them, not knowing if they were safe and happy and wanting them to be. What was college like for Helen; what were her thoughts, her joys and sense of freedom? And Willie: older, beautiful, artistic, creative, married…was she content?

My parents: were they healthy, getting along as empty nesters, enjoying life now as I believed they had when they were younger? My dad's daily, short but comical letters were my only comfort. He never went into detail about anything, just kept pumping his *one-week-at-a-time* theme, *go get 'em son, attaboy Paul* attitude. He sounded as if he thought I was playing a tennis match and losing. Well…I wasn't playing tennis, but I did think I was losing my soon-to-be eighteen-year-old mind that was reeling from this military atmosphere, yawing around the currents of my personal discontent. On my own at West Point, my life was disrupted by rules and regulations, tossed about by chaotic Upperclassmen, while dark thoughts continued to wash over me as the days progressed.

There was absolutely no compensation to be gained from playing squash either. It was a very fast, active sport and quite physical when played with intensity, competitiveness and heart. But it was a short stroke, chopping, wristy game; not a flowing swing where topspin and underspin could be imparted, where you could shape the ball, discern depth and speed easily.

Some of my teammates played a bruising and battering style where you didn't want to be caught with the ball between you and the wall. Steve Darrah would ram his opponent's body into the wall to complete his shot and he'd just grin when the point was over. Tom Genoni used guile and his corner shots caroming away to finish the point. Walt had power and style, plus Darrah's ruthlessness, Ross Wollen's speed and Genoni's guile all wrapped in one tight package. He was our best. Someday I imagined he would be the player on our team to be the Intercollegiate National Champion.

Squash did keep me safely away from the torturous Company tables! It kept me physically fit, reduced some of the traffic jams clogging my brain, but it also ruined my tennis swing. My exquisite, rolling, rocket, topspin forehand was replaced with an abbreviated, half-slap half-hit smack of that little black, hard ball. Instead of reaching back and imparting a dramatic amount of power as I did with a tennis ball, I grudgingly adapted, simply using my forearm, in a mostly half-swing, to hit through it. I became a good player but never achieved the quality of play Walt did. Squash allowed me to eat, feel the fellowship of my teammates and contribute to our team's great record by never losing a match at my position; it just didn't satisfy my personal needs.

October had come and gone, the rain came and stayed. November meant wet, dismal, gray brick buildings framing the campus, overcast dark angry clouds above, lots of rain, smeared cement afoot. Eight weeks into the academic year, I was barely passing my classes, failing to spend enough time studying, grinding my teeth from loneliness. Slumped over the desk in my room, I would dream of anything but West Point.

All my grades ranged between 2.05 to 2.28 which placed me in the bottom sections of each subject. My motivation had dropped, demerits piled up and weekend confinement was a constant reminder of my poor cadet performance. I continued my descent further into a weird, black funk.

The approach of my eighteenth birthday in November—a day of exhilaration and joy for most teenagers—held only the promise of another lonely day, no cause for celebration. My party would consist of cleaning, polishing, studying and mopping. I wasn't going to tell my roommates my birthday was coming up since I wanted nothing from them.

On the eleventh of November, Harvey Fraser insisted I sit next to him at the supper table; his dad must have read my personnel file to find my birth date. Harvey was always doing nice but sneaky things for people, bringing smiles to somber faces. He raised a glass of water to toast my eighteenth birthday, produced a candle and placed it in the center of the dessert pie for me to extinguish. I implored the table not to sing, begging them so vociferously that none of them did. It would have been mortifying!

Harvey's thoughtfulness shifted my mood from dark growling to light brooding. I wondered what my twin was doing for our birthday—*her* birthday—at Gainesville, since we never exchanged cards and hadn't exchanged letters since I left in July. She was probably at a frat party, trolling for a guy! I couldn't blame her; at least one of us was out and about.

Our older sister Wilma's twenty-third birthday was the day before ours, on the tenth. She and her husband were probably celebrating with a night out. Good for them too! Since I knew she was pregnant, I hoped she was having some fun and not getting too nauseous from morning sickness.

The Thanksgiving dinner served in the Mess Hall on the last thursday of November 1961 was a festive affair, but I missed spending the holiday, rich with tradition, with my family. Prior to our move to Florida in 1954, Thanksgiving had been a great Kantrowich/Kashinsky/Harris/Cohen affair in either Brooklyn, Manhattan, or Lynbrook, Long Island. My aunt Gertie always saved me a big turkey wing and then Helen and I would get a good workout gnawing on all the leftover turkey bones. I missed the joy, love, political commentary...even the bitching and the small family squabbles would have been welcome!

At the Mess Hall, the celebration and giving thanks rang a little hollow for me, even with my growing excitement about going to

Philadelphia for my first Army-Navy football game. With the cheerful attitudes of the Upperclassmen, the freedom of being off the reservation, the possibility of interaction with young females and their anticipated reaction to a man in uniform, the atmosphere should have felt intoxicating. In fact, I was truly looking forward to wandering around the city, roaming free, observing life as I had never known yet I was just slow to respond with genuine enthusiasm.

The 1961 game was a thriller, with Navy pulling out a 13-7 win despite our quarterback Dick Eckert throwing a fifty-five-yard bomb and our great fullback, Al Rushatz, blasting the line to score. President John F. Kennedy sat with us the first half, then the second half with the Navy, where he was more at home, having been a Navy man, with his "boat people."

I didn't meet any girls, but after the game, I did make love to a Philly cheese steak sandwich, french fries and fabulous vanilla milkshake. I also ended up half-carrying a totally drunk classmate back to the train station at ten PM. Barfing all over a Tac Officer on the train ride back to West Point didn't help his career any.

So that was the high point of the first semester. With Plebe Christmas/Hanukkah soon to arrive, and Plebes not being allowed to visit home, I anticipated a bleak and long winter. While three-quarters of the Corps of Cadets did go home for the holidays, lowly, dog shit Plebes endured a mass loneliness as our reward for our efforts and achievements to date. I guess that was all part of struggling to learn how to be a man!

CHAPTER 45

HANUKKMAS WITH WESTY

The period of time between Thanksgiving and the holidays of Christmas and Hanukkah were rough and demoralizing. Foliage season had gone with the flocks of Canadian geese flying south, autumn colors were vanquished by the northeasterly wind. Academics were in full swing and getting much more comprehensive, complex and difficult. I was okay with math, because I had studied calculus, trigonometry and solid geometry in high school, and I had a good relationship with numbers. All my other courses—Measurements and Graphics, Astronomy, Physical and World Geography, French, Speech Making and Composition and Tactics—required additional time and effort on my part. I was a numbers guy and the written and spoken words for me were always difficult to process.

The cold weather ripped me like a sharp knife and, as the additional rain made the world grayer and dreary, I sank into a bog of emotional duress. My Plebe Pop and Mom tried to be inspirational, but I didn't have enough access to them as my weekend confinements took all my free time away. As a Corps Squad athlete, I didn't have to walk the Area on punishment tours, but I had to work my demerits off by sitting room confinement on the weekends. Trapped and isolated, I was only allowed to be in my room, the latrine, the

Cadet Library (where I never did go) or the Mess Hall for a meal.

During that time between the winter holidays, we found out that Harvey Fraser had a serious illness. His condition required risky neurosurgery. My thoughts of all the good times he and I had shared at West Point—that football game, the candle for my birthday in the Mess Hall, our quiet and thoughtful conversations about tennis, our lives and dealing with the West Point system—were imprinted indelibly in my mind. I tried to feel optimistic about his future outcome and decided to support him any way I could.

On the day the news broke about Harvey, it had snowed...a lot. I hadn't seen snow in seven years. It was beautiful, white, pure, virginal. The sun created a brilliant, reflective sheen on the surface of the flaky, soft powder and recreated prismatic colors of light through the wet icicles that hung from tree branches and electric lines. I was feeling like a mindless clone of regulation and routine...but I was healthy... all the while this kid Harvey, twenty years old, a happy-go-lucky and beautiful soul, was in serious trouble medically. As I walked around the beautiful West Point campus, I wept for both of us.

The entire Corps of Cadets—except the Plebes and the cadre of Upperclassmen who either had no place to go or were working off assorted punishment tours—went home for the holidays just prior to Christmas. It was quiet and almost peaceful for those of us who remained on the reservation. The days were interrupted only by Reveille and meal formations, no fixed schedule for normal activites, so life was almost tranquil for awhile.

It might have been the twenty-seventh or twenty-eighth of December 1961 when Walt and I had decided, after breakfast, to have a marathon squash session; just beat the hell out of the ball and each other and burn off Plebe anxiety. We had just finished doing exactly that as we lay around the little squash room, maybe 100 square feet, feet propped up in the air, soggy towels around our necks, backs to the open door, dripping wet, out of breath, daily frustrations extinguished.We reviewed points of significance during different games in the extended match. We talked about tennis, West Point, and eventually, what most guys usually talk about: women! In our cases, "lack thereof." There wasn't anyone around the courts before the noon meal. It was quiet, tranquil and a very pleasant moment in time for both of us. We thought we had the place to ourselves. It was a rare moment of relaxed freedom to treasure. A very fine moment indeed.

Just a few minutes later there was a faint tapping of footsteps coming down the hallway, becoming more audible, then stopping when they reached the door of the squash room. In walked Major General Westmoreland, Superintendent and Numero Uno at West Point, dressed in his green uniform with all his medals above his left breast pocket. He looked at me, I looked at him. The general then turned his gaze on Walt, who stared back without saying anything. We were in our private little space, the squash room, where for over twenty-five years, gatherings of squash players had assembled before and after they competed. Protocol is one thing, but this was OUR sacred ground and we thought it should be a "safe zone" for all who entered.

"Atten-hut!"General Westmoreland yelled. We jumped up and stood at attention.

"Slap your silly necks in, come to attention and salute properly!" General Westmoreland barked. It was only then that Walt and I realized we were the ones that should have commanded ourselves to attention. We saluted, then both got our butts chewed out for several minutes. So much for our rare and treasured moment!

When Westy calmed down he said something so funny, I am sure I will remember it the rest of my life. "Do either of you want to play squash with me at 1400 hours?" *Crap! Damn!*

There was a deafening silence as sweat dripped down into my eyes, stinging, causing them to water. Walt said nothing. I bent over to pick up my racquets, and still Walt said nothing. I bent over to re-tie my sneakers' laces. Silence! Not a ripple in the atmosphere. I was embarrassed. My Jewish guilt kicked in. "I will, Sir!" I finally said.

"Kantrowich! You are the Florida guy, right? I remember you!

1400 hours sharp." With that, the general turned and abruptly left. We could hear the clicks from his shoe heels on the poured concrete floor, loud tapping that diminished a few seconds later as he exited that section of the gym. Then there was silence again.

Walter thought it was a riot that I would be playing squash with the Supe! He started laughing and smiling as though he knew something I didn't. Miffed that I'd gotten stuck with the job, I said, "You know Walt, you are an asshole. You could have volunteered." I hadn't realized it at the time, but the Oehrlein brothers always knew what news was in the wind at West Point. They had the inside scoop about our Superintendent's competitive spirit when he had a racquet in his hand.

"My brother Richie told me never to volunteer for anything if I could avoid it," Walt said. "I took my brother's advice...I avoided it!"

CHAPTER 46

figured I could grab a quick nap after lunch and before my squash date with the general. I set two alarm clocks for 1330 hours, figuring five minutes to dress, ten minutes to the gym, so I would arrive fifteen minutes early to meet the Supe at 1400 hours.

Both alarm clocks let me down; at 1400 hours sharp, I was in my bunk, under my comforter, fast asleep. Walt and I really had gone at each other in practice. I was tired and mentally anguished; I could never really gain ground in any one of the many games we played that morning, and I was frustrated since Walt was quite a bit better as a squash player than I; my ego was bruised and battered so sleep was therapeutic for me.

At 1415 hours I sprang awake in an icy sweat. *Shit!* Frantically jumping into my clothes, I dashed to the squash courts. I arrived at the gym at 1428 hours, but there was no one there. Only the echo of my sneakers, racing down the painted cement floor, filled the underground hallway.

In a panic, I raced back to my room to collect my thoughts. I needed to ask Coach Nordlie for his advice. Cadets had no telephones in our rooms, so I had to run downstairs to call him from the Company Orderly Room.

Coach knew I was crazed as soon as his wife handed him the

receiver. "Coach, you've got to help me, I've screwed up big time! Coach, please tell me what to do and I'll do it!" Then I yelled into the receiver, "Please Coach, HELP ME!"

Nothing rattled Nordlie. He replied, calmly, "Paul, call the general up at home, apologize and explain what happened…once you've calmed down, of course!"

Still anxious I said, "Coach, he's going to want to fry my balls…can you call for me?" Leif Nordlie laughed. "Just call him up, you'll do fine! Paul…you'll be fine!"

Immediately I followed the coach's advice. I dialed "O" and asked the switchboard operator to connect me to the general's home telephone.

"Westmoreland residence," replied a female voice that, had it been a pair of eyes, would have twinkled. I could tell this was a very special lady. I introduced myself to his wife and asked to speak to the general.

"Hold on there, Cadet Kantrowich, I'll get my husband for you!" I heard her lightly cup the receiver with her hand. "Oh Westy…phone, dear…it's that nice cadet who was late for your squash game!"

A gruff, gravelly voice barked into the telephone, "Westmoreland here." He listened as I went through my rehearsed two-alarm clock story. Just when I thought I had convinced him of my small mistake, he stopped me.

"Ten minutes, Dress Gray, HERE!"

Whatever he wanted, whatever it takes, I was thinking, to get out of this troublesome mess.

Sweat poured out of me as I knocked on the front door of the Supe's house. The door swung open to reveal a vision of loveliness: Kitsy Westmoreland, a general's daughter and now the wife of a general who was moving up the chain of command. Seeing the expression on my face, she laughed softly and musically. "Please let your chin out, it makes you look very funny! The general is expecting you upstairs in his attic office. Why don't you just head up there?"

I raced up the stairs and knocked on Westmoreland's door. "Come in and report!" he commanded. As I entered his study, he directed me to stand on a small, frayed red carpet directly in front of his large, wooden desk five feet away from where he sat. Standing at rigid attention, I whipped out my best salute ever and said, "Sir, Cadet Kantrowich reports as ordered with the sincerest of apologies!"

He stopped my report dead in its tracks, braced me and chewed me out like an Upperclassman would...only worse. "Chin in, pop that puny chest out," he began, and went on and on until I stopped listening to this grown man, a two-star—soon to be three-star—general, yelling at a teenaged-kid as if I'd just robbed a bank and shot three people. Leadership in action!

Westmoreland ended the meeting with an order: "If you still want to play, thirty minutes, court number one, Cadet Kantrowich. Be there!"

Downstairs, the Supe's wife escorted me to the door, smiling. "I'm so glad the two of you had such a nice chat, dear. Good luck, now!"

I raced directly to the gym and phoned the Coach to catch him up and thank him. I wasn't leaving the gym; I'd be twenty minutes early this time. I paced back and forth. Even though I had played squash for less than two months, I excelled at it. My speed, anticipation, reflexes and power played a role, but my positioning and racquet control gave me a big edge over an average player. While I waited for the general, I plotted my strategy so that he wouldn't feel too badly when I beat him.

After the general arrived, we warmed up the small, hard, black squash ball and started to play. I could discern immediately what type of player he was: lousy! I would have to tank a lot of shots to make him think he was competitive.

Even so, Westy was losing all the points on his own. It took subtle creativity to keep him in each game. In the five-game match, I decided, I would win the first and third, then let him win the second and fourth, keeping them closely contested before beating him in a very close final game. There was no way I would let him beat me.

My design was working well, but the Supe was a poor sport, and he had a nasty, neurotic habit of "hogging the tee." On a squash court, the tee is formed at the intersection of the service line with another line perpendicular to it, forming two boxes where players serve from and into. Controlling the tee allows you the full court to hit your shots into. A good sportsman would never stay too long in the tee area, allowing his opponent to reach for his shot unimpeded. But General Westmoreland's competitiveness was feral. He would hit the ball and then lurch into the tee, pushing, blocking, butting with his arms wide out, not allowing me to pass by him to retrieve my return. He would be in a crouched position, his butt up in the air thoughtlessly hogging the tee.

I tried to solve that problem by keeping the ball along the wall for most of the points, but it was frustrating and my inner hostility towards the general began to grow incrementally. Every time a ball went to the back wall, when I went to retrieve it to hit my return, the general's butt was sticking right there in my face: every single time. I had to hit around him or pull up or pretend to miss.

Westy was a sore loser when down in the score, a braggart when ahead; and he was only ahead occasionally because I was throwing the points. I thought of his rah-rah term, spizzerinctum. Well... there was no spizzerinctum coming from the man that day, as far as I could tell. No vim or vigor, just assholery. He paced, gyrated, blew his nose. His heavy, dark, furrowed eyebrows flashed outward when he squinted his eyes. His prominent chin jutted even farther with grim determination. He had to win this match no matter how he did it, whether by hogging the tee, pushing, or demanding lets (do-overs) for my interference when there was none. He certainly couldn't let a Plebe beat him!

I was a racquet man. As in tennis, I sought the purity, art, science, sport and magic of squash. I respected the game and expected the same of my opponent. This opponent respected neither the game nor me. Perhaps he fancied himself a great military thinker who would never give up the ground gained in a fight but Westy was going to keep sticking his ass in my face, never surrendering the tee!

At twelve-all, fifth and final game, a ball came off the back wall for me to return. My general had his spizzer rectum up in the air as always, blocking my position, hogging the tee. He pumped his legs, gyrated his hips, grunted loudly after hitting his shot. He spread his feet shoulder-width apart for better balance and to further block my return. He had to win, to prove himself better than the scrawny Plebe who had stood him up just hours before.

As the ball caromed off the back wall toward me, I saw, in an intense moment of pure clarity, my entire five and one-half months at West Point flash before my eyes. I felt my pain about the impending loss of Harvey Fraser, for the plight of my former classmate Benny Goldberg and for the other 350 hopefuls from my group who would never graduate from the Academy. I fumed about that southern Upperclassman, "Jack" the jackass who believed that, by finally deigning to recognize me, he could erase all those nights of treating my Jewishness like a disease. I thought of this general, himself treating me as if I were lower than dog shit. These emotions ripped me apart.

The ball had now reached its apex and gravity was pulling it down. I called loudly, "Coming around!" This gave my unworthy opponent time to clear the tee, which, doggedly, he refused to do. To call "coming around" was the gentlemenly call to make, what a good sportsman would do, what any squash player would say, and it was considered proper "squash etiquette" and the right way to play the game. I knew he heard me because I yelled it out in a strong "military" voice!

He did not move!

The ball met the sweet center of my flattened racquet head. It rebounded off the racquet's natural gut strings at a speed commensurate with every ounce of energy I could generate and with the full force of my body weight behind it. A massive amount of kinetic energy was imparted into that small sphere. I couldn't calculate the actual total of foot-pounds of power that squash ball now possessed but…it was certainly powerful enough to firmly embed itself up the general's ass: a hole in one, so to speak!

The general was curled up on the floor, right at the tee, writhing in pain and rubbing his anal orifice. Slowly I approached him, hiding my grin, my hand cupped over my mouth, trying not to gloat. Squatting down over him, my squash racquet parked in front of my mouth as a protective barrier, and with what I hoped was a reasonable imitation of respect and concern for his well-being in my voice, I asked Westy *do you need medical assistance Sir?*

The general's screeching quieted down to a low, miserable, guttural groan. He remained on the ground in a fetal position for a long time. Finally, with slow, agonizing, jerky movements, he was able to get to his knees; pause; stand up; limp through the small door of the squash court; move gingerly to the bench in the squash room; and lie down for ten minutes. We didn't talk; the general, emitting a consistent, quiet moan, was not really interested in frivolous conversation.

I had solved two problems with one squash ball: payback for the general's ridiculous behavior on the court and a sweet release of the insane anger that had been building up in me ever since walking through the sally port of the Academy months before.

Before leaving the squash area, in order to save face for the general, I mentioned *we should call the match a draw since the game had ended without completion.* He did not comment on that.

Westy and I never played squash together again. As the summer months approached, he did try to extract revenge on the tennis court. He hadn't forgotten the squash incident. He did, however, forget who he was dealing with. But that's another story for another time.

CHAPTER 47

MOON OVER THE HUDSON RIVER

wasn't overly worried about my squash match with the Supe. In sports, you quickly learn to slough off events that occur within a match so you can concentrate on the rest of play. If there were to be any ramifications from this incident, it was beyond my control. Apparently, I was one of those guys that either never got the word or was at the bottom of the hill when misfortune was flying downward. *Just add it to my expanding list of screw-ups as a Plebe,* I figured.

As we neared the end of Christmas "vacation," the movie *Breakfast at Tiffany's* came to the Cadet Theater. Not having seen any movies in six months, I thought it would be a real treat. I loved movies! Big screen, buttery popcorn, beautiful women, a good story; it didn't get any better than that.

My roommate Frank and I went to the theater with light hearts and great expectations. This proved to be a colossal blunder. Not the movie, which was terrific—Audrey Hepburn captured almost every cadet's heart, holding us all hostage with her beauty, poise and elegance—the error on my part was in going to the show at all. Its theme song "Moon River," was heart-wrenching to me, making me ache with loneliness, pine for love, any love. I cried buckets throughout the movie. I knew that I could be "waiting 'round the bend" for my "huckleberry friend" for a long time and she was just flat-out never going to appear at West Point; like a Passover seder, where you leave an extra place setting of food and wine for the prophet Elijah... but the guy never shows up!

"Moon River" reminded me of all the misery and empty dreams of the last almost-six months at the Academy. The melody alone took me down a path of loneliness. The lyrics only made the trek longer, more emotionally draining. And I couldn't get the damn song out of my head for days to come; "my huckleberry friend" failed to make an appearance repeatedly. Whether it was 1500 hours during the day or 0300 hours in my sleep, I kept seeing this particular scene, with Audrey's distraught face wrenching my heart.

This was Plebe Christmas, with my morass of heartache expanding. To try to break out of the blues, once again I turned to squash. I met up with Walt in the Mess Hall and he agreed we should practice harder for a longer amount of time. He laughed himself silly when I told him about my match with the Supe.

"I would have pulled the shot," he said in all seriousness after he calmed down. But...I secretly believed he admired me because I hadn't.

"Hey Stein," he went on, "You and I are going to the New Year's Ball." Walt had a lot of nicknames for me. My favorite was "the Florida Flash."

Walt called me Stein since, coming from his solid German heritage, he considered it a typical Jewish name. All the other guys called me "Kantro," but Walt enjoyed calling me "Stein." I knew he meant no offense; Walt didn't have an anti-Semitic bone in his body. He said it as an endearment. I excused him for his lack of ethnic sensitivity. After all, he was raised in New Jersey!

"Are you asking me out on a date?" I answered. "Walt, I didn't know you cared!"

"Not a date, stupid. We'll get the Cadet Hostess to fix us up with some girls from Ladycliff College. Come on, what do we have to lose?"

West Point had an Office of the Cadet Hostess. A whole department was dedicated to her mission: to teach etiquette, train cadets to dance, and match up cadets with acceptable young women for social experiences. The Cadet Hostess was a graceful, elegant, vivacious woman in her late sixties who clearly enjoyed her job and was excellent at it.

At an institution where no public display of affection (PDA) was allowed, it seemed contradictory to fix a young man up on a date and not allow him to hold hands or even walk too closely with the young woman. It was seriously frowned upon even for married officers to exhibit PDA with their wives. In the beginning of the first semester, I wondered why Upperclassmen were walking around holding typewriter cases when they were with their girlfriends. I eventually learned they had a USMA blanket inside the case. The Upperclassman and his date would stroll down to "Flirtation Walk," find a nice soft, clean patch of ground, spread the blanket out and relax together. My understanding was that, when the conversation slowed down, the making out sped up. That's why, if you saw an Upperclassman scurrying around carrying a typewriter case, he was happy and smiling.

Walt's plan was for us to go to the dance and have fun with two gorgeous young women, an evening hopefully with less pomp and more circumstance. Since I loved to dance, it sounded like a wonderful change from "Moon River" and my blues.

We both spruced up in the required uniform, went over to the Cadet Hostess's office to pick up our assigned dates. At the Cadet Hostess's arranged meeting area, we were introduced to the two young ladies. They presented themselves to us, knowing we were to spend an entire evening with them. Both had nice nails, tasteful light makeup and wore pretty dresses…but their excessive weight, the giddy expressions on their faces and their giggling, anxious, high pitched, whiny voices made everything else unimportant. They weren't the visions of loveliness we had expected.

After we were introduced and walked over to the building where the dance was being held, Walt and I excused ourselves to freshen up in the Men's room. It would have been extremely impolite for us to have left our dates high and dry...to slip out the backdoor undetected and jump into the Hudson River to kill ourselves. So, we discussed strategy, the pros and cons, and ramifications of how to approach the rest of the evening; sort of like we did during a doubles match. Coach Nordlie needed us for both tennis and squash, our Country needed us to fight foreign wars, and the two girls outside needed us to be good dates. We might have been the very first dates of their lives, so we needed to be extra chivalrous. Their needs "outweighed" our disappointment, as it were. We adopted the attitude that, regardless of who and what they were, how they acted or looked, they would become Cinderellas to us and we'd make the most of it. We agreed together to go overboard to show our dates a mighty good time.

So...Walt and I made sure we danced every dance, sang along to every song we knew the words to and complimented each of the girls as often as we could. We took them through Waltzes, Foxtrots, Lindys, Watusis, Twists, Locomotives, Swims, Jerks, Mashed Potatoes and Frugs. When they were out of breath and had developed sweat marks under their arms, stringy hair, runny makeup, and the blue bow of my date's dress had slipped down under her stomach making her look pregnant, it was time to call it a night.

We had treated our dates like Belles of the Gala, and, because of that, they were getting turned on and falling in love with us. It was a sad goodbye for them. Both girls gave us their telephone numbers and addresses and made us vaguely promise to take them out again. It was not an honor violation to promise this because, before we both died, we would take them out again IF they were still around and IF they called us and IF we were able to receive the call!

Weeks later, reflecting over that evening, I began to realize my date was probably a lovely person. She was certainly a good sport to put up with me that evening; I knew I could be very shallow at times.

I would have to watch out for that pissy attitude in the future...but I sure could dance!

That was the final social event of our Plebe Hanukamas vacation time, since the whole Corps was due to return within two days. I started to adjust mentally for the start of classes and the return to our "normal" West Point Plebe life. A good night's sleep would have been a big help, but "Moon River" continued to strafe my brain. That night, when I dreamt of Audrey Hepburn, she was wearing a blue bow around her waist and appeared a little pregnant. On her, it looked spectacular!

CHAPTER 48

THE MAN FROM HARVARD YARD

With the holidays over, the Upperclassmen returned from leave in January and the winter doldrums began to set in; this time period on the calendar, called "Doom and Gloom," would remain in effect through mid-March. Everyone was in survival mode, Plebes especially, as the chill of winter, its frost, wind and the frozen tundra of the normally green Plain continued without letup. The misty fog rising from the slick sidewalks blended in well with the dismal season. The days seemed to drag on and on, until, finally, you might hear a bird chirp and see a leaf on a tree, signalling the onset of spring.

At the end of March, squash season was over enfolding into my greatly anticipated tennis time. I was undefeated in squash in my Plebe year, but I took little happiness in my personal success, preferring to claim joy for the team instead, the best Plebe squash team in decades. The game itself continued to leave me feeling unfulfilled; I was greatly concerned how playing squash would affect my strokes on the tennis court.

My battles with the Tactical Department were a different story. Doom and Gloom time was like a boa constrictor around my neck, squeezing out whatever enthusiasm and pride I might have had for remaining a Plebe for as long as I had. Phone calls to my parents every sunday morning sounded like a broken record: "I hate it here, I'm so frustrated, I won my squash matches, I'm barely passing in all my academic subjects, I'm cold, lonely and want to come home!" Both of my parents would always reply, "Try for one more week, just one week and you'll see, it will be better."

Back in confinement most of the time on the weekends, it didn't ever seem to get better. My shoes weren't shiny enough; one single particle of dust was always found on my side of the room; there was always lint in the barrel of my M-1 rifle, even though I got up early to clean it a second time in ten hours; I was always in need of a haircut; and, of course, there was the issue of the improper fingernails. The days seem to drag slowly along, while the nights zipped by. My gray woolen trousers chafed the hair off my legs. Upperclassmen tempers were short and my demerit list long.

Then, two things happened simultaneously. First, spring arrived and with it, tennis started back up. Even with those lousy Davis Imperials, it was a joy to hit the ball once more. I had no feel, no flowing strokes nor proper timing but I was hitting tennis balls outside again…not that hard, black little sucker in an enclosed squash court. Johnny Leyerzaph warned me not to hit too hard in the beginning outdoors, nor to run too fast in the still-chilly air, because I would get shin splints—and I did. At eighteen, I rarely listened, even to good advice.

Secondly, Helen had run into my old flame, Jill David, on the Gainesville Campus. Jill had asked about me and wanted my address. Helen stated (in her only letter to me since I had left for college) that she had reluctantly given it to her.

On the day I received my first letter from Jill, I could not stop my heart from almost blasting through my chest cavity. My conscious thoughts centered only on her. Letters began to flow back and forth between us further reducing my study time. My academic standing was on shakier ground than ever before. I wrote to Jill about how excited I was to be playing tennis again and how I was so looking forward to our first dual match of the year against the Harvard Crimson freshman squad. During practice, however, my game was coming along so poorly that Coach Nordlie would just shake his head and walk away. After practice, he would call me over and ask me what I thought my problem was. My answer was always the same: "I can't get any feel with these damn racquets we're using; and my other problem is, I still don't like this place. Everything is the same, the routine, the uniforms, the formations, the rules, the rooms. I like variety, Coach, in my game and in my life. There's no variety here!"

What I didn't tell him was that I was also a little jealous of Walt Oehrlein. He was hitting the ball so cleanly and effortlessly, making me look like I just took up the game. Also, my level of concentration was poor. It was embarrassing to have such little focus and that needed to be fixed and quickly.

Coach looked at me, put his hand on my shoulder and calmly and quietly said, "Paul, give it one more week, things will change, you'll see. One more week." Had the coach been talking to my parents, for God's sake?!

The weeks passed by slowly until it was a gorgeous Saturday afternoon in mid April, sun shining, blue cloudless sky, the hum of huge crowds out to watch lacrosse, baseball, track and tennis matches, both varsity and freshman squads. The Varsity Corps Tennis Squad played first on the Library courts and were getting shellacked by Harvard. Since there were only six courts, when it came time for my match, I was relegated to a back court near the Bachelor Officers Quarters. Unlike the clay courts we practiced on, the BOQ had hard courts, with no backdrops to provide wind relief or visibility assistance. While Walt was playing on the first court with a grandstand of folks watching, I would be stuck out in the boonies, out of view from the world.

My opponent, the number-two player from Harvard, was Michael Lieberman, who seemed like a nice fellow, but he was left-handed. The lefty spin was reversed for me, so I would be hitting more backhands than forehands, with the ball spinning away from me rather than into my body. I hated lefties even more than I hated damp courts and heavy tennis balls that were hard to get under for a topspin player like myself.

I had a sinking feeling about the whole situation. When Coach Nordlie handed me the three balls and told me I was to play on the BOQ courts, I'd never even heard of them before; I had to ask him where they were. As Mike and I headed over there, we bullshitted about life at Harvard, how great it was. When he asked me how I was enjoying West Point, I had to answer honestly because of our honor code. "Hate this place," I said.

We took our ten-minute warmup. I was spraying the balls all over the place, my timing way off, my shin splints hurt, my elbow was painfull and my shoulder was quite stiff. I could see Mike was a terrific player. It was just going to be one of those days where just getting out of bed seemed to be the wrong thing to do. I thought I was experiencing a left-handed nightmare for sure.

The match started out poorly for me and got worse quickly. I didn't panic or lose my temper, but I was slightly intimidated by Mike's style of play, his ease and fluidity. I saw Coach Nordlie approaching the court from an oblique angle. He was alone.

He came up to the fence with a big smile on his face, even though the Varsity had lost 9-0. Even Richie Oehrlein had lost, which should have caused Coach to despair. Mike and I were switching sides, so Coach was able to speak to me. "What's the score, Paul?"

"6-1, 3-Love, Coach!" I answered quickly. He chuckled. "Great, keep up the good work," he said, waved and started back to the Library Courts.

"Coach," I yelled after him, "Why do you want me to keep up the good work? He is the one that's winning. I'm getting slaughtered! He's killing me!"

I thought Coach Nordlie would have a stroke on the spot. His smile turned lop-sided. His hotshot florida tennis recruit was getting his butt whipped; not what he expected. Coach ambled back to the Library Courts, a slight stagger to his normal lively step, to watch the rest of the freshman team getting blown away. Even Walt was having his troubles, I later learned.

I was greatly upset that I was letting Coach down. I realized at that moment that Coach Nordlie was one person in my life that I did not want to disappoint. He had put so much trust in me, had such confidence in my abilities and had treated me with so much kindness that the only way to repay him was to win tennis matches. I readjusted my tactics and started concentrating with a sharper focus. I forgot about Jill, Beast Barracks, my loneliness, my varying moods of despair, the hardships I had tolerated over the last couple of months. Throwing all negative thoughts aside, I used my trusted weapon, my topspin forehand, with a much greater sense of freedom.

Joy, positive feelings and momentum poured out of me as I kept repeating the mantra from my Richie Peters match a year ago: *One point at a time...this point is the only point I must win. This one point. Whatever it takes to win this one solitary point.*

I blasted Mike off the court 1-6, 6-3, 6-0, winning 12 games in a row. The "Florida Flash" was back! It was amazing how much better I could play when I was able to focus.

When it was doubles time, Harvard Mike and I rejoined the teams still in action. I had a hang-dog expression on my face as I threw my racquets down, rubbed my elbow and shoulder, and plodded over to the water fountain for a drink. I was happy I'd won the match, angry I played so poorly to start off, glad I could rally my thoughts and game back to some semblance of normal. Coach came over to me and said, as a father might to his son, "You did your best, Paul. It's only the start of the season; you'll get better."

"Thanks Coach," I said, "Your words always mean a lot to me." He was genuinely surprised when I told him the score and that I had won the match.

The sun was getting lower in the western sky. With the crowds dissipating slowly, the matches over, Coach Nordlie wore a huge smile as he rambled on. "I'm proud you pulled your match out Paul. You showed a lot of character to do that. That's the fighting spirit I knew you had in you. Fantastic win." Both of his teams had been beaten handily that day, yet he knew how to motivate and keep a positive attitude; that was his leadership in action.

I looked at the coach with a sly grin and quietly told him, "You didn't bring me to West Point to lose tennis matches. I'll always try my best to never let you down." He liked hearing that.

"And Coach," I continued, "Remember, I never give up, ever!" He liked hearing that even more.

I won every match I played that season. Coach Nordlie liked that the best!

CHAPTER 49

PARDONNEZ-MOI, MON CAPITAINE

I was not then, nor will never be, a linguist. I took french that year at West Point because, as I mentioned earlier, I already had two years of it in high school. I thought it would be a tremendous help to me in college where we were required to study a foreign language our first two years...maybe even lighten my academic load a little. French was always such a beautiful language to me: romantic, sensible and easier on my ears than russian, portugese, spanish, chinese, japanese and others.

My french instructor, Captain Lowder, always had a cheerful disposition and, in my humble opinion, spoke and taught the language as well as anyone could. My biggest problem in french class was that I didn't study, nor did I practice speaking the language. Either way, I was creating *un problème* for myself.

In every french class, cadets received an oral and a written grade. Captain Lowder would ask a question directly in french and we had to answer in french. He would then give some instruction about the language and either ask us to read a passage from the text or go to the chalkboard and write either an answer or a statement requested, all in french.

I could read the language out loud beautifully; my pronunciation was excellent, with a Parisian flair. My comprehension was another matter; the words went by so fast that I didn't know what I was reading or translating. I was also slow in hearing the language, even if I listened closely, so I always did poorly when answering any questions in French. My grades were barely passing at around 2.10.

Just as tennis season started, the captain announced that we would be watching a movie with the dialogue in french, no subtitles. Afterwards, there would be a written exam on the film, with all questions asked and answered in french.

Captain Lowder led us to a small theater. The lights were dimmed, the movie began, and I immediately closed my eyes and fell asleep. Movie or no movie, sleeping in class was forbidden! Sitting next to me was my classmate Bill Baker, a swimmer from Coral Gables, Florida and a real pain in the ass. He kept elbowing me in the side every time I would drift off, thinking he was doing me a favor. This continued for about twenty minutes: I would doze, Bill would elbow me, I'd wake up only to doze off again, and again Bill would elbow me.

About three-quarters of the way through, someone shook the crap out of me. My temper immediately got the best of me, and I cursed Bill out, in french, in order to be true to the class I was attending.

"*Sacre bleu,*" I mumbled, eyes still half-closed. "*Fermez la bouche et mangez-moi,* Asshole!" Since I didn't know the french term for asshole, I thought I was being cute.

However, it wasn't Bill who had shaken me. It was Captain Lowder! He wrote me up on a gigantic "quill" (offense), stating I had been "disrespectful to an officer, sleeping in class and neglectful of duty." The usual penalty for this was 50 one-hour punishment tours—walking the Area—and six months of confinement, with any remaining time to be rolled over to the following year. It also meant I would be taken off the tennis team and put back onto and into the indignity of Company tables in the Mess Hall...subjected again to Plebe square meals and *Bugle Notes* poop. Life could not have been any worse.

I got all spruced up to appear before the Regimental Board (who heard serious accusations and offenses) to explain my actions and receive my punishment. This would be a serious blow to whatever efforts I had made to stay at West Point for the last nine months.

Colonel Tarbox was the Regimental Tac Officer, in charge of the Board. His reputation was that of a "hanging judge." That was one notch below the designation of "giant prick." I knew I was in deep, deep shit.

"Sir, Cadet Kantrowich reports to the Regimental Commander as ordered," I said upon my arrival, my voice wavering, my right leg shaking, eyes partially closed from anxiety. When I fully looked up, I was staring into the infectious smile of Colonel "Hot Body" Fraser. Colonel Fraser—a voice of reason, father of Yearling Harvey Fraser, a man of unusually good cheer, a real human being who possessed empathy and compassion for people—had miraculously replaced Colonel Tarbox as Commander of the Regimental Board for that day only.

"What do you have to say for yourself, Cadet Kantrowich? These are serious charges leveled against you by an Officer of the United States Army! This isn't some Upperclass Cadet complaint against you," Hot Body added. The whole time he had a sly grin, almost a smirk; perhaps in lieu of saying aloud, "What the hell kind of a jam did you get yourself into now, Son?"

His son Harvey had recovered from his serious illness right after the holidays; that was a tremendous relief to me. It took him awhile to get back on track, but he was able to stay on as a cadet contingent upon performing all activities and pass all his courses. Harvey proved more than capable in all aspects of cadet academia and physical demands. He also never lost what made him such a great guy which was his kindness and thoughtfulness to others. He appreciated my friendship and I his. I guess he'd spoken to his father at some point about me.

As succinctly as I could, I explained my actions to Colonel Fraser, all of which stemmed from falling asleep during the movie. I swore that I would never knowingly have been disrespectful to any officer, much less the instructor, Captain Lowder.

Colonel Fraser interrupted me. "Do you mean that because you were asleep, you were not in full control of your actions?" he asked. "And that, had you been awake, those actions would NOT have occurred?" "Yes, Sir" I responded. No other member of the seven panel Board spoke or questioned me.

Still grinning, Colonel Fraser slammed down his gavel and announced, "Eight and eight, sleeping in class, next case." This meant I had received just eight demerits and eight confinements; my place on the team was still secure. How Harvey's dad knew beforehand that I was up for a Regimental Board and stood to lose my tennis status was beyond my comprehension. Upon hearing my punishment, I was as grateful to him as I had ever been to anyone in my entire life, except my own dad, of course.

The next day, as I approached Captain Lowder's office, I rehearsed what I would say in apology—in french, so he'd know I was sincere. Upon hearing me grovel, the captain complimented me on my pronunciation and explained that he felt bad about the situation but was obligated to fulfil his sworn duty as an instructor who was responsible for me. He gracefully accepted my apology, adding that he respected me for doing so in person and in his native tongue.

I hadn't realized it before, but Captain Lowder was a real tennis enthusiast and, without my knowledge, had been following my exploits on the courts. I think we each gained a little respect for each other as a result of the incident. Every class, he would ask me to read aloud because he knew my reading was decent. For the oral question, he would always ask me the same question, "*Vous jouez au tennis aujourd'hui, Cadet Kantrowich?*" ("Did you play tennis today") and I would respond, "*Oui, Mon Capitaine, je joue au tennis aujourd'hui!*" (I did play tennis today). He would then ask "*Vous allez triompher?*" (Did you win?)I would always respond, "*Oui, Mon Capitaine, je vais triompher!* (Yes, captain, I won!)

Captain Lowder came to every one of my tennis matches and was my biggest fan at West Point. I usually got close to a 3.0 grade in oral, which balanced out my 1.5 in writing. That allowed me to continually have a passing grade. Because he always taught the last section by class ranking, that is where I had a permanent home. Because of his kindness, I was able to pass his course and, eventually, at least learn to ask where the bathroom was when I was travelling in France years later...*ou est le salle de bain, s'il vous plait!*

CHAPTER 50

JILL AGAIN

That initial letter from Jill dredged up a slew of emotions, adding to the normal chaos already clogging my brain. I didn't know what to think about it or about her.

Spring had arrived, my status at West Point was fragile at best, my hormones on fire and, while tennis eased some pressures, the "system" was still wearing me down. Confinement stifled any possibility of enjoyment; loneliness was crushing my spirit. Jill's letters were like eating a chocolate candy bar instead of starving: incredibly delicious but not very nutritious. They left me with an insatiable desire for more.

Coach Nordlie knew the emotional roller coaster I was having being a cadet. My parents, my substitute Plebe parents Rhoda and Hank, my roommates, my teammates...they all knew what was happening to me, and that I wasn't a typical cadet Plebe. My mind was always elsewhere, my poor performance revealing this character defect.

But it didn't matter. Wanting to quit the Academy but following through with it were two different things. "One week at a time" now became one hour at a time, the clock ticking excruciatingly slow. The beautiful weather, the excitement of spring only exacerbated my flailing mental state. Being with Jill was the only thing, besides tennis, that I was sure I wanted. Everything else was sort of up for grabs.

I had worshipped Jill in high school; she was the essence of my being, the spark of love that electrified all of life. Her smile melted my heart, her confidence boosted mine. The way she walked, talked, dressed, fidgeted; the way she wrinkled her forehead when contemplating something important; her every move overwhelmed my every thought.

Jill was cute and perky. When she put her arm around my waist or her hand on my shoulder, a jet stream of emotions went through my mind, taking bits and pieces of me and accelerating them out into the universe. My tennis game suffered when she came to a match. It's difficult to serve an American twist consistently well when you are sporting an erection.

When she dumped me for that college guy, I took it harder than a punch in the gut. I couldn't breathe, eat, sleep or concentrate. I threw all my frustrations into tennis with unparalleled tenacity. Rather than a blast of excitement, senior year of high school was a time of emotional and sexual confusion.

So, when I received her first letter, "Hi there stranger, how are you?" her words shattered the bonds that were wrapped around my good judgment and common sense. Once again, I was smitten. And she was a great correspondent, writing volumes, mostly about herself, but the letters kept appearing during mail calls. She was a master of sexual innuendo, and I would respond with testosterone-laced metaphors, imagery and bravado, suggesting greater expectations to come. My letters to her became epic works of vital importance. My studies suffered. I didn't care. Jill was like a drug.

We never spoke on the telephone; I never had any money to afford a long- distance telephone call. The only way I could be reached was through the Orderly Room telephone anyway and then, only for emergencies. I saved my one phone call a week to bitch to my parents about how miserable I was.

My darling Jill and I were together again...just not physically. There was my potential summer leave, if I made it that far, and the prospect injected excitement back into my life. We started making plans to rekindle our love. We built our future relationship in our letters, in love with the fantasies of each other that we were creating. I disregarded all her previous infidelities.

I threw myself into tennis with great zeal and passion. Fifteen opponents out of fifteen fell by the wayside and an equal number of doubles, too. Walt, at number one singles, played tougher opponents than I, but in my matches, I was relentless, with a frenzy of topspin forehands, high kicking serves and deft drop shots. Even with those troublesome Imperial racquets, I overcame my lack of feel and whip to dominate play. Paul Kantrowich felt like himself again on the tennis court: stalking, pacing, grumbling and winning—always winning—playing to the crowds that began to gather regularly. Coach Nordlie had no complaints; the whole team was doing extremely well, with Walt, Darrah, Wollen, Shuford and Forrest admirably pulling their share of the load.

My grades had barely improved ever so slightly. Though I wasn't going to set any Academy records for academic excellence, it was what I needed to pass all my courses. My buckling down had been a blessing. It was my lack of leadership skills, poor adherence to the rules and regulations of cadet life, and my personal daily performance, however, that still placed me near the bottom of my class in cadet ranking.

Even though I was racking up the wins on the tennis court, room confinement continued. The Audrey Hepburn movie I had seen remained the only one I would see all year. The only time I was allowed off the reservation was to play tennis matches. The last time I had seen Rhoda and her kids was the babysitting and roasted chicken incident. I spent most of my confinement in my room, writing letters to Jill and wallowing in self-pity.

At the beginning of the tennis season, Dr. Hank had fitted me with contact lenses at the hospital, making me eyeglass-free for the first time in my life. The polymethylmethacrylate, hard lenses he prescribed were new in the marketplace and I was Hank's guinea pig. They hurt like hell as I began wearing them but got more comfortable as the weeks went by. They changed my baby blue eyes into a sparkly, piercing, darker shade of royal blue; I hoped Jill would like that, as well as some of the muscle I had added to my physique.

In anticipation of our summer reunion, my excitement was building. My mind exploded with unrealistic fantasies of sex, marriage, children and a happy, satisfied life away from the military, away from West Point.

While I was in the process of rekindling our long-distance love, I didn't realize that Jill was fueling campfires of casual sex on the University of Florida campus every week with an assortment of young men. In only the second letter my sister Helen ever wrote to me several weeks later, she cryptically mentioned, "Be careful!" But the prospect of having my girlfriend back in my life, it left me too excited to ask what the warning meant.

Now, fully determined and committed to get through my Plebe year, I continued to knuckle down in all areas of cadet life: shinier shoes, cleaner room, tighter bed, better classroom attention, more adherence to all the regulations I had come to abhor. My only goal for the next month was to complete the year of being a Plebe. Jill was my only future destination.

CHAPTER 51

THE RITES, RIGHTS AND WRONGS OF SPRING

Aside from the renewed beauty of the environment, one of the great springtime happenings at West Point was the end of "Doom and Gloom" on the reservation. Gray wool trousers gave way to lighter, heavily starched whites, sports flourished all over the Academy grounds, smiling cadets had a bouncy skip in their steps. The sun was out, the air was fresh, and all the athletes were strutting their Corps Squad stuff. Company sport intramurals were in full swing.

Visitors abounded on the sidewalks between the Thayer Hotel and Trophy Point on the weekends. Upperclassmen's typewriter cases dotted the landscape. Cadets' expectations of the end of the academic year blossomed like the flowers that grew in the window boxes of General Westmoreland's house. The trees and gardens in full bloom, the increase in outdoor activities and the "pass in review" of marching cadets parading in full regalia all blended to create excitement and spontaneity on campus.

Back home, I had always loved saturdays. Saturdays meant a tennis tournament almost every weekend somewhere in South Florida, with a chance to see the results of my hard practice, travel to a different town or small city, no homework, a little beachtime, maybe a date, perhaps a movie or just living life. On saturdays at West Point, we had classes at 0715 hours, room inspections after our last class. In the late morning I had a tasty training meal of steak, a tennis match in the early afternoon and then sweet freedom until suppertime... but confinement in the evening and all sunday after Jewish Chapel.

I always won my wednesday and saturday singles match as fast as I could. This gave me a little extra free time, before my doubles match, to observe the world around me: a burst of much-needed freedom to loll around, talk to civilians, root for my teammates. Since the Library courts were adjacent to the main road that swung around the Plain, there were visitors and sports fans galore to engage with. I also had an opportunity to see our baseball and lacrosse teams in action. It never seemed to rain on wednesday or saturday. It was always a sunny, festive day. It was still my favorite day of the week.

Sundays were a different story altogether. After early morning formation and breakfast, all the cadets would form up for sunday Chapel. The Catholics would climb stairs or march around for ¼ mile. The Protestants would climb the base of the hill or march around for about ¼ mile. The Jews had to march about 1½ miles to the Old Cadet Chapel, which on sundays was called the Jewish Chapel. (Of course, we had to shlep back the same 1½ miles after services.) During services, I always prayed earnestly to God to help me make the right decisions in my new life, to guide me in the direction of righteousness and humility...and to help me pass all my academic courses. (I forgot to ask for world peace and to solve the world's hunger problems.)

After lunch, sunday afternoons and evenings meant confinement for a screw-up like me. While confinement gave me a lot of time to think, thinking wasn't the best activity for me to engage in. The less time I had to contemplate my life, the better.

It always seemed to rain on sundays. My weekly telephone call to my parents on sunday was never particularly uplifting and there was no mail delivery on sundays either. Though I thought about my sisters all the time and missed them, I hadn't spoken to Helen since I left home and didn't even know how to reach Wilma.

It was right about this time in the academic year that I found out a startling fact that jolted me, chilled me to the bone. I learned that, if you flunked out of West Point or if you decided to leave on your own or got kicked out for any reason, you had an obligation to go directly into the U.S. Army for two years. *WHOA!*

At eighteen I wasn't prepared to go into the Army; that wasn't the deal I had made when I was recruited. I wasn't convinced I'd be ready at age twenty-one either, upon graduation, but was sure it would be better to go as an officer than as an enlisted soldier. That was the commitment I knowingly made. This new piece of information certainly woke me up!

If I was going to leave West Point, it would be on my own terms, not the U.S. government's. I shortened my letters to Jill, put an end to a lot of my daydreaming and made a serious effort with my studies. I began hitting the books with as much energy as I used to stroke my topspin forehand.

But those lonely sunday afternoons were difficult. Depression would hit me hard, sometimes flattening me. I would sink into a morass of woe-is-me. My sunday prayers at Jewish Chapel and the pep talk from my parents were quickly forgotten after the long walk back from the Old Chapel. In their place an awareness of everything that was missing in my life seeped in. Walking on the beach, getting a slice of pizza, holding a girl's hand, wearing Jockey underwear instead of these stupid boxer shorts; important stuff in an 18-year-old's life.

Every cadet room had a rectangular, heavy, plastic card attached to the wall, just past the door frame, with a sliding arrow pointing to a location or destination of each occupant in that room. The card was used to mark the location of cadets in confinement. Inspections would take place by the cadet OIC of that company to make sure each confined man was where he should be. If you weren't in your room, an authorized location had to be marked on the card, either latrine, orderly room or library. If your room was inspected and your card was marked for one location, but you were in another improper location, it was an honor violation. The inspection times varied, but I had figured out that usually, after a 1430 hours or 1500 hours inspection, there wasn't another until just before the supper formation. The OIC would stick his head in the room and yell, "All right?" and you would answer the question with the same, "All right!" That constitued the inspection.

Also, on sundays, confined Plebes sat at a Company table in the Mess Hall for 40 minutes of Hell, as there was always a chance for some sadistic Upperclassman who had just broken up with his girlfriend to dump all over us. One sunday afternoon, I'd had a rough going at lunch, so I was feeling hugely sorry for myself. After the room inspection occurred at 1500 hours, I decided to unmark my card and take a risky but quick walk in the rain to get some emotional release.

Ah! It was a Gene Kelly moment, albeit sans singing and dancing, since it had been raining outside and continued to come down hard. It was also a violation of the rules of confinement, but not an honor violation being away from my room. An unmarked card meant you weren't anywhere indicated on the card, so you weren't lying about where you were, you just weren't in your room (or anywhere else you were allowed to be). Nothing would happen if I got back before the room was inspected again.

Twenty minutes later I realized my extreme stupidity. Why risk anything at this point? I turned around, determined to go directly back to the barracks. While I was out in the pouring rain, feeling about as sorry for myself as I ever had, an old, beat-up 1953 Ford sedan drove by, stopped, and a young woman, though older than me, rolled down the window, leaned over and yelled, "It's pouring out! Come on, get in, I'll give you a ride." I did not hesitate.

"You look like you could use a friend right now," she said, eyes sparkling. "My name's Mary. I'm a U.S. Army registered nurse at the base hospital, what's your name?"

I introduced myself and explained that I had been taking an unauthorized walk to clear my depression, realized it was a mistake of judgement and was headed back to confinement in my room. Mary looked at me with compassion.

"You Plebes have a difficult year to go through. It's a hard, tough year and you are in confinement as well?" I explained why, as rainwater sluiced off my raincoat, making a real mess on her cloth car seat. She was very sympathic.

Mary wasn't beautiful, but she had a fresh, clean, scrubbed look, and a light, perfumed fragrance surrounded her. She was a good listener and her eyes twinkled when she heard my litany of woe. With a subtle air of authority, she made a sudden left turn onto a side road and pulled over into a little nook in the woods and parked the car. Looking directly at me she said "You are a cute guy, Paul, and, it seems, we could both use a little cheering up right now. Why don't we cheer each other up a little bit, okay?"

Mary slyly unbuttoned her blouse and proceeded to initiate me into a few of the sexual arts I had only fantasized about. The entire time, I did not think of Jill, even for a moment. All I had space for in my brain was what was happening, our frenzied activity, my body reacting to our primal urges. Was this a dream?

No! I wasn't dreaming. I had finally laid my virginity to rest. Afterwards, she dropped me off in time for me to get to my room before the card inspection; *whew!* Next came dinner formation. It was pouring outside, but the black clouds, congestion and constriction in my mind had all vanished.

So had Mary. I tried calling her the following tuesday and was told by her roommate that she had been transferred to Fort Riley, Kansas and left on monday. I had just missed her.

I thought about Jill, wondered about fidelity, about my confusion around sex and love, and about all the plans we'd made for summer break. Had I been unfaithful? The commitment to Jill was on paper, I reasoned, in letters. It was a discussion, only a future possibility. It was not what was happening in the present.

But Mary, as luck would have it, had certainly been present.

CHAPTER 52

THE MACARTHUR INCIDENT

General George Patton's statue stood before the Library tennis courts, resolute and authoritarian, guarding the corner of the main thoroughfare through the Academy. The statue had been dedicated in 1950. Every time I went to play a tennis match on those courts I would think of this man and the driving force he had been in World War II. His controversial attitudes and performance certainly carved his own section out of military history.

Many other U.S. Army officers have been honored in different ways at West Point over the years. Many of them had etched their own personal character and persona in history and were well deserving. But the favorite son of West Point—aside from Colonel Sylvanus Thayer, considered the Father of the Academy—would be General of the Army (Ret.) Douglas MacArthur.

There had never been a persona so large nor an impact so great in defining the traits of leadership in the U.S. military as MacArthur; even General Dwight D. Eisenhower—who, with his quiet and sensitive nature, became President—took a backseat to the flamboyant, dynamic MacArthur; especially at West Point, where he had been a cadet, returned to the Academy as Superintendent years later and was a living legend. Neither Robert E. Lee nor Ulysses S. Grant could hold a candle to the exceptional, larger-than-life General MacArthur.

And so, in the spring of 1962, the Corps of Cadets and the Academy buzzed like a swarm of bees over a blossoming flower bed. General MacArthur was coming to West Point to receive the 1962 Sylvanus Thayer Award and address the Corps of Cadets at a luncheon. There was to be a parade in his honor, and he would "troop the line" as the Corps stood at attention...an honor reserved only for the highest of visiting dignitaries, usually Heads of State.

I wasn't in that parade because we had a tennis march afterwards, but I was among the Cadets of the Corps in the Mess Hall, where the speech was to be given, awaiting "Attention to Orders" and the introduction of the general who would then receive the award and make his speech. I sat at the Corps Squad table, barely awake. We had finished eating and I was concentrating on my upcoming tennis match and my memories of Mary. It was an extremely wonderful interlude.

MG Westmoreland's introduction, with its long list of General MacArthur's accomplishments and successes, took about fifteen minutes. When I was much younger, I had seen MacArthur's famous "I Shall Return" speech, concerning his activities in WWII, on the *Victory at Sea* television documentary series. I remembered his corn cob pipe. Now I was parked in a chair along the wall, in an inconspicuous spot of the West Point Mess Hall, dozing off from Westmoreland's bombastic buttering up of the guest speaker.

In contrast, General MacArthur was one of the most eloquent and dynamic speakers I had ever heard. He began his speech with a humorous story about that morning. When he was leaving his hotel, the doorman wished him a good morning and asked, "Where are you headed today, general?" MacArthur replied he was going to West Point.

"It's a beautiful place, West Point," the doorman unknowingly remarked. "Have you ever been there before?" This drew quite a laugh and applause.

Speaking without notes, MacArthur discussed the nobility of the professional soldier and how duty, honor, and country were words we should strive to uphold as people; particularly, as soldiers. Duty, honor and country defined us, he said; they made us strong enough to know when we were weak and brave enough to face danger when we were fearful.

What I heard of his speech was terrific, but I was a terrible listener. I got the gist of his message, so I fell asleep, like I usually did in a lecture hall. General MacArthur was legendary by now, so whether I listened to his speech or slept through it wasn't going to change that, but duty, honor and country had to be understood individually for each person. I believed what the general was saying. At the age of eighteen, however, I wasn't mature enough to understand all the ramifications of his words.

The general received his award; I had a little nap. Not all of us were cut out for greatness. In my parents' and my sisters' eyes, I was great. That was more than enough for me.

I am sure MacArthur's speech will be forever carved into the annals of West Point history. It will be read over and over by every new cadet and military person from generation to generation. I believed at the time that, if I heard a full recording of the speech again, many years later, I would realize I had caught all the important parts, even in my semi-comatose state. That's how great an orator MacArthur was.

I began to wonder if I could ever be as passionate as MacArthur was about West Point. To date, being at this institution had not been such a great experience for me. Many of the rules and regulations seemed silly; the attitudes and actions by Upperclassmen were undignified. Some concepts of leadership didn't mesh with my thinking. While MacArthur was in love with the Academy, I doubted I ever would be.

My nodding off during such an historic event did stir up a little guilt. I hadn't comprehended before what the true meaning of West Point would be to someone else for their entire life. I now knew what it meant to General MacArthur, but I was convinced it wouldn't envelop me as it had him. These guilty mind meanderings gave me much to think about; perhaps I would do so later in the evening. After all, it was a Saturday night. I would have all the time needed to reflect while sitting in confinement in my room…alone.

CHAPTER 53

GOING HOME

The first week of June 1962 was called June Week, a very special time at the Academy. It was a week of true joy, happy celebrations, personal transition and turmoil. It provided the perfect time for deep, personal reflection. For a Plebe, June Week was the greatest period of relief. Plebes could take a deep breath for a change. Finishing this crazy, fucking first year was a marvelous ego boost for myself and my classmates; we could finally put it behind us. I wasn't sure if I would ever get over the hazing, the physical abuse, my insecurity and emotional upheavals, but I was determined to give it my best shot and put the present into the past after today.

Plebes had made it through to become Yearlings—sophomores at a regular college. The Yearlings moved up to take on the responsibilities of more leadership as Cows, or juniors. Cows moved up to become Firsties, or seniors, where they'd be responsible for the leadership of the Corps of Cadets.

Firsties were now graduating. Some would marry; most would be moving into the U.S. Army as Second Lieutenants and finding their new duty stations. Some graduates were allowed into a sister service like the Marines or Air Force. It was a great relief that the academic year had ended and there was the promise of a bright and exciting future on the horizon for every cadet. There wasn't one cadet out of the entire Corps that didn't have something or someone to look forward to.

Most of the Firsties were jubilant, joking around and having a grand old time, waiting to throw their white hats into the air at the graduation ceremony attended by family and close friends. The ones who truly loved West Point, who bled West Point black and gold, walked around morose for a short while, as they would miss their buddies and the sense of belonging, not yet realizing they could carry West Point in their hearts and minds, as well as wear it on their hats and jackets. Forever! There would be yearly Founder's Day celebrations around the world, Army-Navy football competition and, of course, war, which usually reunited fellow members within the U.S. Armed Forces.

For me, these arduous eleven months, first as a New Cadet, then as a Plebe, is best described as having been tough, exhausting and harder than anything else I had ever done in my life. Final exams were over, grades were posted; I had passed all my classes and had done what the Academy had asked of me. While my cadet standing placed me in the bottom five percent of the class academically, I was now "The Florida Flash" on the tennis court, with a reputation of being a winner…at least on the fields of friendly strife. I had made more friends than enemies but, without the much-needed assistance from some very wonderful people, my career would have been over after that first day of Beast Barracks. There were too many people to thank, not enough time to do that. I just wanted to go home. Most of my classmates' hearts were now here at West Point while my heart had never left Florida.

Orders were cut to report to Camp Buckner, the West Point summer training camp for Yearlings, during the first week of July 1962. I called Coach Nordlie to say goodbye. I called Rhoda and Hank. I had a short conversation with Walt and some of my teammates. It really was time for me to leave. Leaving occupied all my thoughts.

At the Cadet Store, I had bought my first suit, a blue one; two white shirts; a striped tie, a black belt to match my spit-shined black cadet shoes, all completed my clothes ensemble to travel home in. I was able to retrieve the slacks, shirt and carrying case I came with on my first day of Beast Barracks. They were all the clothes I had; I stuffed them with my toiletries and underwear into my travel bag. I packed up all my cadet paraphernalia, put it all in my footlocker and packing boxes, and stashed them in the storage area of the barracks to be picked up IF I returned in July. My brain was too addled to predict the future. July was a distant thought for now and I wasn't making any decisions about my future today or even tomorrow. All decisions about my future would have to wait.

I was to call my parents to tell them my arrival day and, since I had no airline reservation, also promised to call again from the New York Idlewild Airport when I knew my flight number and arrival time in Miami. They would pick me up. I wanted to see them and my sister Helen before contacting anyone else.

It was a sunny day when I hopped on the Trailways Bus headed toward New York City. First, the bus passed through the front gate of the reservation at West Point, traveled through the town of Highland Falls and then onto the Palisades Parkway heading south. The air seemed fresher, the cloudless sky a more vibrant blue, the birds chirping louder, the landscape greener. My brain seemed less congested as I moved through the bus. I sat taller in my seat. Looking out of the bus window, I saw, with clarity, the meandering Hudson River to my left, sunlight glistening off its calm surface, here and there a ripple, a multitude of boats anchored in the water. My body began to relax.

I had brought two tennis racquets home with me, and I started caressing their smooth forms, sliding my fingers over their strings, fumbling with them as I sat in my bus seat. If I returned to West Point, I would be bringing my own racquets back and saying good riddance to these Davis Imperials. If I returned to West Point it would have to be because I wanted to and not because I had to.

Off the reservation, I could breathe freely again. My mind, however, couldn't relax enough to rid itself of my consternation about the past, my trepidation about the future, or the frustration of needing, yet again, to make huge life decisions.

What would my life be like tomorrow, next week, next month? I had no idea where I was going other than in the present moment, right now on a Trailways bus, heading for a plane to Miami to see my family and my girlfriend. That was all I needed to concern myself with. However, my head was off to the races, worrying about everything else going on in the entire world.

Part of me yearned for the day when, perhaps many years in the future, I could step out of a Manhattan hotel and have the doorman ask me, "Where are you going today, Dr. Kantrowich?" My response would be "Upstate New York, Sal."

He, in turn, might then respond, "If you pass by West Point you should stop there, it's a beautiful place! West Point, have you ever been there?"

As I sat on that Trailways Bus, I envisioned the Long Gray Line marching through history with me standing on the street corner as they marched by. I would politely watch, then wave them on, wave goodbye. I really didn't have enough West Point in my bloodstream to want to be in the U.S. Army now nor return to the Academy for Yearling Camp Buckner.

However, it was June 1962. I was only eighteen years old, still on the march, with a whole month to decide my future.

At this moment in time, I was still a Jew at the Point.

EPILOGUE

After that rough first year at the Academy, I made the decision and did return for my second year. I eventually graduated in June 1965 ranking 583rd out of the 595 in my class. When I walked up the stairs at graduation, Colonel Fraser got out of his seat on the podium and stopped me before I could receive my diploma. He stuck out his hand to shake mine first! What further held up the graduation ceremonies was a group of about ten other faculty members, following his lead, shaking my hand as well before I could get to the presenting dignitary. None of these men thought I would ever graduate! This meant more to me than being awarded the United States Military Academy Athletic Board Award for the outstanding player on the 1965 tennis team, my singular achievement.

Walter Oehrlein and I won the 1965 Eastern Intercollegiate Doubles title together but, once again, I lost to Arthur Ashe and his partner, this time, Charlie Pasarell at the National Intercollegiates that year.

After graduation from West Point, I served almost five years in the United States Army, resigning with the rank of Captain. I served in Vietnam from 1967 to 1968 as a Ranger Advisor out of Tan Son Nhut, lucky to get through the Tet and May North Vietnamese offensives. While I was awarded numerous decorations by both the United States government and the Republic of Vietnam for my service and special achievements, I later trashed all my medals in the dumpster.

It was my way of protesting the war. These were my personal actions, spurred by my own beliefs and not a reflection on anyone else. I still hold to those principles today.

It took me forty-five years after graduation to return to West Point and only then because I was cajoled into it by my tennis buddy and classmate Walter. During that visit I met Coach Jim Poling, who had been coaching the men's tennis team for several years previously; he is truly one of the outstanding tennis coaches in the United States. Walter, Jim and tennis, are the only reasons I have been back to West Point several times since. Still, every time I set foot onto the reservation grounds of the United States Military Academy at West Point, I get a mild tremor in my body as flashbacks of Beast Barracks flood my senses. Some things cannot be forgotten and perhaps shouldn't be.

The Academy, however, has changed over the years and I salute many of these changes, no pun intended. The one aspect that will never change there is the mission of turning young men and women into efficient, dedicated and patriotic leaders for our nation. My message to any young person desiring military life and service to our country is *go for it!* But…be prepared for a lot of "interesting" experiences.

Having traveled widely around the world, I still believe the Unites States of America is the finest country of all. Yes, we have a multitide of major, unsettling difficulties but leaders arise from generation to generation to help prod us forward. The men of West Point, and now I am happy to say women as well, are part of that leadership surge.

Freedom is not free; we must continually work to insure it exists and I applaud our country's effort in doing do. I used to wonder why we must be the world's police force. As I have gotten older, I realize the USA isn't just our country, but a beacon of hope and morality around the world.

That was until recently. I wrote this book to express my feelings about how leadership, used inappropriately, can lead to authoritarianism and chaos. As a country we have made mistakes and drifted off course. We had a President who never considered anything or anyone but himself, breaking down our democratic institutions and bending them to his own will. I feel confident, however, that America will survive and thrive again. Our country's foundation is based on equality and justice, not for the few but for all. This is a pledge we all have made and should never lose sight of. It is what makes our country endure.

West Point Class of 1965, "Strength and Drive", "Son's of the Greatest Generation", has been in my bones since I stepped out of Aunt Miriam's Chevy. I can't change that! My emotions, during my experiences there, even until this day, continue to do a loop-de-loop, both bad and good. However, my admiration for the men I shared these experiences with, has never waivered one bit. It was and is still strong.

I made it through West Point by never quitting, even when that might have seemed the most sensible option. Maybe it was from fear of losing "face" with family and friends. Perhaps it was my stubbornness not letting circumstances control me; or maybe it was simply my competitive spirit. I was extremely lucky, however, to have an assortment of wonderful people to help me as, I believe, I could not have done that by myself.

My reasons for not leaving didn't matter in 1961 nor do they matter today. It's all history anyway. In June 1962, I was still a Jew at the Point and the system needed fixing. I am happy to report many good changes have occurred. Maybe not enough change yet...but still change.

It's now 2021. I can now report, I am a Jew from the Point.

While I experienced a few acts of anti-Semitism at West Point that further exacerbated my experience of being miserable and pushed me to my limits during my Plebe year, the Academy was and is not inherently anti-Semitic.

To paint it as a hotbed of religious discrimination certainly is not my purpose in relating my story. West Point is not like that. The treatment I received there, from a handful of bullies, could have happened anywhere in the United States during the 1960's and even now.

I am happy to report that today, a true Jewish lifeline exists at West Point for any student choosing to use it. There is a beautiful Jewish Chapel and a thriving group of Jewish cadets that welcomes not only the military community but the local Jewish community as well.

As I previously mentioned, from generation to generation, Americans always come forward with their generosity or insight to make our lives better. Here is an example of three men, who happened to be Jewish, who have done just that. I salute them!

A special thanks should go out to Lewis L. Zickel, Colonel, USAR, USMA Class of 1949 who wrote "The Jews of West Point in the Long Gray Line" published in 2009. His comprehensive look and discussion of Jewish cadets goes into detail about personal and collective experiences throughout the Academy's history. He garnered comments from hundreds of Jewish graduates about their experiences. I was one of those graduates who participated, although I did not feel my experiences at West Point brought me closer to Judaism.

Colonel Zickel was instrumental in supervising the design and construction of the beautiful West Point Jewish Chapel that now proudly graces the Academy grounds and helped establish the Academy's first Jewish Chaplaincy. He was a Mensch!

A special thanks also needs to be shouted out to Alan (Class of 1951) and Herb (Class of 1958) Lichtenberg who, in 1999, were responsible for construction of the "Lichtenberg Tennis Center" on Academy grounds. It's one of the nicest indoor tennis facilities in the country and, had it been there during my cadet days…well, maybe I might have eventually beaten Walter in singles!!

GLOSSARY

Cadre: The staff of cadet or Army personnel that manage operations and training.

Corps of Cadets: The entire student body at the Academy.

Corps Squad: Varsity or Freshman sports team.

Cow: A third-year student at USMA.

Duty Officer: The Army officer in charge of cadets during day or night activities.

Firstie: Fourth-year student at USMA.

Hot Body: A Mechanic's Course term for an object having a large amount of energy; a nickname for Col. Fraser from the Mechanic's Course.

Gator: A student at the University of Florida in Gainesville.

Lady: Upperclassmen's epithet directed at New Cadets; a weak man. Also "Little Girl."

Long Gray Line: West Point Alumnae.

MG: Major General.

OIC: Officer-in-Charge.

Plebe: A first-year student at USMA.

Plebe Mom: An officer's wife who assists her husband in helping a Plebe.

Plebe Pop: An officer who helps a Plebe, like a surrogate father.

Smackhead: Epithet used by Upperclassmen to address New Cadets: moron, idiot, stupid person.

MSGT: Non-commissioned officer's rank of Master Sergeant, three ranks above Sergeant.

Supe: The Superintendant or number one Officer at USMA

Table Commandant: Senior Cadet in charge of a ten-man table in the Cadet Mess Hall.

Westy: Nickname for MG William Westmoreland.

Yearling: A second-year student at USMA.

PERTAINING TO PLACE

Academy: Shorthand for the United States Military Academy at West Point, NY.

North Area: Barracks Area north and west of the central or main section of barracks.

Reservation: The land upon which the Academy is located.

Trophy Point: Northern section of campus with a strategic view of the Hudson River.

USMA: United States Military Academy.

PERTAINING TO BUILDINGS AND STRUCTURES

Beast Barracks: The barracks area housing New Cadets during initial summer training. Also: the nickname for New Cadets' summer training period of trials and tribulations.

Poop Deck: Upper-level area of Cadet Mess Hall where visitors, guests and senior cadet staff assemble to eat. Announcements are also made from the Poop Deck.

PERTAINING TO MOVEMENT

Bracing: Body position straight, hands to the sides, chin in, forward gaze.

Double-timing: Running.

Fall Out: Release from present activities. Example: Plebe is bracing and told to "fall out," relax, hang loose.

Hogging the Tee: Not moving from the center of the squash court to allow your opponent access to the ball.

Square Meal: Sitting at attention on the edge of chair seat, chin in, raising empty fork directly from the body's lap area to the plate (to get food), raising arm directly up to chin level, then moving loaded fork in a straight line to the mouth.

Take Seats: Sit down.

PERTAINING TO UNIFORMS, RIFLE AND APPEARANCE

Class "A": Gray pants, dark shirt and tie worn in the classroom.

Present Arms: Salute with right hand tipped to forehead. With a rifle, holding rifle in vertical position direction in front of the body from knees to eyes.

Port Arms: Position rifle out in front of the body with both hands, rifle at a 45-degree angle to the body.

Tar Bucket: Cadet parade bonnet.

Triple "A": Army Athletic Association logo.

Strac: Looking sharp in dress and appearance, ready to go.

MISCELLANEOUS

Brown Boy: Comforter or padded blanket on cadet's bed.

Bugle Notes: Small book of aphorisms, songs, rules and regulations memorized by Plebes.

Doom and Gloom: Depressing time period at USMA from

New Year's until springtime.

Gourd: Chin.

NATO: North American Treaty Organization, international military alliance with USA and European countries from World War II.

Not Bad: Good.

Quill: Certificate awarding demerits to cadets for mistakes.

Poop: Information.

Recognition: Upperclassman's act of befriending a Plebe upon final day of Plebe Year

Spizzerinctum: Old-fashioned word used by MG Westmoreland to describe a spirit of zeal and enthusiasm.

IRP: !Immediate Response Plebe! Speak! Talk! Answer!

ACKNOWLEDGEMENTS

I have been blessed with three beautiful daughters who continually bring me joy and happiness throughout my life. Melissa, Amy and Alison have been my greatest contribution to the world. Six grand-children add even more contentment and excitement. Now, my loving wife Rachel, who is smart and of strong character, brings me balance, love and friendship and keeps my world from spinning out of control. I'll never be able to properly thank all of you for what you contribute to my life.

The idea of *A Jew at the Point* started over thirty years ago. My sister Wilma Chandler, my brother-in-law John Chandler and my eldest niece Jana Marcus, all published writers, kept this spark alive within me until recently, when it burst into a cathartic flame of jumbled words, thought and form. Thank you, Wilma, John and Jana for your continued encouragement and thoughtfulness.

With the patience and empathy of a true saint, John helped me organize and draft this book, guiding me onto a path of learning basic creative writing skills and spending many hundreds of hours of time and effort to help me shape my wet clay of thoughts into a sculptured armature of possibilities. John, my words fall far short of the eternal gratitude and most sincere appreciation I have for you. You are the best! THANK YOU! Wilma, for all things; your beauty and vitality, artistic abilities support and love. THANK YOU!

A shout-out and many thanks, once again, to Jana Marcus (the best photographer on earth, by the way) and to my friends James Harmon, Esq. (WP Class of 1965), Dr. Jon Sethna, Al Raff, Dr. Donald Losman and Walter Oehrlein (WP Class of 1965) for their kindness and time spent reading and commenting on the original manuscript. I took all their comments to heart to make this book readable.

Wilma hooked me up with her fellow Santa Cruzan and editor extraordinaire Carol Skolnick! I immediately felt a special bond with Carol, whose humor, insight and professionalism never ceased to amaze me. Her calming influence quelled my fears and soothed my insecurities; the chuckle and joy in her voice always made me smile. Carol wanted my story told and it was her belief in me that brought it to fruition.I am grateful and forever indebted to you, Carol. Few superlatives could capture the full extent of my praise for you as a developmental editor and advisor.

Large and loud kudos to Stewart Williams, from Pittsburgh, book designer extraordinaire, whose imagination knows no bounds and Scott Uhlfelder, from Los Angeles, one of my great son-in-laws, whose expertise in cinematography, photography and editing were instrumental in shaping and cleaning up the pictures within this book.

Words also fall short, again, in thanking my two best buddies, Dr. Donald Losman and Walter Oehrlein, for their friendship and kindness over sixty years and counting. Walt is a true champion in many more ways than just on the squash and tennis courts. He contributes to the world via a multitude of charitable endeavors, from sport to community and Holocaust remembrance and defines philanthropy in the purest sense. He and his brother Richie, who were both inducted into West Point's Hall of Fame, are wonderful people and deserve all the acolades that come their way.

Donnie taught me what friendship was all about, never giving up on this lost soul. We've shared our innermost feelings as awkward seventeen-year-olds until even now, in our seventies. One of our country's leading economists, Don was influential in helping train countless military leaders from around the world to think in terms of economic understanding and development. His published writings on economics have stimulated many professionals, in that field, to think in broader terms. As a legendary Junior Boys doubles duo from Florida, it seems the older we get, the better we were!

Both Don and Walt were so very helpful in my writing this book. They were kind enough to share with me their own writing expertise and help sort out the life experiences that I reported on. Thanks guys!

Finally, I want to thank my parents Jacqueline and Maurice for all they did for our family, in giving us life and trying their best to instill in us good and strong values. Mom was tough but always put her family first and did the very best she could. Of all the men I have ever met in and out of the military, my dad was the real "man" in my life…a bona-fide hero. We didn't talk much, but he loved me and was always there for me when I needed him most. After I left for Vietnam in 1967, I never saw him alive again; his passing at the age of 61 was untimely and unfair. I carry the memory of both my parents and my twin sister Helen in my mind and heart wherever I am, always.

And Helen…I'm still waiting for a sign from you, as you promised, wherever you've travelled to through time and space!

ABOUT THE AUTHOR

Paul Jules Kantrowich is a 1965 graduate of the United States Military Academy, at West Point earning a Bachelor of Science Degree in General Engineering. He spent the next five years on various Army and Air Force assignments throughout the United States and Europe with a tour of duty in Vietnam from 1967 to 1968 as a Ranger Advisor.

In 1970 he resigned his Regular U.S. Army commission as a captain to pursue an education and subsequent career in Optometry.

He has since had a long clinical career as a Doctor of Optometry, after graduating in 1974 from, what is now, the New England College of Optometry. Garnering many "best in graduating class" awards for his professionalism and expertise as a clinician and contact lens specialist, he was invited to join the College faculty upon graduation as a Clinical Instructor.

Over the last thirty years Dr. Kantrowich has had an Optometric practice in New York City where his emphasis has been on medical health of the eye and contact lenses.

He lives with his wife Rachel in Jericho, New York. Rachel is a Registered Nurse specializing in Pediatric Nephrology at Cohen's Childrens Hospital for almost fifty years. Together, they both love the special time they have with their children and grandchildren and to travel the world.

A Jew at the Point is his first book.

CPSIA information can be obtained
at www.ICGtesting.com
Printed in the USA
JSHW040433200622
27223JS00007B/193